THE POLITICS OF COMMUNITY

THE POLITICS OF COMMUNITY

Theory and Practice

ADRIAN LITTLE

EDINBURGH UNIVERSITY PRESS

© Adrian Little, 2002

Edinburgh University Press Ltd
22 George Square, Edinburgh

Typeset in 11 on 13pt Goudy
by Hewer Text Ltd, Edinburgh, and
printed and bound in Great Britain
by MPG Books Ltd, Bodmin

A CIP Record for this book is
available from the British Library

ISBN 0 7486 1543 1 (paperback)

The right of Adrian Little
to be identified as author of this work
has been asserted in accordance with
the Copyright, Designs and Patents Act 1988.

Contents

For Andy, Pat and Sinead

Acknowledgements

The gestation period of this book has been five years in which the arguments presented here have been rehearsed and refined in a number of conference papers. My first expression of some of these ideas was at the 1996 Social Policy Association conference at Sheffield Hallam University in a paper entitled 'Radical Communitarianism in Europe' (co-authored with Gordon Hughes). Some of the points raised in Chapters 5 and 6 were aired in 'Welfare and Community in Post-industrial Socialist Theory: Beyond Employment' at the Political Studies Association conference at the University of Ulster, Jordanstown, in April 1997. With Gordon Hughes again, I pre-empted some of the debates in Chapters 3 to 6 in 'The Contradictions of New Labour's Communitarianism' at the 7th Congress of the Basic Income European Network at the University of Amsterdam in September 1998. Material in Chapters 4 and 8 was initially expressed in 'Theorising Community and Solidarity: The Politics of Differentiated Universalism' at the Rethinking Citizenship conference at the University of Leeds in June 1999. Last, much of the argument in Chapter 8 was developed in 'Civil Societies and Economic Citizenship: The Contribution of Basic Income Theory to New Interpretations of the Public Sphere' at the 8th Congress of the Basic Income European Network in Berlin in October 2000. The overall thrust of the argument in this book has been enhanced considerably by the comments of participants at these conferences as well as friends and colleagues who commented on early drafts of those papers. Particular gratitude must be expressed to Gordon Hughes and Jim Martin, who both kindly read a complete draft of the book and provided a wide range of useful and critical comments. The book is much better for their practical and theoretical analyses, although I am equally sure that what follows will not answer all of the critical points they raised. Nicola Carr was a supportive Commissioning

Editor and I value greatly her comments and those of the readers who commented on the proposal. Last, I must thank Sinead Hanna-Little, who provided the support that I needed in what, ironically given the theme of the book, was often a rather solitary enterprise. The book is dedicated to her because in everyday life she exemplifies the virtues of community with which the book is concerned.

Introduction

It is a very common error to think that if a word is meaningful then it should have a fixed and wholly determinate meaning . . . [but] if we reject the idea that a word must stand for some kind of object – that which all things designated by the word share – then we shall become more open in our attitude towards language. (Plant 1974: 8, 10)

What is community? This, as we shall see, is not an easy question to answer. A major reason for this is the fact that community is a relatively neglected concept in political theory. It has not received the same kind of attention as ideas such as equality, freedom, justice or rights. However the absence of a clear definition of community has not prevented it from becoming a common feature in a range of contemporary political discourses. Indeed, it is perhaps the lack of conceptual clarity around community that has made it such an attractive tool for politicians, theorists and policy-makers. This book sets out to make a contribution to the process of rethinking community. Whilst it will not be possible to provide an acceptable definition of community for everyone, as the opening quotation from Raymond Plant implies, it is within our remit to problematise some of the existing usages of community in contemporary politics and suggest ways in which the concept needs to be clarified. Moreover it is also possible to identify the implications of rethinking community for political theory more broadly and to identify those theories of community that are most persuasive with regard to its use as a normative objective. That said, it is worth remembering Plant's warning that community 'is so much a part of the stock in trade of social and political argument that it is unlikely that some non-ambiguous and non-contested definition of the notion can be given' (Plant 1974: 13).

It is important to stress that this book is not about communitarianism as a political movement. Whilst the work of political philosophers and policy makers that regard themselves, or are categorised by others, as communitarians will be analysed, the main focus will be on the much wider use of the idea of community by a range of commentators from a variety of ideological perspectives. Indeed, it will be suggested that the process of understanding community more thoroughly is hampered by the automatic association of the concept with the political movement. From this perspective there would appear to be a need to unpack the concept of community in order to achieve critical distance from the way in which it emerges within communitarian discourses. Of course, such a process necessitates an evaluation of the communitarian movement and the political theories that have been associated with it. At the same time we should recognise that the idea of community – and associated concepts – has been used by a range of commentators who do not regard themselves as communitarians.

Once the concept of community has been detached from particular political philosophies and movements, it is much easier to understand the ways in which it can be used. Moreover the range of spheres of contemporary life that are impacted upon by community becomes much clearer. Such is the variety of forms of association, membership and inclusion that the discourse of community appears to be almost ubiquitous. Of course this isn't necessarily a new development. Raymond Plant noted a quarter of a century ago that this most elusive of concepts had become 'something of a vogue word in social description at the present time' (Plant 1974: 1). This suggests that the idea of community has always been a touchstone for those concerned with 'rootedness, cohesion and belonging' and there is undoubtedly an element of truth in this perspective. Nonetheless through the course of this book the contention will be that this process has accelerated in recent years – a trend that has been most notably identifiable (and indeed problematic) in the emergence of communitarianism as a branch of political philosophy and in political movements such as the Communitarian Forum (Tam 1998: ix). The most important effect of this renewed interest in community has been a growing recognition that community is not just a political phenomenon. Whilst the political dimension remains central, the social and economic aspects of community have come increasingly to the fore. As will become clear later in this book, community has become an increasingly important concept for social policy-makers and, more recently, the importance of community to economic policy has also become apparent. This has been manifest in the emergence of debates on social capital and trust.

All of this suggests that any analysis of the contemporary importance of community must deal with the normative implications of the concept. However in analysing the use of community it becomes clear that a gap has appeared between political philosophy and those who advocate community on a more practical level. Thus some commentators such as Frazer (1999) have made a sharp differentiation between philosophical and political communitarianism. This book attempts to provide a bridge between these two strands and suggests that such a contrasting distinction between theory and practice is symptomatic of a serious problem in the way we think about community. Where it appears in political practice and policy-making, community is often deployed in a rather random, haphazard fashion. Often it is assumed that the community exists and merely needs to be empowered. The obstacles to community that exist in contemporary societies are often ignored and the extent of diversity and value pluralism is frequently neglected. At the same time in political philosophy, community is some-times invoked in such an abstract manner that the possibility of practically applying the concept is clearly of secondary importance. In this vein of philosophical communitarianism the critique of liberalism often seems to be a more important endeavour than the construction of any kind of coherent alternative. Whilst this book cannot pretend to provide all of the solutions to these problems, it does attempt to demonstrate how the divorce of theory and practice in the politics of community is fundamentally problematic.

This, then, emerges as one of the major concerns of this book, namely, how political theory can construct a normative model of community that can inform political practice. To this end it is worth outlining some of the main features of community which this books seeks to address. As noted at the outset, community is a slippery concept. Clearly it refers to some kind of association, membership of which is thought to be desirable for one reason or another. However we must recognise that association takes a number of forms and therefore it may be prudent not to be too prescriptive about what constitutes a community. As we will see, the idea of community deployed in this book is based upon the existence or encouragement of certain virtues or principles. According to this kind of definition, community exists where virtues such as friendship, voluntarism and care are exhibited. What this entails is a definition of community whereby individuals belong to a social group either through choice or birth and where their behaviour and status is not based on instrumental gain. Communities can engage in instrumental activities, for example, to raise financial resources. However, when they do so, the basic virtues of community tend to be superseded by alternative rationalities. In this sense the pursuit of instrumental gain, competitive advantage and so on can be undertaken by communities but the virtues that embody communities will be relegated in priority. From this perspective it seems appropriate to differentiate between associations in which we are members for a specific reason or purpose on the one hand and communities whereby we associate for non-instrumental reasons or for no particular reason at all. Nonetheless the latter still command certain behaviour from members and indeed this may take the form of expectations of obligation, reciprocity and so on.

There is no hard and fast rule in all of this. Communities will vary according to their specific practices and different bonds of membership and expectations of behaviour will pertain in each. Moreover we should recognise that, while communities may exhibit certain virtues, they are also likely to encompass many vices as well. As such, the promotion of communities is likely to facilitate behaviour and beliefs with which we may disagree, as well as those which we seek to promote. Whilst the vague nature of such an understanding of community may not assist the elucidation of a political programme to meet this normative model, it nonetheless bears a resemblance to the reality of contemporary societies in which a multiplicity of different communities exist. Clearly this is a non-perfectionist view of community. It does not set out their size, the closeness or otherwise of relationships therein, or the specifics of behaviour in community. All it suggests is that certain types of virtues will be present at one time or another. There is no prescription of morals or standards of behaviour as these will vary from one community to another. There is no veneration of a particular version of association that happened in the past but rather an attempt to legitimise the wide variety of associations that exist today in different groups.

Two questions arise immediately from the meaning of community that is identified above. First, what is it about these kinds of associations and groups that merits the title of community? Second, and more importantly, what is it about them that requires assistance or protection if they already exist within contemporary society? In the simplest terms the first question can be answered by pointing to the idea that the virtues of community, that is the principles that it embodies, do not necessarily exist in other types of association such as pressure groups or trade unions. Associations can contain a wide range of motivations both instrumental and non-instrumental. Communities differ insofar as we belong either through what we are or what we choose to be and because of the types of behaviour that fellow members expect of us. Again the question of definition here is less important than the process of legitimising a wide range of activities and groups that individuals belong to. The problem of definition is, I think, not a serious obstacle if all we are trying to do is support and defend certain relationships that groups of individuals have with one another. If this definition is defensible, then what it means is that a theory of community must be developed that defends and supports a range of forms of association that individuals have with one another.

The second question is, I think, the more pressing, that is, why we should be defending community? It generates several corollaries. If these types of community association exist in modern societies, why should we be trying to protect and legitimise them? Why is there a need to build a normative political theory around something which appears to be in existence anyway? Why engage in such an enterprise? The answer to these questions lies in the hegemony of economic rationality and market discourses in contemporary life. Where communities exist, they do so in the face of the onslaught of commercial imperatives in modern life. Economic rationality appears to spread its logic into increasingly more spheres of contemporary life and becomes ever more pervasive. If it had agency it would demonstrate an unmatchable appetite for proselytising. The expansionist rationality of the economic knows no boundaries and the modern world shows a demonstrable unwillingness in Western societies to construct meaningful obstacles to its further development. The problem in terms of community is that the domain of non-instrumental association is increasingly overwhelmed by economic rationality. In this sense the desire to protect and legitimise community must find a way of rebutting the spread of economic rationality.

This book is concerned with ways of presenting an argument for defending community against the spread of economic logic (at least partially). Such a task is of course difficult and it would be foolish to make grand statements about the extent to which it is achieved in what follows. Perhaps the most that can be claimed is that some of the problems of attempting to establish a meaningful politics of community are identified and possible alternatives are put forward and evaluated. That many people will not be satisfied by the arguments that are expressed is inevitable but, at the least, I would hope that the problems for non-instrumental forms of association in the face of the hegemony of the economic in the contemporary world become clear. Moreover the inadequacy of either philosophical or political communitarianism alone in providing coherent answers to these difficulties should be evident. There are no easy answers in the politics of community, and such is the diffuse and complicated nature of community that we should not expect there to be any. However, if, in the course of the book, the obstacles to the realisation and legitimisation of community become clear and the problems of the contemporary politics of community are recognised, then the argument will indeed have served its purpose. Indeed, when one examines contemporary debates on community there is a temptation to ask its advocates to stop providing answers and to start recognising the questions.

CHAPTER I

Theorising Community

Despite a long and varied history in political and social philosophy, the concept of community is arguably more important and contested now than in any previous era. It remains an idea that is perennially resistant to ideological categorisation and this provides dynamism in the ongoing debates over its meaning. This chapter will explain some of the problems associated with defining community and the resultant problems that emerge in the process of establishing links between the theoretical and practical usages of the term. In some approaches to social theory and political practice community has become something of a holy grail, while in other circles it is a concept that arouses deep scepticism. Nevertheless the principles and desirability of community continue to be invoked across the political spectrum and it is evident in one form or another in most ideological standpoints. In this scenario it seems pertinent to ask if the discourses of community are so varied that the concept becomes just too elastic. Thus we might argue that the clear lack of uniformity in understanding the politics of community renders appeals to community vacuous and redundant. This book argues against this position on the basis that, despite the immense body of literature on communitarianism, the actual concept of community has been under theorised and, as such, that it has been utilised by a wide range of individuals and groups who have no sound foundation for appropriating the concept except political expediency. In short, if community is to continue to feature so prominently in contemporary politics, then it is vital that we establish a clearer understanding of the concept.

Community is a key ingredient in the complex matrix of social organisation and individual self-identity that characterises modern life. The exposition of the theory of community must grapple with the role it should play in social organisation in the context of diversity and value pluralism. In practical terms the book will attempt to transcend arguments over 'the state or the market' by showing that both have a role to play in social organisation if they are supported by solid community institutions. The key to the argument presented here is that the politics of community requires foundations in clear philosophical values and principles. We cannot just assume that communities exist in the requisite form (even though they may do to some extent) or that communities only need to be reactivated to perform some kind of romanticised vision of their role in previous times. Rather communities may sometimes need to be manufactured and policies may have to be directed towards the creation of spaces for them to develop and flourish. In this vein the theoretical exposition of community should be coupled with strategies for their practical enactment. In short, it is vital to establish the appropriate links between the theory of community and practical initiatives for redeveloping social and economic policies on one hand and its implications for political renewal on the other.

Initially it is important to analyse the explicit and implicit appeals to community in political and sociological thought. This approach will demonstrate how the values of community have been employed from Ancient Greek philosophy to contemporary supporters of radical pluralism and civil society in order to propagate visions of cohesive societies. From the beginnings in classical thought much of this theorising has taken the form of discussion about the constitution of the public sphere and the nature of relations therein. This has been evident since the rise of liberalism insofar as debates about individual freedoms and rights have been discussed in relation to the social context in which they are experienced. Moreover, especially in the work of Enlightenment philosophers such as Paine and Rousseau, the theorisation of freedom and rights have been bound up with conceptual arguments about the meaning of the public sphere and the constitution of the good society. The explicit theorisation of community expanded significantly with industrialisation (Reeve 1997) and this was the origin of the link between the concept and 'conservative' sociology. This association is most frequently associated with the work of Tönnies and Durkheim, who studied the effects of industrial societies on traditional associational relationships. Their theories remain influential on thinking about community today, although this is not to say that either the concept of community or the sociological theorisations of it should be endowed with conservative connotations by definition. From these historical foundations we can identify why community remains a central concept in political philosophy and sound reasons to resist prematurely or simplistically pigeon-holing it. By analysing these differing traditions this chapter will establish the complex nature of community and the problems that emerge in practically applying it in contemporary politics.

Aristotelian Thought and Contemporary Approaches to Community

The intellectual heritage of the key principles of community can clearly be traced to Aristotelian thinking on the nature of the good polity. Thus many of the virtues that are embodied in theories of community are based upon classical visions of the values that characterised the public sphere. For Aristotle, the *polis* was the arena in which commonly agreed constitutional arrangements defined an area where higher virtues would be the foundational principles. In this sense the key characteristic of the good polity was to be found in the internal arrangements which defined relationships in that sphere. Thus a 'polis is a composition of elements – the citizens – but, as a composition, its identity is determined not by reference to its constituents but to the way in which they are structured: we speak of the same state by attending to its constitution' (Everson 1996: xvii). Aristotle focused on the broad polity as the venue for the development of higher virtues associated with community at the expense of 'lower' small-scale forms of association such as the family or the village. However contemporary Aristotelian approaches suggest that there is little reason why the virtues which he associated with the good polity could not be cultivated within smaller units or associations. Thus the Aristotelian virtues embodied in his *polis* need not be inapplicable to other less formal spheres of society. In this sense the orthodox political sphere might indeed encompass universal virtues based on common interests but this does not preclude more particularist associations of interest, from also manifesting virtuous characteristics such as friendship or altruism.

Aristotle's perspective is applicable to contemporary theories of community because he highlighted the importance of the internal relations within a *polis*. Rather than focusing on a strict definition of the group of people who constituted the *polis*, Aristotle attached primacy to the values and principles that characterised the mode of association. Part of this is due to the teleological approach which Aristotle employed to identify the importance of the nature of the ideal *polis*. The Aristotelian position recognises that members of the political community or the *polis* may come and go; indeed it suggests that membership of any community or association is always contingent and potentially transitory. In this sense it would be building on shifting sands to predicate a political association purely on the past, present or future membership of that particular grouping. Such an approach would neglect the ways in which associations develop historically and pay insufficient attention to the actual bonds that hold groups of people together. Aristotle recognised that the individuals within the *polis* were only one ingredient in the creation of the good polity. The actual constitutional framework which exists within the political association is, in effect, more definitive of that grouping than the individuals within it at any one given time. Of course, the ways in which the actual individuals relate to one another is important, as we shall see, but the social arrangements which enable them to establish these bonds must be instituted before associative relationships are able to meet their full potential. To expect associations to just emerge spontaneously as in the work of Fukuyama (1996) neglects the social arrangements that are required if individuals are to be provided with worthwhile opportunities to experience fruitful co-operation.

The contemporary identification of the defining features of community should not attempt to match Aristotle's glorification of the *polis*, and political activity, as the location of the highest form of activity in which exclusive virtues predominate. In Aristotelian thought the political community, access to which was tightly defined, was the site in which reason and accompanying intellectual and moral values guided activity. These virtues were, of course, limited and not everyone would be able to acquire them. For Aristotle, women and slaves, for example, could not be expected to develop higher virtues and had to be content with a lesser standing in life. Notwithstanding the anachronistic position of this exclusionary perspective in the contemporary era, such grand claims cannot be made for the micropolitical community. Political arrangements and institutions have changed ineradicably since Aristotle's time and many of the high virtues that he prioritised must also be surrendered on the altar of modern *realpolitik*. Indeed many Aristotelian virtues may only remain central to associational politics such is the modern organisation of the formal political arena. Such is the standing of the domain of macro-politics in Western liberal democracies, that they seem – rightly or wrongly – almost entirely inappropriate for the resurrection of higher Aristotelian virtues. This is not to say that Aristotelian virtues do not exist in the formal political sphere but rather that they are in competition with other less altruistic values and are frequently subsumed by the practicalities of conducting business in the modern political world.

If the macro-political environment is no longer conducive to the *prioritisation* of Aristotelian virtues, we must ask where they should now be most appropriately located and how can we establish environments for certain virtues and values to thrive. We cannot expect the virtues promoted by Aristotle to generate and reproduce without active attempts to create spheres in which they are the fitting principles. It may be tempting to envisage community values sitting unadulterated alongside the realities of the formal political arena or the priorities associated with economic success, but, in truth, experience tells us that altruistic principles are likely to be sacrificed when faced with competition from pervasive economic rationality (Little 1996), the diktats of practical political necessity or the requirements of bureaucratic regulation. Thus some contemporary commentators argue that a sphere for Aristotelian virtues must be manufactured so that they can be protected from the value systems that are accorded greater prominence in modern politics and economics (O'Neill 1998). Unlike Aristotle, the implications of this perspective suggest that there are important virtues to be found in associations which are not in themselves formulated for explicit political influence. Whilst they may of course have political influence and will have internal political relationships, the actual reasons for forming these groups may not be to influence the political agenda. Indeed many of them are likely to be predicated on bonds of friendship, for example, which may not be remotely concerned with the process of influencing the decision-making arena.

Contemporary theorists influenced by Aristotle such as John O'Neill seek to promote an associational sphere located in a micro-political sector which is protected from economic rationality and the logic of market mechanisms on one hand, and regulation from the state and bureaucracy on the other. As such some community associations may be of central political importance through, for example, the local governance of any given area and the decentralised provision of services. At the same time, however, communities in the micro-political sphere may have fairly mundane purposes as their bond of association. Indeed they may merely entail membership of a club or a local charitable organisation. Moreover where they might find common purpose through the intricacies of local politics, communities may also derive commonality through shared sporting interests, religious affiliations, reading groups, associations of parenthood and so on. The point of the principles of community is to establish the independent worth that can and should be attached to these activities. Unlike Aristotle, virtues are not primarily attached to political activities in wider society; they are just as likely to emanate (if not more so) from non-political activities in the micro-social arena.

One of the more controversial (and indeed problematic) aspects of theories of community developed by theorists such as O'Neill and Gorz centres upon the importance of non-instrumental principles as the foundation of communitarian associations. Part of the reason for their perspective lies in their detection of the pervasive influence that instrumental, economic values have in the modern world. Indeed few areas of modern liberal democratic societies can be said to be untouched by economic rationality. Such is the extent of this colonisation of public spheres and civil society that attempts to reverse the trend come up against implacable opposition. Thus it is difficult to assert the primacy of the principles of community in an atmosphere in which they are constantly faced with antithetical values based on instrumentalism and economic or market logic. Nevertheless the challenging nature of the task of reasserting communitarian principles does not invalidate their position – indeed it makes it all the more necessary to formulate a coherent opposition to the process of economic rationalisation. It also feeds into the Aristotelian position with respect to the relationship between the highest virtues and productive activity. For Aristotle, individuals required time and an appropriate environment in which to develop and be taught the virtues. Thus 'goodness lies in activities, and to pursue the worthwhile ones we must be free from others; politics as a worthwhile activity must thus be undertaken by those with leisure, those free from production or commerce' (Williams 1991: 39). From the Aristotelian perspective it is not possible for individuals to develop into rational, moral beings if their time is solely spent in the sphere of necessity, engaging in productive activities to meet material objectives. It is clear then that Aristotle regarded productive activities with a degree of disdain, which was reflected in his disregard for the work carried out by women and slaves. Whilst sharing Aristotle's concern with the impact of economic or productive necessity on opportunities to act upon free thought, this is not to say that the status of work and productive activities should be denigrated out of hand. On the contrary, following the ideas of commentators such as Gorz (1989; Little 1996, 1998), productive activity is recognised as an important source of identity and self-realisation. That said, it should not be eulogised as the highest form of activity in comparison to unpaid activities which are also important sources of worth and status. Thus the argument about the principles of community is about identifying what they are, where they thrive and how to allocate them the same kind of status as is attached to paid work in modern political economy. Overall then, the theorisation of community should be concerned with achieving a balance between perceptions of the importance between paid work and unpaid activities.

From the above it should be evident that there are clear differences between the concept of community as developed in this book and the virtues associated with Aristotle's *polis*. That said, the resurgence of the public sphere must return to Aristotelian thinking for inspiration, especially when concerned with issues such as the promotion of happiness, virtue and the common good. These questions have particular pertinence in periods of technological and social change and the impact that they have on social institutions and political organisation. The changing context of the modern world undermines much of what has traditionally been thought of as the realm of community, and yet it also provides us with opportunities of rethinking the ways in which Aristotelian virtues and the common good can be realised in contemporary circumstances. Nowhere is this more evident than in the opportunities afforded to us by the growth of new technology to renew ideas regarding the ways in which we work and the possibilities of opening up new spheres of free time and leisure (Little 1998). Aristotelian thought clearly implies that spaces and environments need to be constructed for the virtues to flourish, 'so certain economic, social and political conditions must be met if the members of a human community are to achieve their potential as rational and moral beings. One of the political scientist's tasks is to discover those conditions, and base the ideal constitution upon them' (Nicholson 1995: 37–8). All of this presupposes appropriate locations and discourses in which discussion of the common good can take place. Plainly this was a key feature of Aristotle's thinking, namely, that opportunities for *discussion* of the common good were likely to engender the *creation* of the common good. This viewpoint is reflected in much contemporary communitarian thinking which focuses on the empowerment of civil society through processes of deliberation and dialogue. In this spirit Hollenbach suggests that 'to avoid serious public speech about the good life and the good society is itself already to surrender a major dimension of the human good. It will also have the further effect of undermining the concrete conditions necessary for a life of freedom' (Hollenbach 1995: 151). At the same time the advocacy of a multiplicity of communities and the recognition of value pluralism implies that these processes may also generate disagreement and conflict (Mouffe 2000b). Thus, again, the need to avoid eulogising community as a source of consensual governance should be stressed.

Two further points illustrate the continuing relevance of Aristotle's ideas to the process of rethinking community. First, his work provides a corrective to the growth of economic individualism and a simple recognition of the social nature of humanity and thus the possibility of establishing common interests. Second there is a recognition that a vision of equality and social justice does not have to be basely reductive but instead can accommodate and indeed celebrate difference (although the inequalities that Aristotle saw as justifiable do not correspond with the theory of difference that will be embraced in what follows). The promotion of difference within the Aristotelian *polis* is summarised by O'Neill:

> Humans can achieve a complete and self-sufficient good only within the polis. This in turn requires that individuals are able to enter a variety of relationships and pursue diverse and distinct goods. The pursuit of these particular goods will be itself a social enterprise that will take place within different associations. The end of the polis is not some completely separate good over and above these partial goods: its end is rather an exclusive end . . . On this view, the polis does not replace other partial associations, but is rather a community of communities containing a variety of associations realizing particular ends. (O'Neill 1995: 422)

Thus, despite reservations about the exclusions that Aristotle maintained as necessary to his ideal *polis*, he made the important point that the promotion of a common conception of the good need not adulterate the different kinds of associations that individuals form. The common good then can be regarded as a framework in which an understanding is institutionalised that is based upon the importance of diversity and the expression of difference by a range of communities. As will become clear in the later stages of the book, such an approach necessitates an understanding of the political issues that may emerge when diversity gives rise to incommensurable values and disagreement between parties on the most appropriate actions on any given issue.

– COMMUNITY AND MODERNITY –

The concept of community was reinvigorated by the different traditions that emerged from the Enlightenment. One such approach emerged from nineteenth century-sociology and, in particular, the work of Ferdinand Tönnies and Emile Durkheim. Here the focus was on the ways in which industrialisation, urbanism and the rise of the modern state impacted upon traditional forms of community. However, initial fears about the implications of the modern state for civil association were expressed most notably in the work of Tom Paine. He demonstrated considerable faith in the capacity of individuals for self-government in spheres of civil society liberated from the imposed power of the state. Paine emphasised the arbitrary nature of government by monarchs or oligarchies which denied the basic natural rights attached to individuals due to their humanity. Rather he felt that people could come together in non-state domains to co-operate in their common affairs. Thus, not only were individuals rational beings who were capable of making informed decisions about the world around them, but they also recognised the value of pursuing common interests together. Paine's liberal perspective focused on the importance of the separation between the state and civil society and, whilst aware that the eradication of the domain of the former was not possible, he suggested that the sphere of civil society should be broadened to allow people to take greater control over their own lives (Paine 1987; Keane 1995: 116–17). Therefore the primary role of the state was not only to guarantee that individual rights were protected but also to enable people to enjoy their natural rights in self-governed spheres. Whilst Paine emphasised the separation of state and society, it is quite clear that his position implies important links between the two. Nonetheless, despite being one of the earliest commentators to question the appropriate relationship between the state sector and other sub-state levels of public sphere, Paine succumbed to the liberal tendency to see the separation between the state and civil society as rather clear cut. Similarly too many contemporary discourses on the nature of community and civil society actually say little about the state apart from the widespread viewpoint that the decentralisation of power away from state mechanisms is desirable. Whilst that may well be the case, it does not necessarily help us to instigate the processes that could enable decentralisation to take place.

The state–civil society distinction was thrown into sharper focus in the Victorian era and attracted more attention from sociological thinkers, notably Durkheim and Tönnies. Here the political analysis of thinkers such as Paine was coupled with an understanding of the ways in which social and economic change linked to industrialism was altering traditional forms of social organisation. Indeed the ideas of these sociologists alongside the work of Marx would change the profile of theorising about community and call into question the parameters of the modern state. Thus the impetus of nineteenth-century sociology came from the analysis of the relationship between the economy and the state and the implications that it had for various forms of social organisation including civil association. In this sense the notion of community played an implicit role in the major social theories to emerge in this period.

For Durkheim the modernist project was one where a natural division of labour would develop in which individuals acquired organic solidarity. Thus his concern for community concentrated on the 'need for inclusive communities in which social bonds of mutual respect and care were safeguarded' (Tam 1998: 22). As such, Durkheim viewed communities as integrative institutions that would play an important role in the evolution of organic social relations. Their function was to develop and protect certain values that were not to be found in other spheres of social life. In this sense there is recognition in Durkheimian thought that some institutions such as economic bodies are not necessarily conducive to the kinds of human alliances that are embodied by the principles of community. Moreover he also implied that communities have a central role to play in developing a sphere of social existence which is not under the direct auspices of the state. Communities would become spheres of individual freedom. There would not then be control by a prescriptive state deciding the organisation of substate units like communities. Furthermore the analysis of Durkheim also focuses attention on the exact nature of the associations between the state and the theory of community. Thus he stressed:

> the importance of both the state in providing an overarching view of how the values of different groups relate to each other, and representative groups within society in providing a counterbalance to the state lest its views become detached from the concerns of real communities. (Tam 1998: 238)

The relationship between the state and communities is therefore a dynamic and symbiotic one. There is no suggestion that they can exist in a functioning democracy in isolation from one another. This entails some movement away from the Aristotelian position which established more concrete boundaries between the public and the private or the economic and the political.

Ferdinand Tönnies provided a different focus to Durkheim as his key distinction was not between communities and the state but rather community (*Gemeinschaft*) and society or association (*Gesellschaft*). Tönnies suggested that the sphere of community involved small-scale face-to-face relations which seems to link his idea of community with Aristotle's conceptualisation of the village. Society or association, on the other hand, was a broader sphere which, following the course of the Industrial Revolution, had been formed by the process of urbanisation and the growth of the city. For Tönnies this was a questionable development in which community values of kinship and co-operation were eroded. Where community maintained traditional structures and a degree of what has been called spontaneity in the current era (Fukuyama 1996), the sphere of society was increasingly rule-bound and inflexible. This would later become popularised in the sociological mind by Max Weber's notion of bureaucracy (Kumar 1978: 105–7).

The perspective developed by Tönnies remains, to some extent, the dominant one in modern social and political theorisation of community. For example, much contemporary theorising about the politics of difference (Young 1990a) tends to represent philosophies based on community as exclusionary and backward because they are based on rather insular traditions and face-to-face relationships. As we shall see, this model of community is a rather one-dimensional representation of the diverse variety of communities that exist in the modern world. However it is also the case that Tönnies' theory, along with (ironically) opponents of the ideal typical model of small face-to-face communities such as Young, underestimates the extent to which the growth of modern cities has extended opportunities for the development of communities. Certainly cities may have eroded the traditional model of community as espoused by Tönnies and contemporary thinkers attracted by the romantic allure of bygone days, but there is little reason why outdated notions of traditional communities should override alternative visions of community. The orthodox model derived from Tönnies is but one conceptualisation of community, and it seems clear that the representation of community as a purely geographical entity or as dependent upon the scale of the relationships involved must be challenged.

The sociological analysis of community was furthered by the intervention of Karl Marx on the effects of capitalism upon the organisation of the state and the establishment of bourgeois civil society. Whilst clearly Marx's philosophy shared little with more conservative sociologists when it came to political objectives, there was considerable common ground when it came to the analysis of industrialisation. Marx evidently recognised the technological achievements of capitalist industrialisation (albeit, ultimately, in a critical fashion) and based his vision of communist society on the potential of the means of production being harnessed to achieve communistic objectives. That said, he also recognised the effects that industrialisation had had on more traditional ways of life and criticised the alienation that was derived from the organisation of the forces of production under economic arrangements in capitalist societies. Thus Marxists tended to challenge the disruption of traditional forms of life exacerbated by the development of capitalism, whilst simultaneously recognising that the painful disintegration of former traditions was a necessary phase which had to be undergone in the journey towards a communist society. Nonetheless the similarities between the account of life in London provided by Engels in *The Condition of the Working Class in England* in 1844 and Tönnies' perspective (Kumar 1978: 69–70) demonstrate the strength of the orthodox model of community and contribute to the explanation of why traditional models of community retain so much power and popularity today. That said, Krishan Kumar also points to the way in which the sociological position adopted by Durkheim, Tönnies and Marx coincided on the point that, regardless of the virtues of the traditional community, the future of modern societies lay in the growth of the city, not least because cities challenged the rather prescriptive and constraining relationships which were established in pre-industrial notions of community. This is a point that all contemporary analysts of community should bear in mind. Romanticised communities of olden times permeate many political analyses written in different periods – most of these subscribe to myth rather than reality.

Examining the heritage of theories of community it seems clear that the concept does not fit comfortably into any categorical pigeon-hole. Indeed such is the eclectic nature of theorising about community that ideological labelling becomes a rather hazardous business. Of course, this does not reduce the importance of attempting to establish a more thoroughly developed conceptualisation of community; it merely makes it a more difficult task. Part of the problematic nature of this process is the fact that many of the principles attached to community will not be particularly controversial from many different political perspectives. What may be less consensual is the way in which the actual implementation of these principles should be addressed. The values of friendship, trust, voluntary action, benign intentions, and co-operation are unlikely to be challenged with concerted vehemence (except, perhaps, by the most extreme of individualists), but it must be recognised that, if the appeal to these kind of virtues is to be more than a pious wish-list, then a clear understanding of the impact on community of the extent of the jurisdiction of the state and the influence of economic rationality must be recognised. This recognition is more likely to face substantial opposition than the actual virtues of community themselves imply. In no sense, then, is the identification of the principles of community in this book intended to promote a rose-tinted vision of a harmonious civic future. Instead it is predicated upon the opposition and conflict that this process must embrace if a mature understanding of community is to be developed and allowed to form the basis of a thorough reinterpretation of public spheres.

– CONTEMPORARY THEORIES OF COMMUNITY –

Undoubtedly the most prominent sphere in which community has returned to the centre of modern political debates was the philosophical contretemps between communitarians and liberals (or individualists) that emerged as a response to the theory of justice promulgated by John Rawls (1999) in the early 1970s. A group of commentators including Sandel, Taylor, Walzer and MacIntyre came to be categorised as communitarians for the challenge they raised to Rawlsian theory (although some are more explicit than others in actually analysing Rawls himself and most do not use the label 'communitarian' to describe their work). The main features of their critique lay in the rejection of Rawls' individualist approach in his hypothetical model which, in the simplest terms, presents individuals as atomistic and asocial. Communitarians, on the other hand, tend to acknowledge the primacy of human association as a source of self-identity and, therefore, as a fundamental building block of human societies. Clearly then there is a communitarian rejection of Rawls' methodological individualism which forms the centrepiece of his liberal theory of justice. However, despite the dichotomous way in which the liberal–communitarian debate has been constructed in contemporary philosophical discourses, there are also areas of common concern between these two supposedly oppositional perspectives. As such, the source of resolving the conundrum of the meaning of community may lie in the acceptance of some of the arguments on either side of this constructed divide. This is particularly justified because, despite the way the debate is constructed, there is a lack of coherence within the groups labelled as communitarians or liberals/individualists. Again the question of what it is to be a communitarian shall emerge to the fore as the exploration of different theories of community continues to expose differences within the tradition.

The implications of the variations mentioned above are manifold in theoretical terms but it is also vital to examine the ways in which they inform practical politics in the contemporary world. As the pre-eminent guru of political communitarianism Amitai Etzioni has suggested, it is more than a political philosophy but rather communitarianism is most commonly regarded as a global political movement with supporters of all political hues across the world. The analysis will develop from here as we investigate Etzioni's 'political' or 'orthodox' communitarianism[1] and the specific notion of community which it employs. The emphasis will be twofold. First, it will focus on the sometimes distant relations between the sophisticated arguments put forward in the philosophical debate and the approach adopted by Etzioni. Most of the arguments put forward by the latter are couched in somewhat conservative terms which actually counter the liberal ideas held by communitarians such as Walzer. The second point of emphasis will be the populist and potentially authoritarian implications of Etzioni's work which, although he is at pains to suggest the opposite, pander to conservative and sometimes reactionary readings of the organisation of society. This analysis is particularly timely due to the popularity of the communitarianism movement. In the United Kingdom the argument has been taken up by a range of individuals from politicians in the major political parties to campaigning journalists such as Melanie Phillips. Community has also been promoted by members of think-tanks like Demos (see Atkinson 1994) and the Institute of Economic Affairs such as Norman Dennis and David Green. Despite the different standpoints presented by these individuals, they all develop a moralism that ultimately counteracts progressive and liberal ideas. Moreover, in general, the community that they seek to reinvigorate or protect is essentially backward looking and regressive. Rather than attempting to develop a theory of community that fits with the exigencies of the contemporary world, they prefer to don rose-tinted spectacles and eulogise previous ways of life that look increasingly anachronistic in the context of current conditions. Indeed it is just these conditions which necessitate fresh, radical thought on the concept of community.

Whilst the 'moral authoritarian communitarianism' (Hughes 1996) outlined above is clearly the dominant strand of communitarian politics in terms of influence and popularity, there are also radical approaches that offer more sophisticated variations on the meaning of community. Among the most important commentators in this school of thought are egalitarians such as Bill Jordan and André Gorz and radical pluralists such as Chantal Mouffe. The radical approach to community examines not only the relationship between the individual and the state, but also the social and the economic implications of rethinking community. Ultimately it recognises that these issues cannot be easily disentangled from one another. From this perspective the promotion of community is not presented as the panacea for a range of social ills that may be identified in modern societies.

The reason for this is that the radical standpoint does not promote one unitary community but argues instead that individuals need to be members of a range of different associational groups and communities. This goes beyond the search for the subject of the political community that is manifest in the communitarianism/liberalism debate. Certainly the wider political community is a feature of the approach of radical communitarians, but they also stress the importance of other types of community – smaller associational groups, the membership of which provides self-identity and allows individuals to express particularistic differences. Advocates of this perspective often look to the sphere of civil society as an arena that holds considerable potential for individual expression as it may not be guided by the principles which organise market mechanisms or the universal values that underpin the broader political community (Barber 1996). Moreover the radical approach to community recognises that individual self-identity cannot be wholly detached from *communities one is born into* as in atomistic or asocial individualism, whilst simultaneously understanding that identity can also be constituted by communities that individuals *choose to belong to* (Kukathas 1996).

– Economy and Society –

The value of the radical approach lies in the recognition of the complex ways in which contemporary liberal democratic societies are organised and the impact that economic conditions have upon our understanding of community. The question remains as to how different communitarian approaches manifest themselves when it comes to social and economic policies and the extent to which these future policy propositions further a sophisticated and pluralist understanding of community. Having examined orthodox theories of community and then potentially radical alternatives, the third strand of the argument presented in the book focuses on varying policy proposals in the context of the philosophical discourses on community mentioned above. In terms of social policies, particular attention will be paid to ideas which have been put forward to enable individuals to take advantage of opportunities to engage in community-based activities. At the forefront of these new ideas have been the various basic income proposals propagated by a wide range of commentators from Bill Jordan to Philippe van Parijs with a broad variety of justifications. Radical theories of community clearly inform the basic income debate, not least with regard to the potential these policy options have for active citizen participation in non-market-based activities. The critical analysis of these ideas will then feed into the examination of other aspects of communitarian social policy that advocate the community or the locality as the provider of welfare in place of more centralised forms of policy implementation by the state. One of the most innovative areas of concern here is with regard to crime prevention and criminal justice. A plethora of measures linked to varying philosophies of community have emanated within modern politics from curfews for youths to victim-based policies for punishing crimes. It will be argued that many of these ideas have not been substantiated by a firm understanding of community but rather a more limited (and frequently contradictory) desire to, at least ostensibly, minimise the role of the central state. A more developed example that will be evaluated is the idea of restorative justice and reintegrative shaming that has been studied at length by Braithwaite (1989). This should demonstrate not only some of the advantages of community-based approaches to social policy but also the difficulties that can arise in these initiatives.

Despite challenging the popular view that community is only linked to the notion of the geographical locality, the relationship between the centre and the locality is particularly important when it comes to debates over the future of democracy and the economics of community and democracy. Initially these debates will be approached from the position of analysing the usefulness of the concept of community when it comes to organising the economy. A recent trend in political economy has been the growth of theories that imply a strong role for communities in establishing relations of trust in society (Fukuyama 1996, 1999). From this basis it is argued that such trust relations provide social capital that facilitates the healthy working of market economies and liberal democratic politics (Putnam 1993). In theories such as those of Fukuyama and Putnam communities are not so much valued in their own right but rather they are promoted for the economic advantages that they are supposed to engender. These perspectives tend to see no contradictions between the values of liberal democracy and the outcomes of markets, and they fail to recognise that the logic of markets may compromise the values of community. In this sense the desire to strengthen the bond between communities and economies may be a flawed enterprise, and indeed a strong case can be made to disassociate the two (O'Neill 1998). Thus the seamless linkage of community to economy is highly questionable.

Many communities are essentially associations of individuals and groups with common interests that are not active within the sphere of economic activity. In this form of association the individuals within communities do not act according to economically instrumentalist attitudes. Therefore we can argue that some communities may be entities that function in areas that are not permeated by the logic of market-based relations. In other words they are free from the economic rationality that promotes the pursuit of profit, growth and capital accumulation and, according to commentators such as Gorz (1994) and O'Neill (1998), spaces should be established to enable these communities to remain protected from the pervasive economic rationality. However André Gorz has argued that opportunities to participate in non-economic community activities should be coupled with attempts to broaden access to the formal economic arena for all. In other words, this argument suggests that we need to rethink the ways in which we organise time to permit individuals to find fulfilment in the non-economic sphere. At the same time however the promotion of community activities must take place within the context of the creation of opportunities for all individuals to acquire a social identity in the public sphere through access to meaningful work. Clearly then this analysis of community with regard to the economy will take us on to the territory of debates over reduced working hours, work sharing, and so on. However it is also important to note that localities can form very important sources of community values in the contemporary world and there is a sense in which local communities can play an important role in the structure of local economies. Thus communities can become involved in the development of common skills bases for specific industries or strategies for the fruitful utilisation of common resources. At the same time the onus must be on the state to try to ensure that different communities within its sphere of jurisdiction are treated fairly and equitably, and that those with problems (for example, high unemployment, low levels of investment, low skill levels, poor infrastructure) are given the capacity to rectify them. This reflects the idea that communities are not homogeneous havens of the common good but rather they need to be fostered and assisted in their social and economic development.

– THE POLITICS OF COMMUNITY –

The last section of the book will address some of the key debates in modern political theory to evaluate the applicability of the concept of the community to contemporary debates on democratic renewal and the public sphere. Initially the analysis will centre on the notions of individuals, their communities and the state in recent literature on the future of democratic politics. By rethinking the notions of the individual, the community and the state in an integrated fashion then, it is possible to imagine a strong role for community in what Lodziak has termed a new politics of time (Gorz 1989; Lodziak 1995). According to this perspective, the social organisation of time should enable individuals to enjoy both autonomy and the collective expression of will which can be experienced in the associational bonds of community. However this perspective also realises that the requisite conditions for the establishment of these bonds can only really be facilitated on a wider social level. Thus there must be rights and responsibilities which are derived from and attached to an institution such as the state, which has a society-wide sphere of jurisdiction. This is not to say that there must be an all-encompassing state wielding hierarchical powers, but rather that our experience of individual and collective self-determination is reliant on appropriate societal relations. As such the rights and responsibilities which pertain to and guarantee our freedoms must be institutionalised in state bodies which can maintain universalism. Thus it is only in the context of a universal framework that particularist freedoms can genuinely be enjoyed by everyone.

The debate over universalism and particularism has become central in modern political and social theory and has helped to inspire the growth of radical pluralist perspectives which go beyond orthodox or formal pluralism. In fresher, more radical pluralist approaches the domain of civil society has been revitalised as the arena in which our particular wills can be exercised (Keane 1988, 1998). Thus, whilst the state provides universal rights and we each owe obligations in (indirect) relation to those rights (such as those to more free time or work), it is in areas of individual choice and common interest that we express our particularity. We acquire and express identity not only in universal categories such as citizenship and membership of a society but also in smaller projects designed individually or by collective communities or associations of interest. In this sense radical pluralist perspectives attempt to provide a foundation for an individuated understanding of citizenship and community.

Perhaps the most contentious questions raised by this radical pluralist position relate to the ways in which these different groups and associations interact with one another and the impact these ideas would have on democratic structures. Clearly the concept of community used in these theories embodies some advocacy of decentralisation and the principle of subsidiarity (that is, that decisions should be taken at the lowest possible level), although critics may regard the espousal of the facilitating role of the state as evidence to the contrary. Nonetheless it does feed into recent debates on the notion of associationalism and, in particular, the issues that arise from the theory of associative democracy (Hirst 1994). In the context of community we might ask how these radical pluralist approaches deal with issues such as exclusion (White 1997) and the impact that they would have on minority communities. Arguably some of the economic and social policies considered earlier in the book would provide a framework for a healthy and radical pluralism but that they would also need to be supported by political arrangements which encouraged decentralisation and more associational forms of decision-making. That said, at no stage of the argument should it be implied that the state can be replaced or eradicated. Indeed it should be noted that the creation of associational structures requires impetus from the centre as well as from below. It is within the remit of the state to encourage the decentralisation of power and to ensure that communities have the capacity to take on greater responsibility. It would be irresponsible of any government to decentralise power without providing appropriate structures to allow communities or associations to take up the reins. In short, we cannot assume communities are in existence and capable of taking over decision-making. Rather the conditions for the development of communities need to be fostered and the decentralisation of power downwards needs to be planned and implemented gradually. Therein lies the most important role for the state, the creation of the conditions under which radical pluralism can flourish.

The book will conclude by returning to the importance of developing community in non-economic spheres of life. As such it will be important to recognise that not all communities are the same. Some will be closer to prevalent societal beliefs than others. Some will be religious or spiritual, others will be secular. Some will reflect narrow local concerns, others will reflect broader areas of common interest (for example, on the international level). Communities are not the same as associations because the latter often operate within markets and economic relations. For example, groups of business leaders may well have common economic interests and form associations to promote them. Communities on the other hand are formed on the basis of certain principles and shared values which frequently contradict the pursuit of growth and accumulation, the maximisation of profit, ruthless competition, and so on. These are the values of market mechanisms and it is within the economic sphere that they should remain. Principles of community on the contrary may interfere with markets and distort their operation. If we limit the market sphere and develop a broader domain in which friendship, voluntarism, sharing, mutualism and co-operation are the dominant values, then we can say that a process of promoting community is under way. In the contemporary age when markets may generate irrational outcomes in terms of public goods and social need, the sphere and principles of community may establish a sounder foundation for the provision of social welfare.

– A Radical Theory of Community? –

The radical theory of community is likely to attract criticism from orthodox political communitarians who either regard community as coterminous with society or see community solely in terms of the locality. Moreover opposition is also likely to emanate from defenders of orthodox political economy who fail to recognise the ways in which the pursuit of economic objectives may counteract principles of community or public goods. Orthodox communitarians play fast and loose with the concept of community. Because they see the homogeneous moral community as the key actor, they are dealing with an imaginary subject in the contemporary world. Thus they give community an elasticity of meaning that renders it virtually meaningless and redundant when it comes to informing policy proposals. In the hands of commentators such as Etzioni (1993) the Janus-faced nature of his conception of community becomes apparent as his arguments unravel. What is presented as a critique of liberal approaches to social policy concerns rapidly disintegrates into the language of liberal individualism. Thus the state is presented as an enemy in the discourses of 'moral authoritarian communitarianism' (Hughes 1996), whereas in radical approaches community cannot be established fruitfully without state action. Simultaneously, whilst orthodox communitarians call for a return to localised jurisdiction as an embodiment of communitarianism, they promote increasingly authoritarian and exclusionary means of maintaining the community. The radical approach on the other hand attempts to repudiate moral authoritarianism by providing a framework in which community becomes more clearly understandable and grounded in terms of political theory. Moreover it tries to bring out the issues of inclusion and exclusion (and the multiplicity of forms that they take) that are glossed over in much communitarian analysis and demonstrates their importance with regard to radical pluralism.

Despite the critique of economic orthodoxies, it is possible to imagine theories of community that could enable markets to function in a more effective fashion. Of course much economic theory depends upon the ways unfettered markets should work, the impediments to the unshackled performance of market mechanisms, and the ways in which economies should be organised to help them cope with the different demands that are made upon them. The economic experiments of the 1980s in the United Kingdom and the USA demonstrated the inadequacies of this market utopia. Because no economy operates according to these principles, we were led into theoretical cul-de-sacs that provided no alternatives when economic systems did not work as they were supposed to. The economic dimension of the theories of community examined in the book tries to identify the purpose of markets and provide a practical understanding of what we can expect them to achieve. Communitarians vary in the extent to which they feel the need to protect community from the logic of markets, with some such as Barber (1996) arguing strongly that there is a need to insulate community spaces from economic rationality.

This perspective has been taken up by recent radical theories of community. By empowering spheres of community, opportunities emerge to redefine the relationship between markets and the state. The argument here suggests that the demands on the state can be curtailed by enabling more activity with communities and extending their capacity for the provision of social welfare. At the same time the limitations placed around the jurisdiction of the state can also be applied to markets. Radical theories of community imply that we need to delineate a smaller but less cumbersome space in which market mechanisms could operate (O'Neill 1998). This theory of community then is centred upon the idea of moving beyond both the state and the market as providers of social welfare and developing a community sphere which would be responsive to needs in a way that neither markets nor the state can be. At the same time it would provide limitations on the power of the state such that the function of the latter would be reduced to the (albeit important) role of facilitating and overseeing the workings of communities and mediating when these communities come into conflict with one another. Simultaneously the radical theory of community would protect areas of welfare and common interest from the tentacles of economic rationality. It would prevent the principles of economic efficiency, profit and growth from interfering with spheres of life where they should not be the guiding values (Gorz 1989). It would delineate an economic sphere in which these values would predominate precisely because they were the most appropriate form of distributing specific resources. Whilst orthodox political economists will recoil at this vision of curtailing the territory in which economic rationality could pervade, the former perspective might just provide an avenue which would reinvigorate debates about why markets exist and what we actually expect our economies to do for us.

The overall aims of the book then emerge on two levels. On the first level it is concerned with the undertheorisation of the concept of community. Where community is employed it is often as a secondary device to support some other political objective. From this perspective the acreage devoted to studying communitarianism has a flimsy foundation in the sense that the idea of community itself has not been thought through in a systematic manner. Even if the reader does not concur with the arguments put forward here, it is hoped that the need to develop the concept of community is evident and that a serious attempt to address it has been undertaken. The second theme of the book is likely to be more controversial, namely the model that suggests that a space for community should be freed from the rationality associated with economics and market mechanisms. It is tentatively suggested that radical theories could assist the functioning and operation of markets through limiting them and freeing them from other social concerns. The development of the sphere of community could therefore reduce the social demands on market mechanisms. Again whilst this position is likely to attract criticism from more traditional political economy, it is designed to contribute to debates about post-orthodox approaches. It is hoped that, whether the reception is appreciative or hostile, the reader will regard the theory presented in this book as food for thought. Ultimately we need to rethink what communities actually are and what purposes we expect them to serve. Only then will we have solid foundations for communitarian politics, whether radical or not.

– Note –

1. The term 'political communitarianism' has been coined by Elizabeth Frazer (1999) to refer to the work of Etzioni and his followers. I shall also use the term 'orthodox communitarianism' to allude to this position because, as we will see in later chapters, there are reasons to regard Etzioni's position as almost 'anti-political'. In Chapter 2, I will also examine the labelling of Etzioni's work as 'moral authoritarianism' (Hughes 1996).

CHAPTER 2

Communitarianism and Liberalism: The Philosophical Debate

It is widely accepted that the landscape of political philosophy was reinvigorated after the publication of John Rawls' A *Theory of Justice* in 1971. This seminal work recast debates within liberalism and spawned a number of critical responses. This is the foundation upon which the debate has been constructed between liberals or individualists and communitarians. The criticisms of Rawls' work suggested that his liberalism was essentially asocial in the sense that it had, as a hypothetical foundation, a scenario in which individuals would decide upon appropriate forms of political organisation in an imaginary setting where they were behind a 'veil of ignorance'. Rawls argued that in this 'original position' individuals would choose a form of justice that was basically fair. Because this model imagines individuals in a pre-social position without prior social arrangements and institutions, Rawls was accused of developing a liberal theory in which the various ways in which humans interact and form associations was neglected. In this sense much of the criticism directed at Rawls was not of an ideological nature formed by opponents of his liberal project. Instead much of the analysis centred upon the methodological approaches that he employed to support his liberal political philosophy. Critics tended to suggest that the idea of this asocial individual was problematic precisely because it presented a model for political organisation that was inapplicable to the concrete situations in which political arrangements are established. In short, it was difficult to imagine the asocial individual as the primary agent in the formulation of political institutions when, in reality, no individual was asocial in the way that Rawls' hypothetical model implied.

Beyond this methodological issue, the debate inspired by Rawls' work has not been as clear cut as it is sometimes presented. Much recent work has been based upon a perceived division between liberal or individualist positions and those established by communitarians. According to this construction of the argument, there is a clear separation between theories that envisage the freedom of the individual as the primary normative objective and those that focus on the associations that individuals establish with one another and the ways these impact upon political arrangements. This interpretation of the debate is highly problematic for a number of reasons. An initial objection to this characterisation of the debate lies in the observation that a substantial number of the theorists involved in these debates share much of their position with those who are supposed to be their opponents. Few within the liberal camp, apart from the most extreme libertarians, reject the importance of political association and the formation of common institutions. Whilst these bonds may not be accorded the same priority as individual freedoms, they tend to feature all the same. Similarly most of the political philosophers who tend to be located within the communitarian school are essentially liberals. They may be liberals who retain elements of conservative thinking about the importance of communities in maintaining traditional forms of human association. On the other hand they may be liberals who have been influenced by socialist or social democratic perspectives about the centrality of human associations for the furtherance of the common good. Either way, few of the thinkers involved in communitarianism or the promotion of community in all its guises would present themselves as opponents of liberalism *per se*. Whilst they may reserve substantive criticism for elements of liberalism, most of them retain the primacy of community because it offers prospects for fulfilment for people on both individual and collective levels. Indeed it might be pertinent to suggest that community provides an arena in which individuals can establish common attachments that coincide with rather than contradict the pursuit of autonomously defined objectives.

A further problem with the debate as it is constructed in orthodox discourses relates to the nature of liberalism as an ideological tradition and the fact that communitarianism, to the extent that it exists as a movement at all, does not lend itself easily to definition as a political ideology. Whilst liberal political ideology has a long history, communitarianism is regarded as a contemporary response to liberalism. Thus commentators such as Gray (1997) posit communitarians *en masse* as critics of neo-liberalism, Rawlsian philosophy and indeed new liberalism amongst others. However, in practice, the ideas of some communitarians such as Amitai Etzioni tend actually to correspond with elements of individualist understandings of human agency and potential strategies for tackling the ills of modern Western societies. As such we can see that some liberals pay greater attention to community than others and that communitarians frequently employ discourses associated with liberalism. A further problem is generated by the pre-eminent position that the liberal–communitarian debate has achieved in contemporary political philosophy. As a result the immediacy and importance of other traditions within political thought has been undermined. In this sense important political debates have been impoverished by the dominant position held by liberalism and communitarianism and diminishing spaces for alternative perceptions of the key issues at stake. This does little to help with the process of unpacking liberal–communitarian debates, and it is the intention within the course of this chapter to elucidate the ideological background of debates between liberals and communitarians and, indeed, to demonstrate the affinities within, as well as the differences between the two traditions as they are usually interpreted.

– THE CRITIQUE OF RAWLS –

The controversial aspect of Rawls' thought relates to his employment of the imagined original position as the basis of his conception of justice. Thus he envisages a situation whereby individuals involved in the process of formulating social and political institutions are denied access to elements of self-knowledge. In this scenario individuals must decide which arrangements they want to set in place whilst ignorant with regard to how their social position will affect them when those arrangements are set in place. Behind the 'veil of ignorance' we may not know our gender or ethnicity or social class, for example, and how they might mitigate against us in society. These attributes and talents are distributed on the basis of brute luck and Rawls does not believe that this arbitrary system of distribution is an appropriate basis upon which to allocate resources. Thus, for Rawls, in the original position individuals would opt for egalitarian forms of distribution rather than running the risk of being in arbitrary penury should a more unequal system of distribution prevail. In this situation, 'if people don't know who they are going to be, then it will make sense for them to choose fair or just principles to regulate their society' (Mulhall and Swift 1997: 3).

Rawls does not advocate a strong egalitarian ethos directed towards equalisation of outcomes but he does imply that individuals would choose the security of a relatively fair basic distribution over the potential of being a winner in a more competitive system. This leaves Rawls open to critics who reject the psychology which informs individuals in his original position.

Many market liberals would suggest that individuals have a more natural disposition towards embracing risk. Even if this was not a feature of the psychological make-up of most people, market liberals question the idea of overriding the interests and money-making potential of entrepreneurs with a less risky acceptance of a fairer society by the majority. From this perspective Rawls' position might undermine the natural order that is generated by the operation of market mechanisms unfettered from intervention. For market liberals the latter provides efficient wealth creation and thus greater aggregate social welfare as there are more resources in society as a whole. The Rawlsian response to these criticisms is usefully summarised by Michael Sandel:

> the distribution of talents and assets and even efforts by which some get more and others get less is arbitrary from a moral point of view, a matter of good luck. To distribute the good things in life on the basis of these differences is not to do justice, but simply to carry over into human arrangements the arbitrariness of social and natural contingency. We deserve, as individuals, neither the talents our good fortune may have brought, nor the benefits that flow from them. We should therefore regard these talents as common assets, and regard one another as common beneficiaries of the rewards they bring. (Sandel 1992: 21)

For Sandel, whilst it might pertinently be argued that the market liberal perspective is just as unrealistic a foundational model for social, economic and political agreements as Rawls' original position, it is less concerned with the formation of a fair system than is the case with the latter. Where market liberals argue for a natural model of justice as they perceive it, Rawls sets out to envisage a way in which individuals come to agree on institutions that are just because they are fair. They are deemed to be fair because they are based upon individuals being treated as free and equal citizens regardless of the arbitrary distribution of skills and talents.

In terms of the theorisation of community however, the Rawlsian perception of justice as fairness raises a number of problems. According to his communitarian critics, the most notable of these difficulties are the suggestion that the right comes before the good (Sandel 1992), the difference principle and Rawls' treatment of economic inequalities, and the failure of Rawls (and indeed the entitlement theory developed by Robert Nozick) to adequately deal with the idea of desert (MacIntyre 1992). For philosophical communitarians such as Sandel the process of envisaging community is usually a teleological process involving the pursuit of the good society. This suggests that the objective of political theory should be to construct a model of the common good to provide the social context in which individuals would experience their freedom. Sandel is concerned with 'a conception of the self which regards the self as partly constituted by its ends and attachments, discovering them through a process of self-interpretation' (Mason 2000: 21). Rawlsian liberalism, on the other hand, posits that 'the right is prior to the good':

> This [Rawlsian] liberalism says . . . that what makes the just society just is not the telos or purpose or end at which it aims, but precisely its refusal to choose in advance among competing purposes and ends. In its constitution and its laws, the just society seeks to provide a framework within which its citizens can pursue their own values and ends, consistent with a similar liberty for others. (Sandel 1992: 13)

The implications of Rawlsian liberalism suggest that individual rights have greater philosophical significance than broader concerns with the common good of society as a whole. Moreover the pursuit of a Rawlsian theory of justice must override Aristotelian teleology in the sense that the principles of justice supersede any particular ideological perceptions of the best political system in which justice or fairness can best be achieved. It is in this sense then, that, in Sandel's eyes, the right is prior to the good in Rawls' political philosophy. The latter also underestimates the difficulties in establishing a system of justice that enables competing visions of the good to co-exist in a harmonious fashion.

The difference principle plays a central role in Rawls' thought on social and economic inequalities and his ideas for the redistribution of wealth. Put simply, the difference principle suggests that, under prior consideration of achieving the maximal equal liberty between individuals, the second principle of justice is that 'only those social and economic inequalities that benefit the least-advantaged members of society' are to be permitted (Sandel 1992: 20). Thus, whilst equality is a desirable objective up to the point where it does not harm the worst-off, inequalities can exist and are likely to in modern societies. This difference principle provides a rather formal definition of the justification of redistribution in the sense that it is primarily concerned with criteria for economic arrangements. Although Rawls argues for equal access to primary goods which 'comprise liberties, opportunities, income and wealth and the bases of self-respect' (Brown 1986: 56), there is no strong teleological theory of the social and economic institutions and arrangements that are the most appropriate for facilitating his theory of justice. This creates problems with regard to the practical enactment of the Rawlsian vision of justice as there is little indication of the ways in which social, economic and political institutions may impair or enhance justice.

Rawls also builds a 'lexical order' into his theory so that the difference principle becomes the guiding principle only after two other criteria have been met: first, there is the notion of greatest equal liberty and, second, the idea of fair equality of opportunity. In this sense Rawls provides a philosophy in which welfare and redistribution are ordered third in priority after maximal equal freedom and equal opportunities. According to Brown, in practice, this results in a defence of liberal democracy as we know it:

> Rawls wants to offer a justification of societies not unlike . . . modern Western democracies. There will be a 'free-enterprise' economy with private ownership of capital and natural resources. This will be regulated by the state, using mostly macro-economic techniques, in order to promote reasonably full employment and low inflation. For those who are unable to find work or are otherwise unable to support themselves, social security (financed by taxation) will ensure a decent income. In short Rawls is reasonably confident that our structural arrangements are just. (Brown 1986: 58)

Even when Brown was writing his book, this summary of the general trends of Western liberal democracies must have begun to look a little anachronistic. Indeed for twenty years after A *Theory of Justice* was first published, there was a gradual move away from this model of social and economic organisation. The idea that welfare should provide a 'decent income' has long been undermined in countries such as the USA and the UK and the pursuit of full employment was effectively abandoned. The nineteenth-century spectre of 'the undeserving poor' became a popular notion once again as questions were raised as to whether the individuals in receipt of welfare deserved the benefits which they were given. However, such is the elastic nature of Rawlsian liberalism that it was not negated by these social developments. His theoretical ideas could still be used by governments of different political hues to justify cuts in social welfare provision (even though cuts in benefits may not translate into reduced expenditure on welfare, of course). As long as changes in provision did not contradict the difference principle then they could be presented as just in Rawlsian terms. The reason for this is that Rawls did not tie his theory of justice to a strong conceptualisation of needs[1] or to the idea of desert.

The notion of needs plays a rather minor role in Rawlsian thought but tends to feature more heavily in communitarian thinking. The reason for this is that most theories of social justice attempt to engage with not just the redistribution of financial resources but also the actual conditions in which individuals lead their lives. Where Rawls' focuses on the financial wherewithal of the least well-off as the basis of political justice, communitarian social justice highlights a wider range of issues that impact upon the everyday lives of people. On top of this there should be a more explicit concern in communitarian thinking with not just the least well-off communities but also other communities which may suffer inequalities or discrimination for a range of reasons. Therefore communitarians should recognise that we need to construct theoretical positions in which differing needs of diverse communities are recognised and accommodated. Of course, as we will see, many contemporary communitarians fail to deliver on these key points, but this does not negate the importance of theories of community that actually address the question of human needs, whilst rejecting the poverty of the Rawlsian position. In the case of the latter, 'it becomes difficult to see how the Rawlsian approach can adequately operationalise the provision of welfare at an acceptable level to essentially needy groups' (Campbell 1988: 88).

Rawlsian procedural justice relies to some extent upon a model of market liberalism in its depiction of human rationality and economic efficiency. Thus it appears that needs are best satisfied through activity in markets that are freed from governmental intervention with its attendant inefficiency. In this vein market liberals tend to subscribe to the Hayekian view that free markets bring with them 'catallaxy' or a natural order. However the neo-liberal perspective on social welfare has come in for sustained criticism from a wide range of ideological traditions (see the coverage in Little 1998, Chapter 3). In terms of the discussion here, the most important of these critical points are that, first, markets are incapable of understanding human needs or public goods and, second, that the operation of markets tends to distort and undermine our perception of needs. Now Rawls is clearly aware of the problems associated with market liberal systems as he believes in the requirement for redistribution, but his use of proceduralism akin to market liberal perspectives actually undermines the theory of justice because he fails to recognise how social justice is eroded by the model he employs. Rawls is well aware that markets do not react to needs, but he does not see this as problematic because he believes that needs do not play a strong role in the theory of justice. What should be clear is that the Rawlsian theory of justice does not comprise a strong conception of social justice. In this sense again, then, the methodology employed by Rawls is a problematic aspect for those who argue that asocial individualism is impractical and that the original position and veil of ignorance are uncertain foundations for a strong theory of social justice. In the words of Campbell:

> Rawls's system, using as its basis the original position, comes down in favour of choice and opportunity for those with the ability to grasp it, rather than of a sort of full-blooded commitment to satisfaction of needs which is bound to undermine a free-market system but nevertheless seems to be an element in our sense of justice . . . It seems then that, in the event, there is an unresolved tension between the libertarian ethos of the original position and the reflective equilibrium of our considered moral judgements which incorporate treatment in accordance with basic need. (Campbell 1988: 94)

Rawls has also been the subject of criticism from those who believe that a theory of justice needs to incorporate a notion of desert. Desert is a complicated issue for communitarian thinkers because by implication it suggests that something could be withheld from those people who do not qualify for it for some (potentially arbitrary) reason. Indeed, as we shall see, many mainstream communitarians do employ exclusionary ideas with regard to those who do not subscribe to their preferred vision of community. Rawls is troubled by the notion of desert as he believes that it can be erroneously used to introduce entitlement criteria into perceptions of justice and frequently desert is used to justify the unequal distribution of resources. Thus those opposed to redistribution can argue that a given state of distribution is fair and just because the people who have acquired more resources deserve to keep them. This will either be because the process of acquisition of those resources was legal or because the individual beneficiaries have more talent in the system of acquisition than others. For Rawls both of these justifications for desert are predicated upon arbitrary benefits that those who have them were fortunate to come by. In the Rawlsian original position, of course, individuals would be unaware of their precise talents and the riches (or lack thereof) that their talents would bring. As such, under the veil of ignorance, individuals would choose fair shares because they would not want to risk being relatively untalented and therefore be cast into a penurious position. So for Rawls the opposition to desert as a criterion of justice is central to his theory (although he gives over relatively little space to direct discussion of the notion of desert). What he does suggest is that the reliance on market mechanisms as systems of distributing justice cannot countenance issues of desert because the moral notion of deserving something withers when it comes into harsh contact with the laws of supply and demand. Only under the Rawlsian ideal type of justice could it be said that individuals would have the resources which they deserve or are entitled to – and even then Rawls does not go this far in his theory of justice. For him, desert and moral worth 'cannot be introduced until after the principles of justice and of natural duty and obligation have been acknowledged. Once these principles are on hand, moral worth can be defined as having a sense of justice . . . the virtues can be characterized as desires or tendencies to act upon the corresponding principles' (Rawls 1972: 312–13).

Communitarian thinking tends to reject the Rawlsian perspective on desert and moral worth precisely because the worth that is accorded to individuals is disassociated from the social and associational context in which independent worth is ultimately derived. Thus communitarian theories of social justice should recognise that Rawlsian liberalism fails to constitute the actual ways in which people experience their moral worth and thus the context within which we decide what goods individuals deserve. Indeed by positing moral worth as a basis of distributing resources, communitarians are able – if they choose to do so – to move away from individualistic claims of entitlement based on rights. From a more radical communitarian perspective, one might argue that individuals are eligible for welfare benefits by dint of their independent moral worth and their membership of community or society. Unfortunately for Rawls his reliance on 'a conception of the person as antecedently individuated' (Mulhall and Swift 1997: 61) precludes his theory from recognising the ways in which our worth can only be derived from the relationships that constitute ourselves and form our identity. This kind of reckoning is reflected in MacIntyre's communitarian critique of Rawlsian liberalism:

> Individuals are thus . . . primary and society secondary, and the identification of individual interests is prior to, and independent of, the construction of any moral or social bonds between them. But . . . the notion of desert is at home only in the context of a community whose primary bond is a shared understanding both of the good for man and of the good of that community and where individuals identify their primary interests with reference to those goods. (MacIntyre 1992: 58)

The dilemma that communitarians must address is whether we regard all of our sources of worth and our predispositions to be imposed upon us due to accidents of birth. Arguably this is the implication of MacIntyre's perspective but alternative communitarian strategies suggest that our sense of worth is a combination of identities over which we have little control and some that are chosen. What is not in dispute within communitarian thought is the view that individuals need common projects and identities as a source of selfhood. Thus there will be associations from which we might feel we derive certain rights or independent worth and which also contain the source of responsibilities related to membership. The two need not be directly reciprocal but rather they are bonds which may be established in a rather informal or uncodified manner. This has implications for the notion of desert that communitarians might employ because MacIntyre, for example, argues for an 'account of human community in which the notion of desert in relation to contributions to the common tasks of that community in pursuing shared goods could provide the basis for judgements about virtue and injustice' (MacIntyre 1992: 59). This position implies we can make judgements about virtue in communities which feed into our notion of desert. Clearly this could provide ammunition for those who wish to confine welfare, for example, to only those citizens who demonstrate the requisite moral virtues that the moral guardians of society have decided upon. Indeed in the work of modern political communitarians such as Etzioni, it is clear that this kind of moral prescription could be imposed in an authoritarian fashion (Hughes 1996). Arguably a radical theorisation of community should attempt to formulate a conception of the independent moral worth of the individual whilst simultaneously recognising that the identity and selfhood that people develop is grounded in their relationships and associations with the various communities of which they are a part. In this scenario it becomes difficult to envisage virtue and desert being decided by a single moral community.

To complete our analysis of Rawls in terms of the theorisation of the principles of community, it is important to return to the methodology employed in the creation of the original position and the veil of ignorance. The theory of justice that he envisages clearly has origins in the contractarian tradition and is designed to provide a foundation for procedural fairness (Brown 1986: 59). However, the Rawlsian theory of justice is founded on a dubious assertion of psychological motivation and a rather one-dimensional understanding of human association. Not surprisingly, for communitarians such as Sandel and MacIntyre this is highly problematic. Their objections are neatly summarised by Mulhall and Swift:

> [T]he contractual approach to political theory . . . embodies the mistaken view
> that people's ends are formed independently of or prior to society, which is

regarded as the outcome of negotiation between individuals whose ends are already given. For the communitarian, this conception overlooks the way in which it is the kind of society in which people live that affects their understandings both of themselves and of how they should lead their lives. (Mulhall and Swift 1997: 13)

To read Rawls one might be led to believe that humans only associate and co-operate for ultimately selfish objectives – this is supposedly what it is to be rational. Where, one might ask, is the place for voluntarism, charitable activity, friendship and altruism in this scenario for the rational individual? Of course this is not Rawls' intention and he would recognise that humans associate for many reasons apart from those that are rational according to his perspective. The problem created by his antecedently individuated person, by implication, is that these associations and interactions are something that individuals either do out of self-interest or without a rational basis. It then appears irrational for individuals to co-operate except for selfish, individualistic reasons. Again Rawls would not necessarily agree with this but this only serves to demonstrate how problematic the original position and the veil of ignorance are when it comes to practical politics and everyday life. Decisions about social, political and economic arrangements do not take place within the narrow proceduralism that Rawls employs in his conception of justice. Put at the most simplest level, communitarians find it difficult to accept a theory of justice in which the crux of the idea is based on such an abstraction. In the words of Tam, 'from a communitarian point of view, it is the resort to this form of procedural device as opposed to any practical process involving citizens in the community, which casts the most serious doubt on the validity of his whole argument' (Tam 1998: 47). Of course this does negate the importance of theorising the principles of community and to that end the next step in the process is to identify general themes within liberalism that, despite the criticisms of Rawlsian thought above, still have a key role to play in the rethinking of community.

– COMMUNITY AND LIBERAL VALUES –

As suggested at the beginning of the chapter, any attempt to develop new perspectives on community needs to engage with some of the central ideas in contemporary liberalism such as neutrality, diversity and toleration. In this vein, communitarianism must address the concepts that liberals have employed as means of containing difference and value pluralism. The notion of neutrality is one of the most important concepts in this process in modern liberal thought. It refers to 'the view that the state should not reward or penalize particular conceptions of the good life but, rather, should provide a neutral framework within which different and potentially conflicting conceptions of the good can be pursued' (Kymlicka 1992: 165). Instinctively this view, which implies toleration of different perceptions of the good, has much in its favour. Although it may seem at odds with communitarian theories based on Aristotelian teleology, it can still offer us much if the teleological objective is the toleration of difference within a common framework. Thus if our perception of the common good is predicated upon our recognition of difference, then this should not conflict with the existence of a multiplicity of conceptualisations of the good life. Of course, in practice, these different conceptions of the good are likely to come into conflict, and this is undoubtedly where state mechanisms are required to adjudicate in cases of contestation, as we shall see later in the book. The task at hand here, though, is to analyse the extent to which a commitment to difference and multiple conceptions of the good necessitates a liberal conception of neutrality. Moreover we must also ask whether the acceptance of different conceptions of the good conflicts with the predominant teleological approach which is, of course, concerned with an idea of the common good as an attainable objective.

Using the ideas of Joseph Raz (1986), Kymlicka (1992) offers us two different types of liberal neutrality, namely, consequential and justificatory neutrality.[2] The former refers to the idea that the outcomes of government policies should have a neutral impact in terms of not favouring or hindering any particular picture of the good life. The latter seeks to provide a model in which, although government activity is neutral with regard to particular conceptions of the good, it may, *in practice*, help one version of the good over others. In the case of this justificatory perspective, it does not matter if the state acts in ways which favour certain groups as long as there is not an intentional concern to favour those groups. To the extent that any model of neutrality is practically applicable, the latter appears more attuned to the realities of existence in liberal democratic societies than consequential neutrality. Kymlicka suggests that Rawls endorses a justificatory conceptualisation of neutrality (although elements of a consequential approach are also evident). Thus, for Rawls, the 'state does not justify its actions by reference to some public ranking of the intrinsic value of different ways of life, for there is no public ranking to refer to. This kind of neutrality is consistent with the legitimate non-

neutral consequences of cultural competition and individual responsibility'
(Kymlicka 1992: 169).

The Rawlsian perspective is, then, more persuasive in the defence of
neutrality than liberalisms that rely more heavily on consequential models.
However, the major question raised by communitarian thinkers is the
extent to which any model of the state or government policy-making
can be genuinely neutral? Instinctively many analysts of the state, particularly those who adopt a radical approach, will suggest that such is the
distribution of power that it is highly unlikely that the state could ever
operate in a neutral fashion. In this sense neutrality is itself a value-laden
concept. Moreover this also applies to the policy initiatives developed by
governments in liberal democratic states. The arguments with regard to the
state and government vary slightly. Where the state is criticised, it tends to
be on the basis that bureaucracy perpetuates itself and therefore that most
initiatives derived from state institutions tend to reproduce state power.
With governments, on the other hand, the critical argument is that, such
are the sectional interests which governments try to appease (for example,
particular groups or classes in society), there is little chance of them actually
being able to claim justificatory let alone consequential neutrality. Taking
these criticisms on board, it seems that the best that can realistically be
aspired to is justificatory neutrality but that the practical realities of modern
politics make even that idea appear unattainable.

What then are the options for communitarians in addressing these
problems? One approach is to look to the teleological theory that many
communitarians espouse and argue that neutrality is not a desirable feature
of governments or the state anyway because they should follow the path of
the common good. If there is an agreed common good, then the role of
governments is to pursue policies that would have appropriate ends that are
consonant with it. This is a charge that Kymlicka aims at communitarians,
and, indeed, as we shall see, there is a tendency within some forms of
communitarianism to forward morally prescriptive models of the common
good. Even more worrying are attempts to use the critique of state neutrality
to justify a non-neutral *status quo*. For Kymlicka, this is evident in some
more conservative versions of communitarianism that fail to recognise how
cultural traditions have frequently been generated by historically small
sections of the population (Kymlicka 1992: 182). However there is no
reason why this approach to liberal neutrality should be the definitive one
associated with communitarianism. In terms of democratic renewal, a more
radical communitarian approach might be one where the role of govern-

ments would be to achieve the decentralisation of state power. Thus rather than the teleological goal being the pursuit of a singular common good, communitarians could argue that their objective would be a form of political organisation in which a range of communities could express themselves. This need not imply a consequential vision of neutrality and goes some way towards incorporating elements of justificatory thinking. Ultimately, though, radical approaches to community are not predicated upon the appeal to neutrality, even if they may provide sounder appraisals of the issues than is the case in much liberal thought.

Ultimately radical interpretations of a limited, decentralised state may still imbue state institutions with more power than liberals would find palatable. For example, a state organised along the lines indicated by the radical communitarian theories above might allow the expression of the views of a range of groups with unpalatable or offensive standpoints, but not be required to justify itself in terms of actually treating these groups equally in practice. It would therefore be possible to envisage a scenario where communities are allowed to voice their concerns (however unpleasant), but the state is not required to demonstrate neutrality with regard to treating those views in the same light when it comes to actually constructing policy. No doubt this may be deemed unsatisfactory for many liberals but it does demonstrate a blend of communitarian and liberal perspectives. They are clearly not mutually exclusive. The strength of the liberal critique of orthodox communitarianism lies in the recognition of the heterogeneous nature of Western liberal democracies (although Kymlicka notes how this isn't always at the forefront of the work of liberals such as Rawls and Dworkin). By and large they are not comprised of singular cultural traditions or indeed communities. Rather they involve a range of communities with varying concerns from specific local needs to those of different ethnic groups. Not surprisingly this multiplies the likelihood of different conceptualisations of the good. The task for communitarians then is to construct strategies that embrace the diversity of modern societies in the knowledge that in practice liberal conceptualisations of state neutrality are difficult to operationalise.

Ultimately Kymlicka ends up attacking communitarianism (as a coherent whole, it seems) for requiring the state (neutral or otherwise) to ensure the appropriate conditions for human co-operation to flourish. It is a strange criticism that treats the state in all its forms as some kind of evil which 'is likely to distort the normal processes of collective deliberations and cultural development' (Kymlicka 1992: 184–5). Not only does this neglect the complexity of communitarian thinking by implying that there is some kind of unified communitarian conception of the state, but it also perpetuates the unfortunate dualism between liberalism and communitarianism that tarnishes the philosophical debate. In an otherwise well-balanced argument, Kymlicka concludes by resurrecting old generalisations about the nature of thinking about community and implies that communitarian ideas about social relations and the pursuit of the common good should be realised through the lens of liberalism. This kind of approach also appears in the work of another advocate of liberalism, namely, Amy Gutmann. In her critique of communitarian analyses of liberalism Gutmann argues against 'the tyranny of dualisms':

> [E]ither our identities are independent of our ends, leaving us totally free to choose our life plans, or they are constituted by community, leaving us totally encumbered by socially given ends; either justice takes absolute priority over the good or the good takes the place of justice; either justice must be independent of all historical and social particularities or virtue must depend completely on the particular social practices of each society; and so on. The critics [of liberalism] thereby do a disservice to not only liberal but communitarian values, since the same method that reduces liberalism to an extreme metaphysical vision also renders communitarian theories unacceptable. (Gutmann 1992: 130)

Gutmann's argument is based on moving the debate on from that over atomism and the asocial individualism of Rawlsian thought. Instead, she recognises that there are other pertinent issues which liberals need to address: 'the real, and recognized, dilemma of modern liberalism . . . is not that people are naturally egotistical, but that they disagree about the nature of the good life' (Gutmann 1992: 130). As noted above this provides a challenge not only to liberal theories but also to those communitarian approaches that are predicated upon a definitive teleology about the nature of the good life. So, we might ask, where does Gutmann's initial point take us? What does it offer us with regard to the reinterpretation of the debates between liberals and communitarians?

Initially Gutmann appears to recognise that the liberal/communitarian dichotomy as presented in the orthodox philosophical debate is problematic. Indeed there is considerable strength in the argument that '[c]ommunitarianism has the potential for helping us discover a politics that combines community with a commitment to basic liberal values' (Gutmann 1992: 133). Here she implies that a blend of communitarian concerns and liberal values can lead us to a new perspective on these debates. However

Gutmann's stance is less persuasive when she argues that the 'failure to undermine liberalism suggests not that there are no communitarian values but that they are properly viewed as supplementing rather than supplanting basic liberal values' (1992: 133). This is a case of Gutmann, who stridently opposed the 'tyranny of dualisms', reducing the debate to one of communitarianism versus liberalism. Thus she feels that the perceived failure of communitarianism to win the argument against liberalism leaves us only with the possibility of following the liberal path. In subsuming communitarian ideas within an all-encompassing liberalism, Gutmann neglects other less orthodox interpretations of community which emanate from beyond the parameters of the formal debate between liberals and communitarians. She is quite correct to recognise that the principles of community are not incompatible with some of the values espoused in liberal thought. That said, this does not mean that the promotion of community should be seamlessly subsumed within the broad church of liberalism. There is a strong tradition of concern for community within a range of ideological traditions and, as such, it is disingenuous to claim a natural location for communitarian thinking within liberalism. Moreover it does not really help us to differentiate the communitarianism of MacIntyre, for example, from more radical commentators on community such as Michael Walzer.

The problem with Gutmann's perspective, as indeed is the case with Rawls, is that there is insufficient emphasis on alternative arrangements to modern liberal democracies. Indeed there is an implication in Gutmann's argument that, rather than trying to develop a radical communitarian politics, we should only seek to modernise liberalism. Whilst she is receptive to the idea of establishing more democratic communities and is aware of the economic and political ramifications of such a strategy, she does not see the pathway to change emanating from communitarian criticisms of liberalism. In this sense we are left with the process of reforming liberalism and the neglect of more radical forms of communitarian politics than are evident in the dominant academic debates. Gutmann's perspective ignores the ways in which theories of community have attempted to counteract the limitations of liberal theories of neutrality and have provided new models of community and governance. Many of these approaches to community have embraced a recognition of difference and addressed questions of toleration and respect. This implies that theorists of community must demonstrate the ways in which they provide a distinctive method of dealing with issues of diversity and toleration that supersedes the defence of liberal approaches justified by Kymlicka and Gutmann.

_ DIVERSITY, TOLERATION AND _
¯ THE POLITICS OF DIFFERENCE ¯

In addressing these points it is perhaps appropriate to begin with the work of one of the foremost theorists of the politics of difference in contemporary political theory, namely, Iris Marion Young (1990a, 1990b, 1993; Lister 1998; Baumeister 2000). Whilst there is a long history of theorisation of difference and diversity in liberalism, the issue has been reinterpreted in recent times by the contributions of feminists such as Young and radical democrats (see Mouffe 1992, 1993a, 1993b). Young has attempted to construct a theory of social justice in which the diverse views and needs of different groups in society are understood and equally respected. However, instead of pursuing this vision of justice through the lens of distribution, the great strength of Young's work is that it recognises the importance of power to any conception of social justice – even if her disassociation of power and distribution is problematic (Frazer and Lacey 1993: 193–4). She argues that the impact of power relations on social justice takes the form of five sources of oppression: exploitation; marginalisation; powerlessness; cultural imperialism; and violence. For Harvey, this 'multi-dimensional conception of social justice is extremely useful. It alerts us to the existence of a "long social and political frontier" of political action to roll back multiple oppressions. It also emphasises the heterogeneity of experience of injustice' (Harvey 1993: 107). In this sense Young's thought provides us with greater recognition of the practical difficulties of generating social justice than is the case with Rawlsian distributive justice.

Young recognises that groups in society contain significant differences within them. Identity, then, is not given by the fact that we are members of a certain group. The importance of any group will vary to different members of the group. Moreover individuals are likely to be members of a multiplicity of groups that are each in their own way sources of the self as they contribute to individual identity. In terms of community this suggests that we should be careful not to present communities as homogeneous forms of association that have a uniform impact upon their members and that is evident in many contemporary analyses of community. However, Young is a strident critic of theories of community because she feels they are centred on a wrong-headed and anachronistic desire to prioritise face-to-face relationships in small communities instead of her radical, post-modern conception of the individual. This leads her to suggest that modern urban living is more desirable than models of the traditional *Gemeinschaft* community as the former has moved away from the constraints of the latter and enabled new freer forms of identity formation founded on difference. Nonetheless whilst Young's ideas are constructed in opposition to those of theorists of community, her idea of the politics of difference clearly can contribute to new ways of thinking about community. What that requires, however, is to disassociate the actual mechanics of the politics of difference from Young's one-dimensional and prejudiced interpretation of the meaning of community. In this sense we must recognise Young's contribution to the theorisation of social justice based on diversity while simultaneously rejecting her 'reductionist directions in which group identities and communities overwhelm all else. In such worlds the self literally disappears, and tyranny looms . . .' (Fowler 1995: 95). Thus Young fails to recognise the vitality of new conceptualisations of community that embrace the kind of difference which she advocates. In the words of Weeks:

> [C]ommunities are not fixed once and for all. They change as the arguments which shape them over time continue, and as other communities exercise their gravitational pull . . . The social relations of a community are repositories of meaning for its members not sets of mechanical linkages between isolated individuals. A community offers a 'vocabulary of values' through which individuals construct their understanding of the social world, and of their sense of identity and belonging. (Weeks 1993: 198)

Therefore Young's one-dimensional depiction of the community serves to undermine the fact that many of her ideas actually come rather close to the radical communitarian ideas with which we are concerned here (Frazer and Lacey 1993: 204).

Young can also be criticised for failing to devote enough attention to the relationships within groups and the importance of communities in providing membership and contributing to common understandings of social justice. Indeed this is one of the most important shortcomings that derive from her inability to see anything else in theories of community apart from traditional *Gemeinschaft* perspectives. The focus on the relationship between groups and recognition of difference within groups necessitates a discussion of the liberal notion of toleration. The acceptance of diversity in liberal theory has usually entailed that a model of toleration must enter the equation given the likely conflict that might ensue from different groups pursuing their own idea of the good. In terms of developing the theory of community this also implies discussion of whether we need to move beyond the rather limited notion of liberal tolerance and focus on more substantive ideas such as respect. Liberals have traditionally preferred to concentrate on toleration and this relates to the theory of neutrality espoused by Rawls because he believes that political justice 'must allow for a diversity of doctrines and the plurality of conflicting, and indeed incommensurable, conceptions of the good affirmed by the members of existing democratic societies' (Rawls 1992: 188). Critics of liberal neutrality such as Frazer and Lacey put forward a perfectionist theory in which the complexities of diverse societies, social inequalities and differentials of power are taken into account. They argue we need a clearer understanding of the pressing political issues that affect the politics of difference and they attempt to provide a more developed theory of diversity that embraces a concern for equality as well as autonomy. Thus they go beyond advocacy of mere toleration in arguing for 'the positive value of respect for diversity in terms of the creation of a supportive social environment in which citizens share a concern about, and even accept a certain responsibility for, each other's well-being' (Frazer and Lacey 1993: 206). Clearly this implies a more developed conceptualisation of obligation and social context than is the case with Rawlsian neutrality and associated liberal theorisations of toleration.

The position adopted by Frazer and Lacey recognises that in conditions of inequality the notion of toleration may not provide the kinds of equal freedoms with which Rawls is concerned. It is quite possible that societies could exist whereby differences between groups or communities were accepted or tolerated and yet the material conditions in which more deprived communities experience life could deprive them of autonomy. In this sense we can recognise difference and tolerate alternative conceptions of the good without providing the resources necessary for people to follow autonomous courses of action. What this means is that it is possible (even within the Rawlsian model of distribution) for individuals to be provided with liberties to a relatively egalitarian extent but for them to experience simultaneously limitations on their action due to the communities or groups they belong to. There are many practical examples of excluded communities in modern liberal democracies that prove that individuals can be accorded rights and membership of wider political entities such as the state and still face exclusion because of the particular communities that they belong to. For example, we can argue that discrimination against ethnic minorities or disabled people may lead to their social exclusion, even though they may have formal rights and membership of the polity. In this sense it is clear that communities can exist in societies without gaining recognition, tolerance or respect. Indeed, as Fletcher notes, it is patently obvious that 'generalized tolerance carries with it a measure of indifference. Not hating the other often derives from simply not caring about what he or she thinks or does' (Fletcher 1996: 231).

In this light the notion of tolerance does not necessarily entail a strong commitment to allowing others to develop their own perspective of the good and express it in the public domain. Indeed, in both Rawlsian liberalism and the political communitarianism of Amitai Etzioni, tolerance is a virtue to be exercised towards the views and behaviour of people in the private sphere. Both see the public sphere on the other hand as a space that should be dominated by universal values of either procedural justice or the moral community. Moreover there is a continuing suspicion that some liberal theories of toleration gloss over the objection that groups should not have to justify why they should be tolerated. From this perspective the elements of difference should clearly not be regarded as grounds of intolerance anyway, for example in racial discrimination. The point is aptly made by Mendus, who comments that if 'the circumstances of toleration are circumstances of diversity coupled with dislike, disapproval or disgust, then tolerating means putting up with things which we dislike, disapprove of, or find disgusting' (Mendus 1989: 159). This outcome of liberal theorisation of toleration does not ask people to face up to difference and to grapple with a variety of conceptions of the good. Indeed it does not even require us to treat alternative visions as anything to do with the good. Liberal theory implies that we put up with difference rather than recognising the valuable contribution that diversity can bring to public dialogue over the most appropriate social and political institutions in any given society.

The Rawlsian conception of tolerance of different conceptions of the good is really only concerned with permitting individuals to have their own private thoughts about the good. It is not a guideline for policy formation. Thus Rawls implies that 'each man or woman must be free to hold his or her view of what the full good really is. But these comprehensive views of the good life must remain the private convictions of individuals' (Hollenbach 1995: 144). This suggests a rather limited conceptualisation of the importance of difference. Rather than celebrating diversity and using it as a guiding principle for the development of public policies, Rawls leaves us only with the freedom to think what we like in the private domain. If this is the meaning of toleration, then political liberalism is not expecting much from modern citizens. It is a model that still leaves space for prejudice and exclusion when it comes to access to the public sphere. More developed theories of civil society and the public sphere, whilst tending to recognise the potential for conflict, also suggest that it is important that individuals are able to express their perceptions of the good life in the public domain. This differs substantively from the Rawlsian model of toleration based on 'the method of avoidance', which, according to Hollenbach, fails to face up to the realities of modern diverse societies:

> The problems of a deeply interdependent world in which diverse communities not only rub shoulders but must rely on each other for their very survival demand more. They demand positive engagement with those who are other or different. Such positive engagement . . . can be dealt with only on the cultural level, the domain where people's values and imaginative vision of the good are operative in uncoerced, free interaction with each other. This larger solidarity, therefore, is a matter of the kind of virtue that members of the body politic or civil society are capable of attaining. (Hollenbach 1995: 149–50)

There has been a growth in literature on the concept of respect in recent years as a possible alternative to toleration. George Fletcher has asserted that respect as a concept suffers from a vagueness that is not the case with the idea of toleration (Fletcher 1996: 239). This is problematic because, as he himself notes, toleration is frequently a mere smokescreen for indifference. Respect, on the other hand, actually implies genuine engagement with other cultures and different perceptions of the good. It does not imply that we must take on board the actual views of the other or that we even accept the verity of the conception of the good that is deployed. What respect does involve is the acceptance of the right of individuals to formulate conceptions of the good and to express them in the public domain. This does not mean that they will form the basis of public policy but that they will be taken into account in the formulation of policy. Tolerance presumes little of this and assumes moderation and temperance where none may exist. Whilst Fletcher is probably right that respect is more difficult to conceptualise (and indeed operationalise) than toleration, the former is a more appropriate concept to a developed theory of community than is the case within the model of tolerance that appears in orthodox liberalism.

The rejection of liberal toleration as the basis of a coherent understanding of how diverse communities with different conceptions of the good can co-exist in one society also derives from the critique of state neutrality above. The latter feeds into conventional pluralist arguments about the role of the state in which it is a mere arbiter between different individuals and communities. This orthodox pluralism fails to take sufficient account of power differentials between different groups and the difficulties that weaker communities can face in attempting to influence the public agenda. Moreover the liberal conceptualisation of the state also fails to provide a substantive theory of membership by relying primarily upon rights-based frameworks that assume membership of society on a rather formal basis. It fails to recognise how certain individuals and communities can be excluded from substantive social membership through a range of factors from discrimination to lack of access to resources and services. Thus a range of impediments can impact upon the extent of membership that individuals encounter and this experience suggests that the state is not the model of impartiality and neutrality that is often assumed in liberal theory. However this point does not entail the imposition of prescriptive ideas of what the state should do nor does it imply that we should attempt to limit toleration. To be clear, the criticism is not of tolerance *per se* as a way of helping diverse groups to live together, but rather that liberal theories of toleration do not go far enough when it comes to practical issues of equal access to the public sphere for example. This implies that the state must be pro-active in areas such as the redistribution of resources to help groups to achieve public recognition and respect. It suggests that the state must play a substantial role in actually achieving the appropriate conditions in which difference can flourish. We cannot assume that the state is a neutral instrument as it stands or that it will ever fulfil this hypothetical role.

To put this argument in the context of community, we have seen that groups or communities can be internally cohesive whilst still suffering from degrees of exclusion within wider society. Thus groups are capable of achieving solidarity within their own ranks whilst, at the same time, being powerless in the face of a lack of solidarity within society as a whole. One potential alternative may be for the state to try to impose a model of solidarity (Mendus 1989), but that would not provide a model of the state based upon communitarian ideas of governance. Such a model would undermine the power of communities through the imposition of top-down strategies that (even if they were capable of imposing some kind of solidarity, which is highly doubtful) would do little to empower communities. Essentially theories of community need to focus on collaboration between institutions of the state and community networks to seek both empowerment of groups outside of the direct jurisdiction of the state and the development of greater respect within different communities. As we shall see, this approach implies that solidarity cannot be imposed or asserted.

Rather, it must be developed gradually and manufactured through ongoing dialogue between institutions of the state and groups and associations in civil society.

The creation of solidarity is a continuous and imperfectible process rather than a development that can be derived from state imposition. In short, solidarity and respect for difference cannot be created by the state alone but, at the same time, it cannot be manufactured without the state either. In this sense we should promote an extension and development of, rather than wholesale rejection of, toleration. This position is articulated by Susan Mendus as a model for a socialist theory of toleration: the 'demand for a *construction* of socialist unity from different solidarities is thus, in itself, a demand for toleration. It is the articulation of a desire to belong to the wider community . . . [T]oleration is a moral necessity of a socialist society, not just a requirement of expediency' (Mendus 1989: 157). This perspective is based on the view that a concern for community need not exclude the importance of contributions from within liberalism. Under their liberal guise these concepts may be problematic, but this does not mean they should be rejected wholesale. Rather, contemporary theories must move beyond homogeneous conceptions of community and embrace notions of difference that improve upon liberal political theory. In this sense such theories may address a range of ideas and perspectives that have been marginalised in the orthodox liberal–communitarian debate.

CONCLUSION: TOWARDS A NEW POLITICS OF COMMUNITY

The pre-eminent position accorded to the debate between liberals and communitarians has not helped to elucidate the variety of different theoretical positions with regard to community that exist in modern political discourses. To label all of those concerned with community as communitarians overlooks the complexity and variety of perceptions of community (Kymlicka 1993). In the orthodox liberal–communitarian debate communitarians are frequently presented as conservatives insofar as they wish to protect communities that are already in existence. Beyond the literal sense however, there is little reason why communitarianism should be labelled conservative by definition. The recognition that there may be elements of traditional communities that are worth preserving or are inescapable in terms of selfhood does not, in itself, preclude us from also having a concern with the construction of newer forms of community at the same time.

Indeed if we do attach independent significance to the principles of community then it seems perfectly coherent to have a concern for both orthodox forms (for example, the local community) and more radical variants (for example, the gay and lesbian communities). Thus a concern for community may indeed be literally conservative, but this does not make it conservative in an ideological sense. Concern for previous forms of community need not be an exclusive condition in which the manufacture of new spheres of community must not enter the equation. The promotion of community can be forward-looking and need not result in the veneration of social practices and institutions (many of which are harmful to the principles of community) merely because they have a lengthy historical precedent, as is the case in some variants of conservative thought. In short, there is no reason why conservatism should have the sole claim on concern for historical tradition. A developed theory of community must evaluate which historical practices and institutions are worthy of preservation or resurrection and which tend to undermine the principles of community.

Clearly the attempt to empower sub-national communities, groups and associations implies decentralisation and strict limitations on the state. The principles of community certainly point to impositions being placed upon the sphere of jurisdiction of the state and a concomitant downward devolution of power. However the role of the state provides complications in terms of the distribution of power. There are forceful arguments regarding the promotion of traditional forms of community, but it is less clear how power is to be redistributed from the central state to sub-state bodies. Ultimately the relocation of power can only develop through a process of public dialogue between sub-state groups and state institutions to ascertain the complexity and implications of decentralisation. This, of course, assumes a willingness among governments and state institutions to commit themselves to decentralisation and there are few examples of processes of genuine empowerment in modern liberal democracies. That said, lip service is certainly paid to the concept of community, and there is a variety of economic and social policies that could contribute to such a process. It is vital to recognise that, despite the track record of centralisation, this process of decentralisation actually involves the state. There is no point in wishing away the state or indeed the fact that decentralisation is likely to meet with resistance from the institutions that are being challenged. There must be recognition that the promotion of community requires processes of negotiation that must deal with conflict as much as harmonious change. Thus the process is gradual and there is no optimal form of governance to be achieved. Rather the process of promoting community is ongoing and requires substantive dialogue between the sub-state bodies involved and institutions of the state.

The feminist critique of the liberal–communitarian debate has raised the most substantive queries regarding the failure of either side in the discussion to address questions of power (Frazer and Lacey 1993). Commentators such as Young (1990a, 1990b, 1993) and Lister (1998) have made significant contributions to debates over difference and the extent to which diversity supports or undermines concerns with equality and universalism. These are central concerns of new theories of community. Frazer and Lacey reinterpret the liberal–communitarian debate in the light of the importance of sub-stantive issues related to equality and the particular position of women. In terms of applying liberal and communitarian ideas, Frazer and Lacey do not merely subscribe to a hypothetical, idealistic sphere of debate to realise a common good but rather argue for a position in which there is 'actual debate between real, embodied, socially-situated persons. Only in such debate can the ethical impulse to recognise each other's claims by listening attentively to them, respecting the difference of others whom we identify as in some deep sense having the same moral status as ourselves, be realised' (Frazer and Lacey 1993: 207). This process would seem to involve an understanding of difference and the rights of individuals to develop their own conceptions of the good. By arguing for a 'deep' sense of identification in our understanding of others, it suggests that we should go beyond merely tolerating difference (which may be predicated on a lack of genuine concern for the perception of the good developed by the other) and instead promote the notion of respecting diversity and parity of esteem. Again this suggests that we have to actually engage with the ideas of others in the public domain rather than merely (and possibly resentfully) recognising their right to hold alternative views. This perception of community and respect does not pretend that agreement will always ensue from public deliberation and recognises that conflict will sometimes have to be resolved. In this scenario there remains an important role for the state in deliberating between competing claims. Because the liberal notion of state neutrality has been rejected, the engagement between theories of community and dialogic approaches must recognise that even the adjudications of the state in situations of conflict may well generate even further contestation. Whilst this is undoubtedly a much more untidy version of contending with diversity than liberal perfectionism would allow us, it much more closely resembles the practical realities of the celebration of difference which some liberals sweep under the carpet of state neutrality.

New theories of community need to address the limitations of conservative communitarianism and the paradox of toleration within liberalism in the process of understanding how we respect the conceptions of the good life developed within different communities. From this perspective then, a society based upon the principles of community would be one that would attempt to allow individuals to enjoy the communities that they are part of and enable the inclusion of all. However, this could only be achieved within a realistic vision of a society based on difference, that is, one which is capable of managing the conflict and contestation that diversity can generate. In the words of Barry, 'what is required is a set of rules of justice . . . that provide everybody with a fair opportunity of living a good life, whatever their conception of the good may be, while leaving room for the kind of discretion in shaping one's life that is an essential constituent in every conception of the good life' (Barry 1995: 206–7). Obviously all of the above is presaged upon the existence of a multiplicity of communities and the acceptance of a variety of conceptions of the good life. This perspective provides a timely counter to two of the major problems in modern theorisations of community. First, there is the equation of membership of community with membership of society at large or the nation-state. This outlook misunderstands the nature of communities and the multiplicity of associations that provide individuals with a sense of belonging. Second, the equation of community with society runs the risk of imposing what is regarded as the majority view of the common good on society as a whole over alternative minority views. This can lead to moral authoritarianism and the creation of a situation where difference is not tolerated, let alone respected. This is always the danger with communitarian theories because the notion of membership of community also implies that others may not be members or be excluded. However, radical approaches suggest that a more coherent conceptualisation of community need not be exclusionary. Before explaining why this is the case however, it is important to evaluate critically forms of communitarianism that, even if they are not formulated with social exclusion in mind, could lead to exclusionary outcomes.

– NOTES –

1. For a discussion of recent theories of human need, see Little (1998: Chapter 4).
2. These concepts of consequential and justificatory neutrality are also known as neutrality of effect and neutrality of justification respectively (Mason 2000: 25–6).

CHAPTER 3

Political Communitarianism: Towards Moral Authoritarianism

Undoubtedly the most influential communitarian commentator in modern politics has been Amitai Etzioni, who has left his imprint on policy initiatives in both Europe and North America. Such has been his influence that sometimes communitarianism as a political movement has been treated as synonymous with Etzioni's brand of thinking. This chapter sets out to examine the pre-eminent position that Etzioni has achieved as a political commentator and to identify the strengths and weaknesses of his approach to community. This analysis will demonstrate how many of Etzioni's ideas are morally prescriptive and, when placed in the light of political reality, potentially authoritarian. Simultaneously we will also encounter some of the problems associated with traditional sociological approaches to community as these perspectives have been applied within contemporary contexts. The focus here will be on the ways in which political communitarianism might engender, rather than rectify, social exclusion. Thus the inclusive principles that usually underpin communitarian theories are often marginalised when it comes to the practical application of these theories in the sphere of politics.

In Chapter 1 there was a brief discussion of the sociological thought of Tönnies and the uses of his *Gemeinschaft/Gesellschaft* dichotomy in outlining the differences between community and society. Whilst there is considerable strength in the approach of setting out the differing meanings of community and society, not surprisingly many of the ideas seem anachronistic when viewed through a contemporary lens. That said, Tönnies is still regarded as one of the most important contributors to sociological thought in this area, alongside twentieth-century thinkers such as Nisbet (1969). Put simply, the dominant interpretation of community in sociological thought was that it was a traditional bond between people that was eroded by the urbanisation that had accompanied industrialisation. Thus since 'the essential nature of industrial society involved an explosion of the division of labour which splintered people's lives into separated roles, industrialization logically threatened community . . . The loss of community was associated especially with the growth of industrial cities which were contrasted not just with the past, but with the countryside as well' (Abrams 1978: 11). Yet we might ask why this kind of approach was, until relatively recently, the dominant sociological position. Why should community usually be associated with rural association? What is it about the city that supposedly undermines community? Has community and the virtues that it was supposed to embody disappeared in the contemporary world?

In answering these questions initially we should restate the kinds of values and principles associated with community such as co-operation, altruism, voluntarism, friendship and mutual respect. Clearly there are plentiful examples of the ways in which these principles may have been embodied in traditional communities. However it is equally apparent that traditional communities were not the peaceful rural idylls that one might assume from the orthodox sociological approach. Indeed, as Abrams points out, this depiction of traditional communities was generally axiomatic and indeed has become a rhetorical device to assist the representation of the breakdown of community in industrial societies. But, even if we did accept the sepia-tinged model of traditional community, that still does not explain why urban life, in itself, has eroded the principles of community outlined above. This has become a central problem in the sociological analysis of community. If industrialisation and urbanism have done anything specific to community, then the key effect has been to change our understanding of the word. If we move beyond the local, geographical understanding of community to an approach based on specific values, then the simple dichotomy between the traditional image of the local and rural on the one hand and the 'city of strangers' on the other becomes highly questionable. Thus the 'problem of solidarity is . . . one that should be separated, as a matter of principle, from the problem of the effects of spatial arrangements on social relationships' (Abrams 1978: 13). The implications of this are clear. There is considerable evidence that many of the values of community outlined above are alive and well in contemporary industrial or post-industrial societies whether in the rural or urban setting (Little 1998). In other words the equation of the demise of community with urbanism and industrialisation neglects the existence and importance of community activities that take place in contemporary societies.

The traditional sociological approach implies that when community is stripped of the local spatial dimension, it becomes such an elusive idea that it becomes virtually meaningless. If that were the case however, what would become of ideas such as friendship, altruism and co-operation? Would these phenomena fall off the agenda of sociological theory? Of course, the answer to these questions is negative as these ideas remain central to sociological and philosophical analysis. One way out of the impasse created by the critique of traditional sociological critiques of community has been to subsume the virtues outlined above as features of social solidarity. Without wanting to neglect the importance of solidarity as a central social objective, it is a different concept from community (although the two are interrelated). Solidarity is usually depicted as a social phenomenon that refers to a measure of cohesion and inclusion. However solidarity, in itself, does not necessarily imply diversity and frequently its usage does not focus on ways that we mediate relationships between different groups. Certainly in recent years there have been a number of theoretical proposals for 'solidarity in difference' (Lister 1998; Young 1993) but little by way of examination of the communal relations that hold groups of people together. The focus has tended to be on how diverse groups with different conceptions of the good can be accommodated within modern societies rather than the relations within the groups themselves (Young 1990a).

When we do examine what holds groups of people together then a range of different principles can be in evidence. First, we can point to bonds of solidarity whereby people form groups and associations, such as trade unions, because they perceive common interests. In this example unions provide potentially greater power for their members through the pursuit of objectives in numbers rather than as isolated individuals. At the same time membership and solidarity in unions emanate from mainly instrumental concerns rather than the principles of community. A second example of relations of solidarity applied to society as a whole is provided to some extent by an emphasis on shared citizenship. However, even if rights were experienced on substantive rather than merely formal terms, the notion of citizenship does not necessarily provide real feelings of membership. The foundation of citizenship in liberal democracies tends to focus on formal status but we need to recognise how that may not give rise to sentiments of membership and belonging. Certainly liberal democracies can evoke nationalistic emotions in some sections of the citizen body, but these feelings are unlikely to be universal in the context of the diversity of contemporary societies. In this sense neither instrumental theories of solidarity (such as in membership of trade unions) or those associated with formal status (such as citizenship in liberal democracy) satisfactorily embody the kinds of relations which tend to be associated with theories of community, even though, as we shall see, some communitarians are keen to articulate their ideas in those terms.

Other important sources of solidarity that need to be differentiated from community are economic associations. It is quite possible that bonds of solidarity can emerge within the economic context as individuals and groups coalesce to further shared objectives. However, in terms of achieving economic success, values such as competition and greed may be the basis of achieving solidarity in the market place. In this sense, the pursuit of economic success, and the bonds of solidarity that it may generate, may need to override communitarian virtues such as altruism and reciprocity. This would imply then that it is within spheres of common interest that are not predicated upon economic values, instrumentalism and the need for competition that community values can best be achieved. This does not mean that associations founded within communities cannot partake in economic activities – they patently can and frequently they do succeed in the competitive world in which economic enterprises must engage.[1] However once associations are engaged in the sphere of economic activity, they cannot, *as a priority*, base their activities on friendship and altruism. This does not mean that the latter values will not be part of community economic enterprises, it is merely to point out that competitive activity in markets entails that different principles will frequently take priority. Thus the demands of economic success tend to predominate over the less aggressive and competitive virtues that communities tend to exhibit in this situation. To summarise then, most theories of community are based upon specific virtues and principles of community that are accorded special status (Frazer 1999, Chapter 2). The vast majority of communitarian approaches imply that these philosophical principles are not accorded the appropriate significance that they deserve in modern capitalist and liberal democratic societies. However, this understanding of the erosion of the principles of community is not usually developed in such a way that fundamental challenges are directed towards the social, political and economic arrangements in these societies.

– COMMUNITY AND COMMUNITIES –

The pursuit of the appropriate political, economic and social arrangements that would allow the principles of community to flourish is not aided by the representation of community as akin to society as a whole. The latter perspective has become something of an accepted truth when, in reality, there 'is no overarching value of community to which all political movements can reasonably pay lip-service. Conceptions of community, and public policies aiming to promote it, will vary radically according to the political principles they express' (Gray 1997: 77). In this context the notion of a unitary, homogeneous community is an anachronistic idea in contemporary, diverse societies and yet it is one that predominates in political debates and the output of major political parties. One of the major culprits in this development has been the political communitarian movement and, in particular, Amitai Etzioni. Whilst the work of Etzioni and his supporters may be littered with caveats and disclaimers regarding the suggestion that they do not embrace diversity, they ultimately tend to retreat behind an idea of a unitary community based on majority concerns. Moreover the depiction of community employed is often presented as a clarion call for the return of traditional values such as those of the family and hard work, for example, to combat the ills that present themselves in late modern societies. Gray calls this the *'project of return'* and argues that this is 'what community *is not'* (Gray 1997: 81–2). Thus orthodox political communitarianism combines a backward-looking perspective on dealing with contemporary social change with a nostalgia for traditional forms of community that arguably never really existed in the way that they are presented now:

> The diagnosis of decline and deficit is followed, perhaps inevitably, with the prescription of nostalgia. Politicians of all persuasions, from social democrats to conservatives, share a preoccupation with the notion of returning to the past, of rekindling the half-warm memories of family, work and community. After all, the essence of the widespread appeal of Etzioni's communitarianism is the attempt to bolt on to a shattered society all the steadfast certainties of the past: a world where everyone pulled together. (Young 1999: 49)

The traditional community espoused by orthodox communitarians focuses on methods of reasserting the primacy of the family (often defined in somewhat conservative fashion) as the most important unit within society as opposed to the abstract individual who reigns supreme in liberal thought. Moreover the traditional family model is frequently combined with the Protestant work ethic (especially for men) in a strategy to counteract the changes to family life and patterns of work in contemporary Western societies. Thus the orthodox agenda cherishes the values of individual and familial responsibility alongside the disciplinary effect of hard work. For women, this responsibility often appears as motherhood and domestic labour in orthodox communitarian discourses, whereas work for wages is predominantly a duty to be undertaken by men.

Orthodox political communitarianism is problematic because it neglects the importance of economic policies in the establishment of appropriate conditions in which communities can prosper. Instead of examining the obstacles to community, they tend merely to assert its primacy. Family, work and community are placed at the forefront of social arrangements without any challenge to the ways in which economic arrangements impact upon these social conditions. In this sense brands of communitarianism that fail to engage adequately with the interaction between market mechanisms and the regulation of state institutions are unlikely to achieve genuinely communitarian objectives. In the words of Gray, 'communitarian thought must engage with economic policy, as it affects the needs of people at work as well as those of the growing population that is excluded from work' (Gray 1997: 83). For Gray, this necessitates a move away from neo-liberalism, classical socialism and social democracy. This shift from traditional work-based thinking on political economy is particularly pertinent in rethinking the theory of community. However this does not mean, as Gray seems to believe, that we are left with communitarian liberalism, for there is a considerable body of work that attempts to move beyond work-based political economy (Little 1998). In terms of community then, the challenge is to develop theoretical positions and public policies that accord appropriate significance to non-paid work and other activities that take place beyond the boundaries of the formal economy.

Orthodox political communitarianism can be criticised for the definition of community that it employs as a foundation as well as the means of achieving that goal. Arguably we need to address the importance of diversity and the idea of individuals as members of a multiplicity of communities that sometimes overlap with and at other times contradict each other. The dominant orthodoxy within communitarianism, however, tends to invoke a conception of a homogeneous community that is devoid of the kinds of confrontation that diversity makes inevitable. John Gray argues that this seamless community is a fiction which undermines diversity. Thus the 'reactionary project of rolling back this diversity of values and world-views in the pursuit of a lost cultural unity overlooks the character of our cultural inheritance as a palimpsest, having ever deeper layers of complexity' (Gray 1995: 109). What orthodox political communitarians tend to neglect, then, is the multiplicity of relationships that help to formulate identity. It is in a multiplicity of different communities that we form as different individuals as no-one will have the same combination of sources of identity.

Orthodox communitarianism has its philosophical roots in the work of Alasdair MacIntyre, for example, who presupposes a kind of heteronomy in which 'individuals find themselves simply defined by a history and tradition from which no proper distancing is possible' (O'Neill 1998: 75). Communitarians challenge the model of individuals as utility maximisers seeking maximum fulfilment from a menu of choices from which they can pick and choose. Whereas MacIntyre suggests that our identities are bound and predetermined, the latter perspective implies that we can adopt identities and then dispose them at will. Neither position is satisfactory for a developed theory of community. MacIntyre and other communitarians are correct to point out the importance of the traditions that we are born into in the formulation of our identity but wrong to suggest that we are necessarily constrained by them. For example, we might be born into Catholic families but that does not mean that we will automatically remain as Catholics. We might choose to reject Catholic theology, adopt an alternative system of belief or reject religion altogether. Nonetheless the conscious act of doing so – that is, the process of engagement with our sources of identity – suggests that there will remain some imprint of that which we have rejected. Similarly we may be born into particular ethnic communities but the extent to which that influences our identity is largely down to our commitment to that community. Even if we choose to largely ignore our ethnic heritage as a major defining factor in our lives, there remains some link due to our common experience of our treatment at the hands of others. In other words, we can govern the extent to which some forms of community influence our lives even if we cannot totally escape them due to their unavoidable part in our individual process of identity formation. This kind of position has advocates within communitarian thought, such as Charles Taylor (1989), who see the importance of choice but do not present the process of choice as one where autonomy overrides all else.

The main problem with communitarians such as Etzioni and MacIntyre, however, is that they fail to accord sufficient significance to what might be called communities of choice as opposed to communities of fate (Hirst 1994: 49–56). Although Hirst does not differentiate explicitly enough between communities and associations, he notes the importance of freedom of individual choice in deciding which associations we become part of in the process of identity formation. Thus he argues that it is from:

the right to be a voluntary member of an association [that] we derive the most basic right in an associative society, that is, the apparently paradoxical right of exit, to be able to leave an association within a relatively short and specified period of time and without a significant fine or equivalent financial loss. (Hirst 1994: 51)

Several issues emerge from Hirst's depiction of association. The initial problem emerges from the way in which he subsumes community within the idea of association. This would suggest that he regards communities as merely forms of social association that differ little in principle from other kinds of association, such as being a member of a trade union. Whilst the latter is an important form of association, it is not by definition imbued with communitarian values in the sense that, as Hirst rightly notes, individuals may be members because they believe it will further their own personal rights rather than holding strong communitarian values about fellow members of that union. In this sense communities differ from associations because they are definitively not characterised by self-interest or economic considerations.

The other significant aspect of Hirst's thesis is the importance he attaches to being able to leave associations. This argument can be extended to the theorisation of community. It is indeed vital that individuals are able to leave communities, especially as the values and beliefs of that community may change over time, thereby potentially making the ideas of the community incompatible with those of the individual. In that scenario, to suggest that individuals must be bound by the communities they are part of smacks of authoritarianism and, more dangerous, reductionist versions of nationalism. At the same time the idea that we can just come and go may be true of some forms of association but the principles of community under consideration here suggest otherwise. In communities there is a degree of commitment and mutual responsibility that makes them slightly different from the more general category of associations that may not require such commitment. Moreover the notion of financial penalty for exit that is highlighted in Hirst's position is not a major consideration when it comes to the sphere of community. The latter is not predicated upon economic or financial interests or considerations. Thus, in short, some of the instrumentalist features that Hirst regards as part of the membership of groups are applicable to associations but not to communities. He is correct to argue that associations are communities of choice but this does not mean that all associations are communities and that the right of exit overrides the kinds of commitment that we tend to expect of members of communities.

Despite the criticisms raised above, Hirst defends his vision of associative democracy from critics who challenge pluralism on the basis that groups in society are constantly pursuing power and the opportunity to subjugate the ideas of other groups. Thus he rejects the view that 'in a multicultural society of conflicting identities, of communities *as* identities, the public sphere and the freedoms of civil society become nothing more than a medium for different groups to seek to capture the public power for their own purposes' (Hirst 1994: 53). Clearly this kind of instrumentalism is not reflected in the theory of community examined here. Indeed, arguably it is the acceptance of difference and competing claims in the public sphere that enables communities to pursue their objectives. Thus the establishment of social arrangements based on the importance of communities has its foundation in respect for others, thereby enabling them to express their own conceptualisations of the good. Clearly this involves an understanding that oppositional viewpoints will be aired in the public domain and a recognition that the opportunities accorded to communities in this scenario clearly suppose self-limitation and moderation when it comes to dealing with alternative conceptions of the good.

This approach to community is evidently opposed to conceptualisations of the homogeneous community as the basis of social and political arrangements. Clearly, though, despite his promotion of the moral community implying a degree of homogeneity, Etzioni does suggest that he has an understanding of a multiplicity of forms of community:

> Communities are webs of social relations that encompass shared meanings and above all shared values. Families may qualify as minicommunities. Villages often are, although not necessarily so. Some neighbourhoods in cities . . . constitute communities. Well-integrated national societies may be said to be communities. Communities need not be geographically concentrated . . . True communities are not automatically or necessarily places of virtue. Many traditional communities that were homogeneous if not monolithic were authoritarian and oppressive. (Etzioni 1995b: 24–5)

From this passage it would appear that Etzioni is aware of some of the complexities of community that undermine the idyllic depiction of the homogeneous community. He is correct to identify the multiple forms that community can take and that community should not be thought of solely as the domain of the small scale and geographically local. Moreover he is also right to point out that some of the traditional communities that are espoused as models for community organisation were authoritarian – indeed, taking this point further, we might argue that many traditional communities were not particularly communitarian when it came to exclusionary tendencies, bigotry, homophobia and so on.

However we need to ask questions about the representation of 'well-integrated national societies' as communities. This sows the seed of doubt about Etzioni's perception of community as it implies that relationships in which we do not have a strong commitment to others can still be thought of as communities. Thus we can exist in the same national society as others and yet we may not be particularly committed to the other individuals within the polity. Equally members of that polity may exclude or discriminate against us. In reality these types of broader social relationship are better mediated through concepts such as citizenship, which recognise that there are large-scale forms of social organisation that require certain rules and regulations which are legally enforceable.[2] In terms of relationships, citizenship implies formal organisation to accommodate different groups of people with a variety of perceptions of the good but the same rights. Community, on the other hand, implies greater spontaneity and a less structured system of understanding our relationships with one another. In this sense community differs from citizenship in the sense that the former involves ideas of rights and obligations as is the case with the latter but in the sphere of community those relationships are less structured and less directly reciprocal. This formulation of the meaning of community relationships helps us to understand how Etzioni's ostensible pluralism and recognition of a multiplicity of communities does not translate into a genuinely pluralist perspective in practice. In short, despite the numerous caveats that he expresses regarding depictions of his ideas as morally prescriptive, Etzioni's ideas contain the seeds of authoritarianism and this trend is all the more evident when political parties or movements attempt to translate orthodox communitarian ideas into public policies. In other words, despite the rhetoric to the contrary, orthodox political communitarianism tends to provide a recipe for moral authoritarianism (Hughes 1996).

– MORAL AUTHORITARIANISM –

Part of the problem with the translation of communitarian philosophy into political practice comes when theoretical ideas have to be applied to contentious social problems such as law and order and criminal justice.

Indeed it tends to be the case that when communitarian ideas are put in the context of public policy that we see the dilution of the radical potential of communitarianism and the resort to more orthodox (but arguably less communitarian) perceptions of community. In the words of Hughes:

> Within this popular variant of communitarianism, there is a vision of a unitary, homogeneous community sustained by strongly-held moral certainties, celebrating in turn monoculturalism and setting, albeit at times implicitly, a morally prescriptive agenda for the social exclusion of marginalized and 'deviant' categories of people. (Hughes 1998: 110)

From this perspective the communitarian project of challenging the sources of social disintegration in contemporary Western societies becomes one of remoralising society and reversing the concentration on individual rights within liberalism. It appears that the orthodox model relies upon the idea of a deficit of the appropriate virtues that allow society to cohere. Faced with this deficit, orthodox political communitarianism becomes a crusade to reinstate lost values and traditional forms of cementing society together. However, as Frazer notes, it 'is a big leap from [the] emphasis on the interconnectedness of human individuals to a full-blown prescriptive theory of community' (Frazer 1996: 92). Thus the development of the theory of community places central importance on the actual principles that embody communitarian relationships and must be careful to avoid the prescription of the specific communities in which these bonds exist. If this can be achieved, then there is no need to engage in the often exclusionary and ethnocentric practice of selecting which communities are particularly worthy of the name.

A further query to be raised about the promotion of traditional *Gemeinschaft* communities, and one that commentators such as Etzioni are well aware of, is the potential of those communities to stifle difference through the creation of an atmosphere of homogeneity and intolerance. This critique of community has been apparent in Iris Marion Young's attack on 'face-to-face' communities as venues that are incapable of encompassing choice and diversity (Young 1990b). The point is accurately expressed by Anne Phillips:

> Small communities are not necessarily the most democratic, nor are they necessarily the most tolerant of people who want to challenge their current conditions. Through centuries . . . dissident individuals have felt themselves hemmed in by small, homogeneous communities – or by small communities

which imagined themselves more homogeneous than they really were – and the anonymity of the big city has offered the classic escape route to those at odds with dominant conventions. (Phillips 1996: 120)

This throws up numerous problems for orthodox communitarianism but also for those concerned with the importance of diversity and the construction of a theory of community that attempts to accommodate a wide variety of lifestyles and conceptions of the good life. There is little reason to presuppose that traditional models of community were more capable than modern cities of providing opportunities for such diversity to flourish. Indeed the opposite might well be the case because individuals living within small, traditional communities do not necessarily have to grapple with the accommodation of different groups because in everyday life they may be unlikely to encounter people other than those of their own ethnicity or religion. Similarly, even though small communities will have an in-evitable mixture of people of different sexual orientations, for example, many people may feel unable to express themselves because of the prejudice, exclusion and danger that they may come up against. Of course this may also be the case within cities, but the latter do not embody the imposition of homogeneity in quite the same way as in the model of the traditional community. Thus, whilst it may well be the case that people in cities are not particularly adept at dealing with the differences they encounter, there is no denying the existence of diversity and a variety of lifestyles that may not be the case in the traditional community. Moreover cities may provide more spaces for people to express their individual identity and may enhance opportunities to develop solidarity with others.

The theorisation of community should recognise the fact that the small, traditional, geographical community is only one form of community and perhaps a more likely form than others to involve exclusionary notions of homogeneity. Following the work of Marilyn Friedman, Phillips differenti-ates between 'chosen' and 'found' communities in the same way that Hirst notes differences between communities of choice and communities of fate. For Anne Phillips, 'instead of being bound to an involuntary community of place, people can create or join new communities based on shared pre-ferences, goals or ideals' (Phillips 1996: 120). Importantly Phillips retains the word community in this argument, and this suggests that a recognition that communities contain specific types of relationships can be retained alongside the important idea that communities can be constructed or manufactured. In this sense there is a positive recognition that public policies can be employed to generate the conditions in which community relations can thrive. For orthodox political communitarians initiatives should be directed at the resurrection of the traditional model of community whereas, from a radical perspective, social and economic policies should be directed towards shoring up the communities that already exist as well as developing conditions to allow new communities to establish themselves. This is clearly predicated on the basis that communities do exist in modern societies and, contrary to common wisdom, that we have not witnessed the death of community in contemporary society. This is not the same as a communitarian utopia. The recognition of community may point towards the obstacles that communities face in contemporary societies. For example, communities may exist – and indeed derive unison – in the face of prejudice and homophobia against them. The experience of adversity, then, may help people to bond and unite through the common treatment they encounter. Importantly, then, the existence of these types of association do suggest that the death of community thesis has been overstated in both academic and practical political discourses and the public mind.

If it is the case that communities still exist in modern societies, we might ask what form they tend to take and how they are reflected in modern urban settings. Some communities take rather orthodox forms in terms of being linked to certain geographical areas and the protection of local interests. Others may be formed on the basis of common sporting or religious attachments or sexual communities may be established. The latter are celebrated by commentators such as Young (1990b) as examples of associations that thrive because in a society of strangers there is less chance of these bonds being stifled by the homogeneity of others. In this sense she argues that urbanism has allowed new forms of association to thrive in a way that was not possible within communities. But what are these associations if not forms of community? These groups do not form out of the ether but rather are prime examples of the ways in which modern cities can actually engender communitarian relationships because, within large urban spaces, a wide range of potential communities exist, given the variety of individuals therein. It is not because we are among strangers that cities allow more open expression of sexual communities than in traditional models of community, the reason lies in the fact that there is a much greater diversity of people in cities with whom to establish common bonds and form communities. Thus, whilst in orthodox models urbanism undermines community, a more radical approach suggests that cities can provide opportunities for a diversity of communities to develop and express themselves. Cities, in this sense, can provide a more open and diverse public sphere than is the case in the traditional model of community. There is little reason why communitarianism should be morally authoritarian if we establish that the traditional model based on face-to-face geographical relationships is only one form of community. This strengthens the argument that we need to examine not only the relationships between groups but also those within communities. This is important because, in invoking traditional forms of community, orthodox communitarianism promotes homogeneity and creates difficulties for some communities (especially minority groups) in gaining social acceptance and especially in finding access to the public sphere.

– COMMUNITARIANISM AND SOCIAL EXCLUSION –

Orthodox political communitarians are careful to rebuff suggestions that their work leads to exclusionary outcomes and Etzioni's work, in particular, is full of caveats regarding that kind of interpretation of his work. Indeed he is careful to note differences in cultural traditions and the importance of enabling a variety of ethnic groups to maintain their particular outlook on life (Etzioni 1996: Chapter 7). However, even where he does accept a multiplicity of communities, he is particularly keen to stress how they must recognise that they are part of a wider integrated whole that will impact upon their behaviour and beliefs. Whilst this is important, it does not attempt to deal with ways in which ethnic cultures are only one form of differential community and that, indeed, ethnic groups may contain within them many different communities. It is especially worthy of note that each member of an ethnic community will be a member of a range of other communities, some of which may not be recognised within Etzioni's schema. Thus his recognition of an ethnic mosaic does not really grapple with the sometimes conflicting forms of diversity involved in different communities. In this sense 'what he is suggesting is a multiculturalism held together by the glue of basic agreement. In the image of the "mosaic": the cultures are held separate, their traditions valued and preserved, their separate entities are held together by the contractual glue of mutual respect and a rather basic collection of common values' (Young 1999: 163). The problem that arises here is that Etzioni accepts cultural difference and believes in individuals privately following their own objectives as long as they are prepared to accept a wider public agenda that supersedes their own individual interest. In short we are free to follow our own private goals but they will exist within a picture of the common good defined by the moral community that will predominate in the public sphere. Like Rawls then, Etzioni's understanding of diversity is privatistic and doesn't guarantee the expression of difference in the public domain.

What emerges, then, is a privatistic understanding of difference which accepts that individuals will not all follow the same creeds but that asserts a more important universal principle of commonality that overrides the particular. In other words we can do what we like in our own private worlds but must adhere to the dominant overarching moral consensus (if it can be called that) when it comes to the public sphere. There are implicit problems with this privatistic perspective as it neglects the importance of access to the public sphere:

> Policies of community renewal must not ignore the public sphere. An open public sphere is as important at local as at national level, and is one way in which democratization connects directly with community development. Without it, schemes of community renewal risk separating the community from the wider society, and are vulnerable to corruption. (Giddens 1998: 85)

Giddens implicitly suggests, then, that there are dangers that arise from approaches that involve the recognition of communities (and diversity) but do not necessarily guarantee access to public spheres. Herein lies the danger of Etzioni's agenda when, despite recognising that different groups exist, he proclaims that the dominant moral agenda must ultimately be accepted. The suspicion remains that whilst Etzioni is prepared to acknowledge the private right of individuals to follow their own particular creed, that is superseded in the public sphere by the duty to accept socially held conventions and beliefs. The question this engenders is who decides which beliefs will be the dominant ones in the public sphere? The answer, for Etzioni, seems to lie with the majority, even though dominant groups in society may well retain somewhat orthodox and sometimes dangerously conservative moral beliefs. Where Etzioni retains the private right to follow one's own perspective on life, in the public sphere this wanes in front of the dominant moralism. In practice this can lead to the kinds of prejudice and homophobia that exist within modern societies. The acceptance of difference in the private sphere without a concordant recognition of a multiplicity of views in the public sphere offers little by way of translating the existence of different communities in society into a society which is based upon the importance of diverse communities as the basis of social organisation. It merely hides behind the curtain of privatism which helps to explain the animosity of many diverse groups towards the formal public sphere of practical politics in modern societies. In short, Etzioni's ideas suggest that the rights of individuals to develop their own private conception of the good must be sacrificed on the altar of the duty we owe to social cohesion in the public sphere. We can believe what we want as long as it does not impinge upon the overall public good of the moral community, even though the latter may well be inadequately defined or exclusionary. Thus, once we reach beyond the inclusive rhetoric of Etzioni's perspective on difference, his moral authoritarianism provides us with a recipe for social exclusion.

Of course public spheres are likely to be governed by specific universal values, but this does not mean that they will or should be definitively exclusive of minority perspectives. For example, values that are not in themselves exclusionary, such as mutual respect, may be the universal values that we establish as the foundation of relationships in the public sphere. This stands as an alternative to the dominant communitarianism of Etzioni and his supporters that, behind a shroud of diversity and choice, promotes homogeneous understandings of community. The latter is potentially exclusionary because, as in the work of economists such as Hayek and social commentators like David Green (1996), 'on the one hand, there is a plurality of values but, on the other hand, there is a homogeneity of the "successful" cultural values developed during the process of human evolution' (O'Brien and Penna 1998: 216). This helps to explain the correlation between the brand of communitarianism espoused by Etzioni and the ideas of defenders of neo-liberalism. Underneath a shroud of diversity and choice, neo-liberals promote an individualistic ethos in society which leads to exclusionary outcomes. Similarly Etzioni's repudiation of individualism in his communitarian theory rests heavily upon his critique of rights-based liberalism.

To counteract this focus on individual rights, Etzioni calls for a resurgence of duty and responsibility. Thus individuals must be encouraged to take responsibility for the welfare of themselves and their families rather than relying upon the state to provide benefits in accordance with social rights. Ironically, given the anti-individualist stance that Etzioni adopts, his position firmly locates responsibility for social cohesion upon individuals and families. In inverting the liberal focus on individual rights, Etzioni provides us with individual responsibilities as the cement that holds communities together. The point is that a strong role for the state in integrating society is criticised from both orthodox communitarian and rights-based liberal approaches. However, this overlooks the important role that the state plays in providing services and the ways in which state orchestration of welfare may be more effective and efficient than communities in providing some services. In the absence of state coordination we are left with individuals and whatever intermediary associations they form as the basis of social cohesion. The outcome of this method of placing so much onus on individuals is arguably responsible for the phenomenon of exclusion and I would suggest that it is an ineffective and inequitable strategy for the eradication of social disintegration and discrimination.

Social exclusion emanates from both forms of individualism noted above because it provides a convenient scapegoat for social problems. Both argue that where individuals perpetrate crimes or engage in anti-social activities, they are themselves or their families always morally responsible for that behaviour. Similarly the social problems that may be most evident in poor, run-down urban communities demonstrate a lack of moral fibre among the individuals in those communities. Not surprisingly this simplistic analysis of the origins of social problems has aroused considerable suspicion from criminologists concerned with the notion of community that is employed by commentators such as Etzioni (Hughes 1998; Young 1999). For Hughes, Etzioni provides us with a conservative moral authoritarianism because his theory is focused on the homogeneous community as opposed to diversity, nostalgia for the past, a neglect of power structures, a critique of personal rights in the promotion of duties, a rose-tinted glorification of past communities, and a rejuvenation of traditional family forms to remedy social problems (Hughes 1998: 109). Hughes argues that this is exemplified in Etzioni's homage to Utah as a model for communitarian objectives and similarly Young picks up on the way in which the 'American dream' (with all its exclusionary aspects) has problematically appeared as a desirable model for communitarianism:

> The United States is a quite exceptionally exclusionary society. The notion of the ethnic segregation of suburban development scarcely causes criticism. Indeed the word 'community' comes to be used as the singular form of a plural entity and even Amitai Etzioni's . . . much vaunted 'communitarianism' is not one of integration but of overarching values and shared sentiments. (Young 1999: 22–3)

It seems remarkable that Etzioni can brazenly argue that diversity and cultural pluralism are important and still defend models of social organisation in the United States that reflect high levels of social exclusion. For example, the United States has witnessed the rise of gated communities whereby the reasonably affluent and usually white communities segregate themselves in suburban settings in order to exclude the urban squalor, poverty and crime outside. It is no surprise that the latter are disproportionately populated by members of minority ethnic groups that also face disadvantage in the parallel world of the formal economy and the limited provision of welfare in the American system. However, Etzioni sees fit to defend the constitutional workings of the US regime:

> American society has both constitutional and moral safeguards against majoritarianism that communitarians should very much respect. These safeguards basically work by differentiation, by defining some areas in which the majority has not had and ought not have a say and those in which it does and should. We are not a simple democracy but a constitutional one. That is, some choices, defined by the Constitution, are declared out of bounds for the majority. (Etzioni 1995b: 23)

There is clear evidence here of Etzioni's rather limited conceptualisation of the public sphere and neglect of issues related to power. In defending the United States against accusations of majoritarianism, he points to the Bill of Rights and the freedom of speech enshrined therein. Thus he argues that the United States, and the model of community he employs, are not majoritarian because minorities and individuals are able to exercise their right to free speech for example. Similarly he hails the fact that minorities have the right to vote and that everyone has a right to trial by a jury of their peers (Etzioni 1995b: 23).

What does this mean with regard to the public sphere and social exclusion? It gives individuals the right to say what they want but no compunction on the rest of us to listen to or respect what anyone says. The right to free speech does not equate to a right to contribute to the decision-making process in any meaningful sense, save being able to vote. And the right to vote takes place within electoral processes that are not open to deliberative or discursive processes in any contemporary Western systems – representative democracy tends to be dominated by opinions supported by substantial numbers of people and most decisions are handled by elites anyway rather than diverse communities. In this sense Etzioni's conceptualisation of the public sphere is essentially privatistic. We can say what we want, it seems, but there is no sense in which we must listen to others and deliberate on possible courses of action. Just as we do not have to listen to others so they have no good reason to listen to us. In this scenario the right to free speech does not entail social inclusion in the decision-making process. Rather it provides us with the opportunity to spout our opinions without a proper process of dialogue. If this form of freedom of speech is indeed Etzioni's vision of safeguards against majoritarianism, then it is a limited and unsatisfactory form of access to the public sphere, and one that does little to facilitate social inclusion especially for minority groups.

Part of this problem emanates from the multiplicity of definitions of community that exist within philosophical and political discourses. Etzioni is well aware that different levels of community are encompassed within the one term and it is the task in hand here to try and clarify what we mean by communities in a much more specific sense than is frequently the case (although that specific sense leads to a very broad definition). Etzioni is culpable to some extent in the slippage between the use of the terms community and society. On one hand he acknowledges that 'contemporary communities . . . are part of a pluralistic web of communities' (Etzioni 1995b: 25) and that we have multiple membership of a range of communities some of which may provide rather different types of association. At the same time he is prepared to argue that 'well-integrated national societies may be said to be communities' (Etzioni 1995b: 24). This kind of conflation of the terms society and community is commonplace but highly problematic when we have to identify the relationship between membership of community and social exclusion. According to perspectives such as that of Etzioni, in a 'well-integrated' society we may see a model of community. Reading between the lines, and given his eulogy for Utah mentioned above, we might suggest that Etzioni believes that fairly homogeneous societies are more likely to fit the model of community that he supports. Whilst this may seem innocuous enough at first glance, and indeed commonsensical, the practical implications of this position are more problematic. If Etzioni favours the broadest extension of communitarianism possible, then, from his perspective, this suggests that we promote the most well-integrated society that is achievable. Following his argument then, it would seem that the greater degree of homogeneity that exists, the more likely we are to see communitarian social relationships.

In the context of modern developed society such visions of homogeneity are somewhat anachronistic. Beneath the ostensible pluralism of Etzioni's thought, a rather conservative belief in the primacy of unitary societies seems to hold sway. Of course, given that these models of unity and homogeneity do not exist in contemporary Western societies, orthodox political communitarians must attempt to modify this belief in cohesion to make their ideas applicable to the practical world. But this problem is eminently avoidable. If we apply a narrow theory of community whereby we acknowledge that societies are made of a range of groups and associations, only some of which are established on the altruistic, voluntary foundations that characterise communities, then we are closer to developing a theory that is applicable to the modern world. Moreover rather than trying to model society on the relations of community, we can then identify society as the broad entity in which the conflicting and sometimes contestatory communities and associations must co-exist. Within the domain of society there is a role then for the state and governmental bodies (sub-national, national and supranational) in mediating the relationships between different groups. In this scenario the extent to which a society can be deemed communitarian would be reliant upon the extent to which democratic power is devolved downwards towards communities and the ability of social institutions to contain conflict between different groups.

Etzioni's perspective varies from this model insofar as he argues that societies will be more communitarian if they are able to find moral consensus on as broad a level as possible. Thus he states that:

> Most people are able to maintain a commitment both to their immediate community and to more encompassing ones . . . Indeed, a strong case can be made that what might be called upward shifting of moral commitments, to ever more encompassing communities, is the earmark of a community which is most progressive. Such a community is likely to be more committed to widely shared values, such as peace and social justice. (Etzioni 1995b: 25)

On the surface Etzioni's case that the establishment of values in a community may make the wider establishment of these kinds of values within society as a whole more realisable seems reasonable. However it fails to recognise how membership of communities differs from membership of society as a whole and the way in which contemporary liberal democracies tend to be characterised by incommensurable value pluralism. Thus it must be understood that many communities in modern societies maintain views that are basically incommensurable due to their essential differences. Whilst it is important to attempt to spread the values within communities to wider society, such projects will never yield perfectionist results. Society then becomes the sphere of containment whereby difference is accepted but controlled through democratic processes.

In more pragmatic visions of community, societies can never mirror the kinds of values that exist within communities. Thus it may be a more worthwhile strategy to try and build upon the idea that the freedom to enjoy membership of the range of communities that we do is predicated upon the acceptance of and respect for the voices of other communities within the public sphere. From this perspective we may be closer to the representation of society as a public sphere in which a range of diverse voices will and should contribute. This stands in contrast to the existence of communities and their levels of public participation in societies such as the UK and the USA today. Communities exist and perform all sorts of worthwhile activities but their recognition in the broader public sphere (limited as it is) is minimal. Elites and representation dominate over the possibility of increasing access to deliberative forums for a range of communities (frequently minorities). Put at its most basic level, it is perfectly possible to be a member of a range of communities in Britain today but still experience social exclusion. It might be said that it suits the system as it stands for people to be engaged in a range of different private associations as long as the decision-making process is dominated by elites and majority concerns.

– THE POLITICAL IMPACT OF COMMUNITARIANISM –

Undoubtedly Etzioni has developed a more sophisticated communitarianism over the course of his work in terms of trying to accommodate diversity. However within his perspective there continues to lie a rather conservative kernel that tends to emerge when the implications of his ideas are drawn out. This basic conservatism is even more apparent when politicians have attempted to formulate public, social and economic policies from the foundations that Etzioni provides (this will be covered in more detail in Chapters 5 and 6). Perhaps we should not be surprised that political practitioners from many traditions have found inspiration in communitarian ideas. Within the mainstream, politicians such as Blair (1996) and Willetts (1994) have espoused communitarian ideas from their respective social democratic and conservative viewpoints. Moreover there remains considerable attraction in the idea of community for many political radicals from anarchists to communists and other perspectives in political thought such as romantic nationalism. It is this kind of ideological elasticity that makes community such a continuously influential idea in modern politics, but, of course, for the same reason it is also a concept that seems rudderless at times, without an agreed reference point. It is in this context that this book sets out to re-evaluate the principles of community, but before moving on to this explication of the key points of community in terms of political practice, it is important to examine the ways in which the concept is employed in modern political discourses.

Not surprisingly, when it appears in popular political discourses the call for community tends to be predicated on the romantic and backward-looking nostalgia for previous forms of social arrangements that are deemed preferable to contemporary societies. In a way this seems inapt when politics itself increasingly resembles a commercial enterprise in which philosophical ideas and the promotion of the common good are supplanted by less ambitious and more short-term concerns. Tam expresses his concern with the lack of vision in modern politics associated with the demise of the left–right divide:

> The commercialized promotion of political parties has displaced the development of morally coherent political programmes. Instead of being brought together to deliberate over their common good, citizens are encouraged to behave as self-centred consumerists, deciding what personal gains to purchase with their votes. What is on offer is constantly repackaged to suit what the largest number of voters seems to favour, however prejudiced or ill-informed those views might be. (Tam 1998: 33)

Clearly there is a nugget of truth in Tam's statement insofar as modern politics is less concerned with philosophical principles and more focused on the pursuit of votes. However, this has not merely emerged as part of an evolutionary process. Rather we need to recognise that political parties are themselves culpable in this development. In many ways it suits parties to pander to somewhat simplistic individualist motivation when it comes to attracting votes. Despite the fact that people do have concerns for ideas such as liberty and equality and the practical application of these universal ideas, these kinds of principles have become less prominent in political debates that become dominated by visions of voters as rational utility maximisers. This simplistic packaging of politics suits political parties and enables them to focus upon less sophisticated and more pragmatic bundles of policies than might be the case if common goals linked to a complex theory of community were the sole objective.

The rhetorical use of community in contemporary politics marks a shift away from engagement with political conflict. In other words, this is the phenomenon of community as 'anti-politics'. The appeals to community in modern political discourses, imbued as they are with nostalgia and visions of homogeneity, are essentially attempts to depoliticise our approaches to social and economic issues. By attempting to explain social problems somewhat simplistically through the demise of the traditional, naturalistic community, politicians arm themselves with a convenient remedy that is not imbued with ideological baggage. In this organic argument the return to the traditional way of doing things in community becomes the recipe to cure our ills. In political terms this may then be couched in terms of a rather conservative vision of modern societies and the methods through which we could deal with the attendant problems of contemporary life. This is precisely the reason why the principles of community need to be freshly examined and the theoretical virtues upon which they are based must be reiterated. Modern political discourses reduce community to a convenient sideshow that can be wheeled on in times when the moral fabric of society appears to be breaking down. A more radical approach, as we shall see in the remainder of the book, involves the redefinition of community and pro-active attempts to create the appropriate environment in which spaces for community and communities themselves can be manufactured.

Unlike self-styled communitarians such as Etzioni and Tam, most commentators who invoke communitarian strategies do so on the basis that they understand the concept of community more accurately from their own ideological position than do others. Etzioni and Tam, on the other hand, tend to present their ideas as non-ideological politics. They see themselves as somehow pure and protected from political analysis that is tainted by ideological posturing. This depoliticises the important decisions that have to be made about social institutions and the way they impact upon sub-social associations and groupings of people. Ultimately this betrays the conservative heritage on which orthodox political communitarianism builds. Conservatives, such as Burke, have always been prepared to countenance change, especially if it was predicated upon reverence for historically proven ways of doing things. Similarly orthodox political communitarians have expressed a willingness to challenge accepted social arrangements, especially those emanating from the operations of the welfare state and discourses of individual rights. However, this is rarely accompanied by a recognition that tinkering with social institutions is unlikely to bring about communitarian societies without a direct engagement with economic affairs.

Orthodox political communitarianism also attempts to gloss over value pluralism and, instead of recognising incommensurability in the public sphere, it encourages difference only in the private domain. In this sense it attempts to neuter political debate over moral issues and imposes a manufactured consensus where no such consensus exists. The question that remains is whether the orthodox depiction of community in political communitarianism is the most coherent and persuasive account. To ascertain the answer to this question it is important to analyse now more radical theories of community and their contribution to our understanding of communitarian politics.

– NOTES –

1. For example, there is plentiful evidence of community organisations successfully participating in local economies and providing valuable services in their environments. For one such attempt to articulate these concerns, see Wright (2000).
2. For an attempt to reconcile a version of left communitarianism with the defence of nationality and the broad political community, see Miller (2000).

CHAPTER 4

Radical Theories of Community:
Beyond Orthodox Communitarianism

From the argument on political communitarianism developed in the previous chapter we might ask whether it is worth pursuing a radical agenda on community. After all, if it is dominated by moral authoritarianism or the different types of 'political communitarianism' described by Frazer (1999), one might reasonably ask whether the concept of community has been become so elastic that it has become meaningless. Moreover we might say that communitarianism has become so imbued with conservative messages or inscribed in reactionary discourses that it has become redundant for radical argument. Whilst such an argument is wholly understandable, it is problematic. There are certain values that can be attached to community such as friendship, mutualism, co-operation, and so on, and the normative politics of community need to be addressed if we believe that those principles are essential foundations of solidarity and social inclusion. In the light of this, it would be negligent to surrender those principles to conservative arguments or traditional perspectives on what constitutes a community. In other words, it is vital that radicals establish their own conceptualisations of solidarity and the common good to demonstrate that community is not a concept which is owned by traditional orthodox communitarians.

In recent years a more radical variant of communitarianism has emerged to challenge the hegemony of moral authoritarian forms of communitarian thinking. Where the latter derives impetus from conservative instincts and traditional definitions of community, radical communitarianism can be identified in new theories emerging from the work of many feminists, radical democrats and pluralist socialists. Not all would recognise themselves as radical communitarians, but, in essence, these commentators have a concern for communal relations, the dynamics of a multiplicity of groups living in diverse societies, and the recognition of a plurality of communities of which individuals are members. Clearly, then, this moves us beyond the narrow definition of the singular community and attempts to reconcile the existence of a plurality of communities with more traditional ideas regarding the importance of membership, commonality and solidarity. In so doing this radical perspective suggests that these values of community make a fundamental contribution to the formation of self-identity. Thus radical communitarianism blends a pluralistic concern for the individual with a recognition that individuation, that is the meaningful realisation of individual self-identity, takes place within a social context or environment in which a variety of solidaristic relationships are established.

Radical communitarianism does not establish a singular set of ideas to define the characteristics of the relationship between individuals and the groups of which they are members as communities. Variations exist between those who concentrate on the real existence of communities and their forms of solidarity, such as Jordan (1998), those who criticise the political usage of the term community but still recognise the importance of notions of commonality (Frazer 1999), and radicals who argue for agonistic forms of democracy that are capable of containing conflict (Mouffe 2000b). Moreover elements of radical communitarianism are discernible in the work of some liberal egalitarians such as Philippe van Parijs, who puts forward the idea of 'real freedom' (van Parijs 1997), and communitarian liberals such as John Gray (1997). The contention in this chapter will be that these thinkers do not always put forward identifiably radical communitarian ideas but that there is an explicit concern with certain values which can be regarded as communitarian. Thus radical communitarianism is not a homogeneous perspective but rather reflects a range of concerns and traditions of thought that can be bound together in a loose fashion. In this sense radical communitarianism reflects community itself insofar as it is plural and informal and resistant to easy categorisation. Radical communitarianism is difficult to pigeon-hole and asks us to rethink fundamental issues in political theory such as the primacy we attach to the individual and the meaning of equality in a diverse world where individuals take on a multiplicity of identities. In political terms radical communitarianism implies that democratic systems must be engendered that recognise and accommodate difference. To use the words of Mouffe, there must be:

> a vibrant clash of democratic political positions . . . Too much emphasis on consensus, and the refusal of confrontation, leads to political apathy. Worse still,

the outcome may be a crystallization of collective passions which cannot be contained by the democratic process, with the consequent collapse of agonism into an explosion of antagonism that may tear up the very roots of civility. (Mouffe 2000a: 127)

From this perspective then, a radical view of community implies a healthy attitude towards politics whereby it becomes the sphere where we pit our own identities and commitments against those of others. At times there may be negotiation and compromise that is acceptable to all, in other debates the incommensurability of values may lead to our winning or losing the debate on specific issues. Radical communitarianism does not put forward a perfectionist model of the public sphere but recognises that sometimes conflict cannot be simply overcome through the process of rational debate.

– Towards a Radical View of Community –

One of the most important radical writers on community in recent years has been Bill Jordan (1998). Jordan's work is rare in the sense that, whilst most communitarians bemoan the loss of community in the modern world or look to ways in which traditional notions of community may be resurrected (Fukuyama 1999), Jordan has focused on how communities and values of commonality have remained resilient throughout the onslaught of liberal individualism. Thus contrary to the idea that communities have been eroded by individualist values or market economics, Jordan recognises that there has not necessarily been a demise of community. Instead what we may have witnessed is not the end of community but rather the formation of new arenas of community. Activities based upon communitarian values whereby individuals co-operate for non-instrumental ends or on a voluntary basis have not disappeared from modern life, but they have been relegated in prominence due to the dominant, hegemonic position that has been accorded to the operation of market mechanisms. In societies that are dominated by economic rationality (Gorz 1989; Little 1998; Hughes and Little 1999), activities based upon communitarian values frequently become neglected in public policy-making. Indeed, as Jordan has noted, we may well even criminalise some activities with a communitarian ethos because they are performed on the black market. In this context it is difficult to promote the idea of community. Under the hegemony of economic rationality, community activities are, at best, to be performed by those who are either beyond the tentacles of the labour market (for example, the retired), unable to meet the requirements of work (welfare recipients) or those with sufficient temporal and financial resources to contribute to their communities after paid work. Jordan's favoured approach is to enhance community development by enabling individuals to make a greater civic contribution and participate more in community activities. In so doing he wants to encourage much greater recognition of the informal economy and the benefits that accrue to local communities from activities carried out beyond the sphere of markets.

Jordan's radical communitarianism is founded upon his long-term critique of the paternalistic and bureaucratic welfare state. Thus he has suggested that state welfare has been oppressive of those dependent on its largesse and 'may crush or distort the lives of those who receive it' (Jordan 1976: 213). Against the dominance of political elites and the bureaucratic machinery in decision-making processes, Jordan proffers the view of the social condition that all humans are fundamentally cooperative actors due to their embeddedness in social groups. From this basis he argues that 'individuals seeking their own wellbeing are able to associate co-operatively with each other' (Jordan 1992: 213) and thus that we need to develop a 'bottom–up' theory of social order in which we prioritise interpersonal bonds 'based on a rough understanding of reciprocal roles and responsibilities' (Jordan 1990: 4). The comments above may point to a fairly orthodox communitarian position in Jordan's theory but what makes it stand out from the communitarian philosophy of, say, MacIntyre is his concern with the material conditions in which community is experienced. Thus, rather than merely advocating his theoretical position, Jordan attempts to outline the real obstacles to communitarianism and the associated goals of democracy, membership and participation. In this vein he states that there needs to be a 'theory of social relations which takes account of the ways in which people share their lives in a community' (Jordan 1992: 159) and that we must give ethical priority to decisions over the distribution of resources that will allow all to participate in these decisions and the shared life of the community. The material basis of Jordan's thought is appealing and the model of participation he provides is a worthwhile goal. However, there is also a tendency to present full membership and participation in somewhat idyllic terms and a failure to recognise the conflict and antagonism that is likely to be generated in the context of diverse societies containing a wide range of communities.

Although coming from a less radical perspective than Jordan, John Gray's critique of orthodox communitarianism and liberal individualism reaches some similar conclusions (Gray 1997: chapter 2; Carling 1996). Whilst

Gray is rather difficult to pin down on a particular political agenda, his advocacy of what he calls 'communitarian liberalism' has radical credentials. He defines this perspective according to three main principles:

1. Individual autonomy is best understood as a common good, which suggests that it involves responsibilities as well as choices.
2. The benefits of market exchanges are limited to specific contexts and may threaten autonomy beyond those spheres.
3. That markets should not be used as systems of distribution beyond those spheres where they are appropriate.

For Gray, these principles do not accord specific privilege to either libertarian perspectives based upon negative liberty or egalitarian theories of justice. What is most notable here is the way in which Gray, in trying to identify a radical form of communitarianism and not previously renowned for his opposition to market mechanisms, now expresses his 'communitarian liberalism' in terms of limiting the sphere of markets. Thus he argues that:

> The central application of the communitarian liberal view to public policy is that market freedoms have instrumental value only, as means to individual well-being, and they have this value only when they do not weaken forms of common life without which individual well-being is impoverished or impossible. (Gray 1997: 17)

Importantly then, Gray not only suggests that there are limited areas where markets are the most efficient form of distribution, but also that they may be positively harmful in other areas of life where different values permeate relationships than those which are economically rational. Unlike commentators, such as Fukuyama (1996), who present social virtues in terms of the economic benefits that accrue from them, Gray implies that communitarian principles need to be protected from the impact of markets. Civic virtues are ends in themselves rather than mere contributory factors to economic prosperity. In this sense markets have a history and are embedded in specific environments and contexts. Here Gray is explicit that this necessitates the limitation of markets:

> Legitimating the market requires that it be curbed or removed in institutions and areas of social life where common understandings demand that goods be distributed in accord with ethical norms which the market, of necessity, disregards. Public acceptance of a dynamic market economy requires that the ethos of market exchange be excluded from important contexts – contexts in which non-market institutions and practices are protected as a matter of public policy. (Gray 1997: 18)

Whilst this passage hints at radicalism, insofar as it suggests that markets may be detrimental in certain spheres of life where civic, communitarian values are more appropriate and should therefore be limited, the last sentence implies that Gray remains attached to a notion of a dynamic market economy that may still undermine community. The extent of radicalism in communitarian thinking is very much a matter of degree. It is not really sufficient to argue that markets need to be limited – the restraint of markets could be operationalised in more or less radical ways. Such is the dominance of markets in contemporary discourses that their hegemonic position will not be sufficiently challenged by a theory that suggests simply that they should not interfere with communitarian values. In other words the limitation of markets will take place to a greater or lesser extent depending upon the size of the sphere of community that is delineated.

Further light is cast on Gray's oblique perspective in a paper entitled 'What community is not' (1997). Notably he explicitly states that 'there is no overarching value of community to which all political movements can reasonably pay lip-service. Conceptions of community, and public policies aiming to promote it, will vary radically according to the political projects they express' (Gray 1997: 77). Whilst he is on sure ground in pointing out the ways in which different communities will express themselves as communities, Gray's view that community does not encompass any particular values is more problematic. If there are not particular values or principles that we seek to protect in the advocacy of community, it becomes very difficult to identify the basis upon which it should be protected. In other words, if it is not possible to discern specific values that inform market transactions and that are different from those of community, then it is not clear how we would be able to justify the limitations of markets that Gray appears to favour. If there are no objective grounds on which to challenge the logic of market exchange, then it is unlikely to take place. Likewise if community is not associated with any particular values, then the protection of community becomes a rather difficult procedure to enact. Sceptics may well ask why we should seek to prioritise and protect an entity that is not attached to any specific principles. Stating that communities and markets operate according to different rationalities does not get us very far if we are not prepared to identify what it is that comprises those rationalities.

Gray is on surer ground in rejecting the 'project of propping up traditional forms of social life or recovering any past cultural consensus' (Gray 1997: 81). Here he is rejecting the nostalgia and romanticism which permeates moral authoritarian approaches and recognising that in contemporary Western societies (and increasingly other parts of the world, too) mono-culturalism is unusual. Instead of appealing to the community, we must validate the existence of a multiplicity of communities. Gray, quite rightly, recognises that the promotion of community as part of a process of the remoralisation of a delinquent public is a recipe for exclusion. It points to the likely promotion of the particular morality of a singular community with which many within any given society might not concur. For Gray, the pursuit of community 'is concerned with contriving . . . a common frame-work of institutions within which diverse communities can live, not with any ideal of a single, all-embracing community' (Gray 1997: 81).

A similar scepticism regarding the dominant political discourse of com-munity within communitarian thinking permeates the work of Elizabeth Frazer. It was expressed in the book *The Politics of Community* (1993), in which Frazer and Nicola Lacey articulated feminist concerns with the contours of the orthodox liberal–communitarian debate. Nonetheless, despite their critique of the philosophical orthodoxy, their analysis does offer some useful pointers in the construction of a radical perspective on community, not least the necessity of recognising the relationships of power that can skew the nature of community life. This perspective has been taken up by Frazer in her later work, *The Problems of Communitarian Politics* (1999), although where in the earlier work she explicitly advocated a 'dialogic communitarianism', she now seems much more opposed to dis-courses of community. So much so that she openly states that 'conceptual and theoretical problems with "community" are very far-reaching . . . They resonate in discourses, and have particular (not progressive) rhetorical effects. They impact in policy and practice in perverse ways' (Frazer 1999: 3–4). Part of the reason for Frazer's scepticism about communitar-ianism derives from her identification of a slippage between the different concepts of community that are deployed within that tradition. Thus she argues that community is sometimes used to depict a set of relations between people, sometimes it is used to describe an entity – often a geographical location – or a surrogate thereof, and sometimes community is presented as a thinking subject (Frazer 1998: 118). It is the subjective and often vague usage of different definitions, sometimes overlapping and sometimes not, that informs Frazer's new, more critical stance towards community. More-over her later work reiterates the common concern that communitarianism may threaten individual freedoms and in its political manifestation may lead to exclusionary outcomes. Thus, in a prescient comment, Frazer states that 'communitarianism needs to be supplemented both by a supra-communitarian theory which explores the relationship between communities, and by an intra-communitarian theory which looks critically at the welfare and status of individuals within communities' (Frazer 1998: 121). It is just those two projects that the remainder of this book seeks to address not just in philosophical terms but also in the realm of practical politics.

For now it is worth exploring whether the concept of community can be rescued from the rhetorical meaninglessness that Frazer identifies and, if so, what impact this may have on radical perspectives. She is correct to note that the concept of community has been somewhat undertheorised in relation to other political concepts such as equality, freedom or rights, and this may be a partial explanation of why it is used in such a poorly defined fashion. However we must ask if this negates it as a useful political concept. After all, Frazer's objection that community is used loosely and has become a 'feelgood word' (whilst true) can also be applied to other concepts in common political discourses. Freedom and rights are frequently employed in vague terms that often have very little bearing on real social practices. Other ideas such as equal opportunities are deployed with no less 'rhetorical force' than community and frequently serve to obscure rather than clarify the meaning of equality or the practical realities of opportunity. Thus, whilst Frazer is right to point out the misuses of the concept of community in popular political discourse, this is hardly a unique misappropriation of philosophical ideas in the world of practical politics. This truism does not negate the fact that freedom and equality are central political ideas and the same extends to community. That it requires clarification is beyond dispute, that this position is idiosyncratic is less than clear.

As we noted in the previous chapter, the main problem in moral authoritarian communitarianism, or what Frazer refers to as political communitarianism (as opposed to philosophical communitarianism), is the tendency to prioritise a vision of *the* community. This notion of a singular moral community around which we can all coalesce has been the subject of much criticism from radicals who argue for the existence of a multiplicity of communities and the establishment of a framework in which a plurality of communities can co-exist alongside one another. As we shall see in the last part of the book, there is dispute about whether the differences between communities can be accommodated through a perfectionist process of dialogue and debate, or whether incommensurable objectives will generate inevitable conflict that must be contained through democratic measures but cannot be resolved. For now it is important to recognise that, despite the limitations of 'normalizing communitarianism' such as that of Etzioni, when it comes to the conceptualisation of the community, radicals have argued that contemporary communitarians must try to grapple with the 'pluralization of cultures'. In this vein Rose contends that whatever 'closure it may seek to impose . . . this inescapably plural field invites an agonistic politics of ethics, one that argues for the powers of "other communities" and "other subjectivities", for an experimental ethical politics of life itself' (Rose 1999: 194). It is on this territory that the work of Chantal Mouffe (1993a, 2000a, 2000b) has had a clear impact upon the development of radical forms of communitarianism.

According to Mouffe's radical democratic perspective, we need to encourage a range of different groups, including communities, to engage in a multiplicity of forms of democratic enterprise. Thus there is a need to understand the conflicts generated between particular groups and to enable their expression in numerous political settings and environments. This would then comprise what Mouffe terms 'agonistic pluralism' (see Mouffe 2000b: Chapter 4). Against models of deliberative democracy and procedural theories of democratic renewal such as those of Rawls and Habermas, Mouffe contends that we must move away from the idea that the differences between conflicting, particularist communities can be resolved through 'rational, universal solutions'. This is presented as something of a dangerous fiction which amounts to 'just one more futile attempt to insulate politics from the inescapable reality of value pluralism. Democratic theory should renounce all such forms of escapism and instead confront the challenge that recognition of value pluralism entails' (Mouffe 2000a: 119– 20). Thus the recognition of value pluralism or a radical view of multiple (sometimes incommensurable) communities becomes a starting point for renewing the democratic process rather than a problem that democracy must overcome. Such a process will reflect distributions of power and particular communities would be defined in terms of their relations with one another and the forms of power they hold. Thus 'if we accept that relations of power are constitutive of the social . . . then the main question for democratic politics is not how to eliminate power but how to constitute forms of power more compatible with democratic values' (Mouffe 2000a: 125).

According to this scenario then, we should not engage in futile attempts to create political systems that are capable of eradicating the antagonism that emanates from value pluralism and particular communities. Rather Mouffe's 'agonistic pluralism' is concerned with regarding others or our opponents as legitimate adversaries rather than fundamental enemies. In this sense our adherence to certain principles which underpin our debates is more important than the vain pursuit of consensus. At times agreement may be reached, but that does not negate the essential conflict that acts as a foundation of the political. For Mouffe, 'compromises are, of course, also possible; they are indeed part and parcel of politics; but they should be seen as mere temporary respites in an on-going confrontation' (Mouffe 2000a: 126). It is in the shift from conflict with enemies to conflict with legitimate opponents that Mouffe identifies a move from a politics of antagonism to a politics of agonism. This provides a radical impetus to the study of community. It suggests that a healthy democracy will be one whereby different communities with particular views are able to express themselves in political debate. The participation of communities would happen with a full recognition that the outcomes of political debate may not be optimal or consensual but that their specific vision of the common good would be legitimised as a valid contribution to political discourse. The ultimate arbiter in such a model would, of course, be the state.

Mouffe's perspective provides a dynamic structure for the co-existence of a range of particularist communities and a refreshing understanding of the nature of democratic processes when it comes to accommodating difference. Most importantly, she recognises the inevitability of power and the barriers that it can construct against full participation by all. Similarly Bill Jordan recognises that major obstacles are thrown up against certain communities in contemporary liberal democracies, especially those that are marginalised due to prejudice or low income. This throws up practical problems for the realisation of the kind of 'agonistic pluralism' that Mouffe advocates. Where the latter highlights issues of power that may undermine the participation of certain groups in the democratic process, the task for radical communitarians is to identify ways in which excluded communities can be engaged more directly in political debate. Ironically, as we shall see in the coming chapters, the strategy favoured by many radical communitarians is to provide individuals with a guaranteed income in order to generate 'real freedom for all' (van Parijs 1997). This suggests that the pathway to providing political legitimacy to a multiplicity of communities is to empower the individuals therein by providing them with sufficient opportunities for full social participation. In this sense the radical theory of community must, by definition, engage with issues of social and economic policy. Before doing so however, it is important to engage with new debates over citizenship and the ways in which the discourses of universalism and particularism can help us to rethink the distribution of social and economic resources.

– Community and Citizenship –

Traditionally the liberal conception of citizenship has involved notions of membership and inclusion with regard to large political units such as nation-states. This membership has usually been understood through a matrix of rights and (to a lesser extent) duties that establish a relationship, between individuals, their peers and social institutions such as the welfare state. Implicit in this conception of citizenship is an underlying belief in equality of status whereby the existence of a range of social inequalities is permissible if individuals are included in the social whole by the status that is accorded to all individuals as citizens. Thus, from this orthodox liberal perspective, citizenship provides universal recognition for everyone accepted as citizens in a broad political unit (although, of course, the conditions that govern the status of citizenship is highly variable between different political units). However this model of citizenship has been increasingly difficult to main-tain as a representation of the reality of Western liberal democracies such as the UK and the USA. The constitution of the formal relationships between individuals and states still embodies facets of universal citizenship that vary from country to country, but, to some extent, the erosion of various citizenship rights, such as those to social security, has necessitated a new evaluation of the meaning of citizenship. The waters of this process have also been muddied by the growth of theories associated with the politics of difference developed within feminism and radical pluralism (see, for ex-ample, Young 1990a, 1990b; Mouffe 1992, 1993a; Shanley and Narayan 1997). Here the question has been raised as to how universalising concepts such as citizenship can encompass the diversity of modern societies and the attendant needs that different social groups encounter. In this context it is important to evaluate the role of community in these debates and the extent to which communities might play a role in the development of a differ-entiated universalism (Lister 1997, 1998).

The task for radical communitarians is to explain how the promotion of community can accommodate difference in a meaningful fashion and overcome the exclusionary outcomes that emanate from some discourses of political communitarianism. The theory of differentiated universalism requires a politics 'in which the achievement of the universal is contingent upon attention to difference' (Lister 1998: 84). However this attention to difference with regard to community requires that not only do we focus upon the relationship between universalism and particularism that animates citizenship debates, but we also examine the ingredients of an environment in which the principles of community such as friendship, compassion and mutual obligation are allowed to flourish. One of the traditional objectives of citizenship has been the establishment of common bonds and values that create social solidarity. Given that difference can generate the kind of antagonism identified by Mouffe (2000b), it might be argued that social solidarity is likely to be undermined under conditions of diversity. A response to this point might suggest that we need to develop a new understanding of solidarity, namely, one that is based upon the recognition of difference and the opportunities that are afforded to all by the encouragement of diversity in a range of communities. As such, although conflict and tension between the universal idea of citizenship and particular communities cannot be eradicated, the extent to which they can be contained may be used as a gauge of a model of citizenship that is founded upon differentiated universalism. In itself then, dispute or conflict need not contradict social solidarity and indeed the capacity for containment can be regarded as an indicator of a radical and mature pluralism.

Orthodox political communitarianism is problematic because, although it is clothed in quasi-universalist language, it provides a recipe for the exclusion of those who do not subscribe to the dominant moralism that informs the project. In this orthodox model the term community becomes subsumed as if it equated automatically with the beliefs of the majority of the populace of the nation-state.[1] In effect, community comes to represent an organic view of the family writ large to encompass the wider unit of society as a whole. In this orthodox version of communitarianism, the community does not facilitate difference but rather overrides it in the pursuit of a manufactured commonality between divergent groups of people. This has led Lister to comment that it amounts to a false universalism and that 'as presently constituted, the ideal of community would therefore appear incompatible with the kind of politics of difference with which an inclusive approach to citizenship needs to engage' (Lister 1998: 80). From this viewpoint one might be tempted to ask whether the baggage that has now been attached to the notion of community has led to its redundancy for radicals involved in redefining citizenship.

Whilst recognising the danger that Lister identifies, it is important to recognise the distinctiveness of community and its usefulness for radical theory. Arguably there are no other concepts that embrace the values and principles of mutualism, voluntarism, co-operation, care, compassion and friendship so tellingly and to such great effect. Where liberal notions of citizenship tend to be tied to a framework of rights and duties (often understood in rather vague and abstract ways), community implies relationships that transcend formal reciprocity, relationships in which participants do not ask 'What do I get in return?' even though they will derive benefits. Similarly, where the world of work is predicated upon labour contracts and the uneven distribution of power among the main actors, activity within communities reflects common interests and the benefits of co-operation. Frequently the values of community derive from compassion and a desire for usefulness rather than economically rational thoughts of 'What is in it for me?' Thus the radical rethinking of citizenship needs to employ a theory of community that does not pander to the instrumental values that are imbued in economic relationships. Even commentators who defend the expansion of market mechanisms and the limitation of government can contend that 'for the members of some group who cooperate with one another for a common purpose to form a community in the relevant sense, the common purpose for the sake of which they cooperate has to be of some intrinsic or noninstrumental value to them' (Conway 1996: 141). Conway's comments imply that even market liberals can accept the idea that the greatest promise for the protection of communal values lies in the creation of a social sphere in which the economic ethos of growth, accumulation and the pursuit of profit do not predominate. This suggests that the voluntaristic, co-operative relations of community are inimical to the rationale of market mechanisms or the regulation of the state. The promotion of these values implies that communities can form the basis of new layers of governance that would complement rather than replace government or the market (Barber 1996: 283).

The implications of this perspective suggest that there are principles associated with the idea of community that hold considerable power and are not easily transferable to other sites of life-activity. These principles of mutual respect and co-operation are the very foundations upon which diversity can be encouraged. Indeed radical communitarianism would imply that it is only through the establishment of these kinds of values between different communities that they can genuinely flourish within communities. As such, these principles of community endorse and validate the differences between communities, and it is only through the recognition of a multiplicity of communities that the concept of community (and the values it embodies) can play a central role in the redefinition of citizenship. Without the values of community, citizenship is reduced to either liberal formalism, which offers little by way of critical thinking for the future and a return to somewhat abstract ways of understanding the concept, or it becomes nothing more than a recipe for isolated individuals making lifestyle choices without the anchorage of common projects and identity derived from collective self-determination. This kind of dislocation of individuals from common projects undermines the politics of difference that radical reinterpretations of citizenship are predicated upon.

It is also the case that difference *within* communities need not contradict universalism. In this sense it would be erroneous to suppose that the actual relations within communities could be exemplars of universal virtues given the different qualities and abilities that different members of communities have. Thus, within the parameters of community, differences between individuals do not matter as long as they don't prejudice our capacity for membership. Where different abilities and qualities may foster inequality in economic transactions, for example, or where relations of citizenship are founded upon rights and duties that require formal universalism, the universalism embodied in radical conceptions of community accepts difference as a desirable feature that does not undermine the equal status of the members of any given community. In this sense, 'equality in democratic rights in a community is quite consistent with inequality in excellences. A community that is not differentiated in the standing of members is consistent with a community that is differentiated in the particular virtues that an individual can exhibit' (O'Neill 1998: 105). From this perspective, such are the potentially benevolent relations that may exist within ideal-typical communities that they encapsulate the capacity for recognising difference without prejudice more than is the case in economic relationships or in formalistic liberal notions of citizenship.

In terms of citizenship, and following the work of Dean (1996), Lister argues that the concept of community must be able to assist the creation of 'reflective solidarity' in which common bonds are created between people that are predicated upon the understanding of and respect for our differences (Lister 1998: 84). The focus on 'reflective solidarity' reinforces Young's (1993) perspective that solidarity is based upon the relationships that are established between different groups of people. Whilst, of course, this is a key means of manufacturing solidarity *within society* as a whole, it is also important not to underplay the significance of relations *within communities* themselves, not least because individuals are likely to be members of a variety of different communities. Thus intra-community relations are important because we should 'conceive of identity as constituted by the intersection of a multiplicity of identifications and collective identities that constantly subvert each other' (Mouffe 1993b: 79). In this scenario we need to clarify not only the nature of intergroup relationships, but also the bonds within communities and the ways in which they contribute to solidarity. At the same time the radical rethinking of citizenship in accordance with the politics of difference must be careful to avoid straying into the territory of liberal individualism and the portrayal of people as utility maximisers choosing to join communities or groups for personal gain only. Rather it must be remembered that civic groups 'frequently have a purpose oriented on what they take as a wider public good; often they do not regard themselves as merely working for the collective self-interest of their members' (Young 1995: 209).

In her advocacy of differentiated universalism, Lister argues for a politics that embraces a conceptualisation of citizenship as universal and yet permits individuals to enjoy their rights and status in particularistic ways. Indeed she suggests that although there is potential conflict between universalism and particularism, it is a tension that should be taken on board and used to further the rethinking of citizenship (Lister 1998: 82–4; see Spicker (1996) for an alternative reading of the universalism/particularism debate). The question that arises, then, is whether the universal status that forms the basis of citizenship (for those regarded as citizens) can accommodate the particular needs and interests of different groups. Moreover how can this tension contribute to the creation and maintenance of solidarity and social integration which has traditionally been founded on notions of commonality and equality of status rather the celebration of difference? For Lister, the answer lies in the universal recognition of 'the equal moral worth and participation and inclusion of all persons' (Lister 1998: 83). Viewed from this perspective, a conceptualisation of citizenship that does not couple universalism with particularism would appear to be in denial of the different ways in which individuals see and experience the rights and duties with which they are (or should be) endowed.

This type of argument is developed in more detail by Hollenbach (1995), who advocates a 'community of freedom in civil society' based upon his engagement with Aristotelian politics and Roman Catholic social thought. Although he uses a rather broad definition of community (he includes economic associations for example) and is overly optimistic about the emergence of forms of solidarity, Hollenbach suggests that there is a specific ethos involved in internal community relations that negates the conception of the neo-liberal individualist. On this foundation he argues that the 'strong communal links found in the diverse groups of civil society must have greater public presence' (Hollenbach 1995: 147). Thus he believes that communities are founded on Aristotelian virtues of mutuality, co-operation and friendship, and that these aspects of communitarian politics can be harnessed to influence broader social units such as the state and the economy. Although he is in favour of the principle of subsidiarity that would potentially devolve power to communities, he believes that this can only develop within the broader context of an accepted notion of the common good. Of course, the values and principles of the common good are debatable and therefore Hollenbach's model provides only one example of this strategy. For this reason, Hollenbach's argument for the need for a fusion of universalism with particularism founded on the creation of 'intellectual' and 'social' solidarity needs to be addressed.

In promoting 'intellectual' solidarity Hollenbach is referring to some form of discursive or deliberative democracy. Lister too, building on the ideas of Habermas and Benhabib, advocates a commitment to dialogue and communication as central to the production of a politics of solidarity in difference (Lister 1998: 77–8). The commitment to increasing dialogue and spaces for political debate is important but this should be accompanied by a realisation that the outcome of such debate is unlikely to be harmonious agreement. Thus the idea of 'intellectual solidarity' is attractive, but the political realities of incommensurable value pluralism suggest that consensus is not a feasible outcome of every issue of debate. A more realistic politics of solidarity in difference would follow the kind of agonistic model outlined by Mouffe. Nonetheless, whilst we should be sceptical of the overall outcome of dialogue, this does not undermine Hollenbach's advocacy of 'intellectual solidarity' as a concept in which the weaker notion of toleration of difference could be replaced by a more thorough idea of solidarity. For Hollenbach, this strong community of solidarity would in turn lead to 'freedom of reciprocal dialogue'. Thus:

> Where conversation about the good life begins and develops in intellectual solidarity, a community of freedom begins to exist. And this is itself a major part of the common good. Indeed, it is this freedom in reciprocal dialogue that is one of the characteristics that distinguishes a community of solidarity from one marked by domination and repression. (Hollenbach 1995: 151)

Again the overall thrust of the argument provides a useful foundation for the radical theory of community, but we need to be explicit in our recognition that 'the freedom of reciprocal dialogue' will tend to generate contradictory interpretations of what the common good actually means. The commitment to such open and pluralistic expressions of different conceptions of the good cannot presuppose agreement, but it could facilitate the opening up of new spaces for political engagement.

A radical view of community and citizenship then would be concerned with the creation of structures for dialogue as the basis of intellectual solidarity. The existence of such structures would not do away with disagreement and conflict but could provide an environment for their exposition instead. Importantly, even if Hollenbach promotes an overly broad conception of what a community actually is, he is more aware than most that we need to understand the bonds within communities as well as the relations between them if we are to generate a genuine politics of solidarity. Indeed his second category of solidarity, the notion of 'social solidarity', extends not only to the positive depiction of communal structures, but also the need for bonds to be established with those who have traditionally been marginalised from decision-making processes in liberal democracies. In this sense Hollenbach believes that civil society must be opened up to groups in society that are currently excluded due to a range of social circumstances. This is what he refers to as a process of creating a 'community of freedom in civil society'. To put it another way, a spirit must be enshrined in the framework of civil society that would allow a range of communities the freedom to express themselves. Viewed from this perspective, the principles and values of community provide the structure that permits the flourishing of a diverse range of communities. Solidarity, in this sense, is founded on one hand by the bonds that hold groups of individuals together for non-instrumental reasons, and, on the other, by the recognition within society that opportunities to experience particular communities rely fundamentally on the recognition that others must also be accorded opportunities for particularist forms of expression. Thus, according to the perspective of differentiated universalism, solidarity is predicated upon a universal structure that identifies the centrality of difference and, more concretely, recognises the importance of establishing a framework in which particular differences are allowed to manifest themselves.

The radical rethinking of citizenship reminds us of the need to engage with the continuing tensions between notions of the public and the private, society and community, the state and the economy and the ways in which these different categories interact with and influence one another (Kenny 1996). The theory of community has for too long been associated with geographical definitions of belonging and traditional understandings of the bonds that hold people together. In traditional terms there remains an overbearing focus on the conflation of communities with an overarching political community that embodies an Aristotelian notion of the common good. Whilst concern with the common good remains a central feature of the radical perspective, this does not mean that it can only be expressed within the parameters of the orthodox debate. Of course, the notion of political community remains a central concept in the understanding of citizenship (Mouffe 1993b), not least in the context of debates over more cosmopolitan democratic structures. However we overlook micro-politics and the associational bonds that people form at our peril, for they are the means through which people experience and enjoy common interests in everyday life. Whilst notions of citizenship and universal rights and duties provide a framework for belonging and membership, it is the actual experience of that status on a micro-level that creates commonality and social solidarity.

Clearly then, individuals acquire status and identity through membership of a range of groups and associations that provide different kinds of belonging, and some of which are predicated on community values such as voluntarism, friendship and co-operation. Communities will not always be concerned with big social and political issues and the representation of specific interests in the decision-making process. This moves us beyond one-dimensional instrumental understandings of why people are members of groups. On the contrary people may acquire their most important bonds with others through small-scale, and indeed sometimes mundane, forms of association. Thus communities, as construed by Kukathas, are essentially 'partial associations':

> A community is essentially an association of individuals who share an under-standing of what is public and what is private within that association. This definition of community captures the idea . . . that it is something about the relationship among people (rather than merely their propinquity) that makes their association a community rather than just a social grouping. (Kukathas 1996: 85).

This captures the importance of the internal relationships within communities as well as intergroup relations. Solidarity is generated through the attachments we make as individuals with one another due to common interests and non-instrumental motivation. Influential commentators such as Young rightly argue that a politics of difference must be created in which a polity is created based on 'social equality among explicitly differentiated groups who conceive themselves as dwelling together without exclusions' (Young 1993: 135). At the same time, however, there must simultaneously be a recognition that our ability to build such a politics of difference needs to be founded on the ways in which we all derive our identities from being members of differentiated groups. As such, the institutionalisation of universal rights and duties in a radically conceived understanding of citizenship must also recognise the importance of allowing individuals to establish a range of bonds of solidarity in the different communities of which they are members.

Nevertheless the question remains as to why the solidarity that we might experience as members of communities should necessarily entail that we should extend opportunities for solidarity to others in different communities. For radical communitarians, the answer to this may lie in the recognition that our ability to enjoy the communities of which we are members relies upon other members of our society enabling us to do so. From this perspective it is reasonable to argue that we should extend the capacity to form and be part of different communities to other members of society. This is clearly part of the reason that many communities in modern societies are effectively socially excluded because bonds of understanding and mutual respect are frequently not extended *between* groups in the contemporary era. Part of the reason for this lies in the instrumental attitude to communities and associations that has been generated as a response to pluralist thinking on the role of groups in modern life. Communities and associations are represented as mere interest groups in competition with each other for the furtherance of particularist goals rather than bodies that rely upon each other for the opportunities to come together and express common interests. For Mouffe, orthodox liberal pluralism underestimates the political nature of the relations between different groups: 'to deny the need for a construction of . . . collective identities, and to conceive democratic politics exclusively in terms of a struggle of a multiplicity of interest groups or of minorities for the assertion of their rights, is to remain blind to the relations of power' (Mouffe 2000b: 20).

Essentially, radical views on community and citizenship suggest that there is a need to understand that a differentiated universalism must be founded on mutual recognition and the extension of opportunities to enjoy difference to all equally and universally. Thus difference and particularism can only be posited as the foundation of a radical rethinking of citizenship, if the bonds and values within the communities of which we are a part are extended to encompass our relations with members of other communities. In this sense solidarity as a universal social virtue must be based upon the principles and values that characterise relations within particularistic communities.

– CONCLUSION: AN EGALITARIAN THEORY? –

Radical theories of community clearly contain an egalitarian concern insofar as there is a recognition that there are communities in liberal democratic societies that are effectively excluded from political participation and debate. An extreme example of this would be the limitations on political rights that are often imposed against immigrants or asylum seekers. On a less direct level, members of minority ethnic communities may feel disenfranchised by the limited representation of their communities in formal politics and the low priority accorded to the issues that they are most interested in. Thus exclusion may emanate from the nature of political and social structures that limit access to the public sphere or may be as a result of the hegemonic power over public discourses that reflects the interests of elite groups in society. As such, the main thrust of radical theories of community is to construct political structures in which the voices of excluded communities are heard and dominant powers can be challenged. In this sense commentators such as Mouffe rule out perfectionist models of equal outcomes due to power inequalities but seek more democratic forms for political participation that might enable excluded groups to influence public debate. On a more material level radical commentators such as Jordan and Gorz have recognised that more equal access to political spheres requires social and economic policies that empower the deprived and disenfranchised. Too often communitarian philosophy has neglected the social and economic spheres and orthodox political communitarianism has tended to ignore the arguments of the radical perspective outlined above. However, in all its forms, radical communitarianism does not impose a strong egalitarianism either with regard to economic situation or social provision. As noted by Frazer, this reflects one of the ambiguities of the concept of community that critics find particularly problematic:

> There is a common theoretical dispute whether relations within community must be equal, or whether inequality and hierarchy of status, material resources, power and authority are consistent with community. Although equality is often associated with the socialist traditions, while hierarchy is associated with con-

servatism, it is more remarkable that in many practical and theoretical contexts both the ideals of equality and hierarchy coexist and their coexistence is expressed in and by the concept community. (Frazer 1999: 79)

Frazer is correct to identify that within the discourse of community different views of equality and inequality are expressed and that there is not a simple distinction to be made between equality and hierarchy. Thus the assumption that inequalities in terms of skills and abilities necessarily translate into hierarchical relationships within any given community is not conclusive. Similarly even in a hypothetical scenario where people in a community were equal in terms of talents, for example, this is no guarantee that hierarchy would be avoided. The dichotomy between equality and hierarchy is not particularly helpful in trying to grapple with the form of egalitarianism that emanates from radical communitarian politics. At the same time, Frazer is right that there is nothing within communitarianism *per se* that rules out the possibility of hierarchy. Perhaps, as we shall see in the following chapters, the model of complex equality associated with Michael Walzer (1983) is the most coherent form of equality for communitarian theory (Miller 1998; Miller and Walzer 1995). According to Walzer's perspective, equality of status remains a key concern. However, this does not preclude the existence of inequalities of excellences and positioning with regard to various social goods. Nonetheless, in the scenario of complex equality, there will be no inherent link between inequalities in different social spheres. Thus the fact that one person has greater educational ability or technical capacities or sources of income than another does not translate into a justification for inequality in a different social sphere where education, technical capability or financial resources are deemed to be irrelevant. For example, we may decide as a society that, in the field of health, the inequalities that pertain in other areas of life should not affect our equal access to care on the basis of need. For Walzer, different distributive logics pertain in different spheres of life. This theory entails the view that 'although members may enjoy unequal standing in certain particular respects . . . overall they regard and treat one another as equals' and, more concretely, 'equal membership of a political community is the precondition for all the more specific practices of distributive justice that citizens may engage in' (Miller 2000: 105).

The radical theory of community does, then, embrace a notion of equality. In the case of Walzer this is a complex equality where we recognise that there are varying distributive logics in different spheres of life. Literally, then, there are different spheres of justice. However radical theories of community also understand that the ideal of equality is bound up with the debate around what Charles Taylor (1992) calls the politics of recognition. In an important statement Taylor argues that the politics of difference cannot be merely reduced to a process of procedural justice and liberal neutrality. As such, he argues that the meaningful recognition of difference requires that equal value needs to be attached to differing conceptions of the good. But he identifies the problematic dimension of this aspect of equality because the fact that we have chosen to be members of certain communities or are born into them in no way guarantees that they will have equal value to others. In other words, the mere existence of difference does not entail equal recognition. Thus, for Taylor, there need to be some prevailing values that underpin our differences:

> To come together on a mutual recognition of difference – that is, of the equal value of different identities – requires that we share more than a belief in this principle; we have to share also some standards of value on which the identities concerned check out as equal. There must be some substantive agreement on value, or else the formal principle of equality will be empty and a sham. (Taylor 1991: 52)

This idea of a shared value of equality is an aspiration for democratic politics that clearly does not prevail in contemporary liberal democracies. Indeed the pursuit of that value is often undermined by the manufactured consensus of the middle ground. Taylor's advocacy of the recognition of difference based on equal value is perfectly compatible with the kind of agonistic pluralism put forward by Mouffe. In this sense, recognising equal value for different visions of the good does not presuppose ultimate agreement or consensus and need not descend into a morass of relativism. Respecting differences in others allows for disagreement with their views – this radical view of egalitarianism promotes difference rather than sameness. This clearly moves us beyond formal notions of liberal neutrality 'and one of the crucial ways we do this is sharing a participatory political life. The demands of recognizing difference themselves take us beyond mere procedural justice' (Taylor 1991: 52). Thus understanding, and respecting, difference in political discourses is itself an egalitarian perspective. However, this philosophical egalitarianism must be addressed in terms of material conditions as well. It is all very well having one's differences recognised, but this may mean little if, for example, our material conditions prevent us from having equal access to the spheres of political debate. It is for this reason that, before turning to the appropriate political structures for the furtherance of community, we should clarify the social and economic conditions that allow principles of community to come to the fore.

– Note –

1. David Miller provides a more radical interpretation of the link between nationality and communitarianism. Whilst Miller wants to avoid prescription of the make-up of the national political community, his overall message remains within the boundaries of orthodox communitarianism. To this end he argues in favour of what he calls 'the left critique of multiculturalism':

> [I]f people define their identities through a plurality of specific communities without at the same time *giving priority* to an inclusive politically organized community, there is a danger that the social fabric will begin to unravel, with the different communal groups becoming increasingly alienated from and hostile to one another. (Miller 2000: 104–5, emphasis added)

The reason why this differs from the kind of radical approaches outlined here is the priority that Miller attaches to the overall national political community and the underlying message that such a community can overcome the difficulties of hostile groups living alongside one another (see also Miller 1995).

CHAPTER 5

Community and Economy: Rethinking Work?

The political relations of community cannot be dealt with in isolation from the social and economic structures that exist within any given polity. This has given rise to numerous studies in recent years that have explicitly tried to link political economy with communitarian relations or the lack of them. Notable contributions here have been linked to commentators such as Francis Fukuyama (1999) and Robert Putnam (2001) and their engagement with the idea of social capital. The latter is envisaged as a means of understanding the ways in which community can contribute to economic success and sustain market economies. At the same time critics such as André Gorz (1999) and Richard Sennett (1999) have pointed how the operations of markets can have a deleterious impact on communities. Thus they argue that, in the climate of flexibility in the new economy, markets and communities do not sit harmoniously alongside one another (see also Rifkin 2000). Moreover they imply that such harmony is unlikely to emerge from the trajectory of modern political economy and the ubiquitous discourses of flexibility and globalisation. In the light of these developments, this chapter suggests that communitarians have been slow in grappling with the problems of the new economy and, where they have done so, that their position has not been persuasive. Thus only alternative forms of political economy offer the kind of economic change that might facilitate radical theories of community.

The most notable advocate of community as an important factor in economic success in recent years has been Fukuyama (1996, 1999) in his work on social capital and trust. The thrust of Fukuyama's argument is that successful capitalist economies tend to emerge in societies in which there are strong bonds that encourage people to trust one another. Thus Fukuyama argues that social capital is a similar phenomenon to physical and human capital: 'social capital produces wealth and is therefore of economic value to a national economy . . . Social virtues like honesty, reciprocity, and keeping commitments are not choiceworthy just as ethical values; they also have a tangible dollar value and help the groups who practice them achieve shared ends' (Fukuyama 1999: 14). Fukuyama's thesis suggests that un-bridled individualism is detrimental insofar as it generates a contract culture informed by mistrust. This is economically inefficient and undermines common bonds. Whilst Fukuyama is in favour of the cultural benefits of community, he does seem preoccupied with the economic success that accrues from shared values, norms and experiences. The key point here is that community is portrayed as not only compatible with economic logic but also fundamental to the formation of a culture in which capitalist economies can flourish.

Similar arguments to that of Fukuyama have emanated from within the communitarian movement itself. Whilst Etzioni has tended to focus on the social and political benefits that accrue from communitarianism, others such as Henry Tam (1998) have tried to link communitarian politics with economic concerns for work and business. Here again the argument that there is no inherent conflict between community and economic rationality is prominent (see also Miller 1992: 85). Thus the particular social norms and values which emanate from strong civic bonds can contribute to successful market economies. Within this approach there is little recogni-tion that the requirements of market economies may be detrimental to community values – the relationship seems to move in one direction only. In recent times, however, these orthodox communitarian arguments have been criticised by those who see economic needs as potentially harmful to community virtues (Gray 1997). The latter criticises orthodox commu-nitarianism for presenting a backward-looking politics: 'It cannot be a call for moral regeneration which passes over the ways in which, in the absence of intelligent public policy, free markets can weaken social cohesion. That is what community is not, and cannot be, for us' (Gray 1997: 81). This kind of argument is developed in a more sustained and systematic way by John O'Neill (1998), who puts the case for a reduced sphere of market exchange which would enable other non-market, non-instrumental virtues to flourish in alternative parts of social life. Moreover such a restriction of economic logic and market transaction would for O'Neill allow greater scope for individuals to exercise autonomy and join in forms of collective self-determination. As such O'Neill's project centres upon rectifying the neglect of non-market associations in which there has been a 'failure to address issues of market colonisation, of the invasion of market norms into non-market spheres . . .' (O'Neill 1998: 3).

O'Neill reaches radical conclusions in his provocative thesis. He states categorically that because 'the market has a tendency to extend its boundaries it is corrosive of the conditions for human well-being'. For this reason, he suggests that markets need boundaries and that 'the realisation of human well-being now requires a non-market economic order' (O'Neill 1998: 63). Undoubtedly this takes a radical stance towards market and non-market relations, but this is not merely the preserve of radical commentators. As we have noted, similar fears emerge from Gray's thought but they also permeate many analyses of new developments in the nature of advanced capitalism. Notable here is the work of Richard Sennett (1999), who has argued that the growth of flexible working practices in capitalist economies has had a fundamental corrosive effect on human relations. Thus he provides a useful corrective to modern economic discourses regarding the need for flexibility, and he points to the ways in which such economic developments cannot be divorced from social and political structures. In this way he demonstrates the flawed logic of the promotion of economic flexibility. Rather than enabling people to take greater control over their lives, flexibility ultimately limits human freedom by making increasing short-term demands upon people: 'the new order substitutes new controls rather than simply abolishing the rules of the past – but these new controls are often hard to understand. The new capitalism is an often illegible regime of power' (Sennett 1999: 10). These concerns connect with the theoretical reflections of André Gorz, who has argued for many years that the economic developments of the new economy in contemporary capitalism and the attendant discourses of flexibility will have dire consequences for social integration (Gorz 1989). Gorz's thesis has been that the sphere in which market mechanisms predominate should be limited in order to allow greater space and resources for individual and collective self-determination (Little 1996).

This chapter will compare and contrast the perspectives on work and the economy that have emerged within orthodox and more radical communitarian arguments. What should become clear is that many orthodox approaches employ fairly traditional views on work, such as the desirability of the pursuit of full employment, and that these views offer little challenge to the organisation of modern capitalist economies. Radical theorists of community, on the other hand, tend to argue for more fundamental economic reforms in which restrictions are placed upon the operation of market mechanisms. This dichotomy between orthodox and radical approaches throws up a central question in the very nature of communitarian politics: are communities and the values that they incorporate compatible with the operations of markets and their economic logic? One answer to the problems associated with this question can be derived from Michael Walzer's theory of complex equality in which barriers are created between different spheres of life which have their own rules and structures (Walzer 1983). Thus, in terms of the economy, there could be a space that is governed by economic rationality and the logic of markets.[1] However, the order that emanates from this rationality should not endow power in other spheres that are governed by alternative virtues and procedures. The aim of complex equality is then a scenario 'in which different goods are distributed according to the distinct understanding of different institutions and practices, and not by some other external institution' (O'Neill 1998: 176). This would allow for a role for markets and the appropriate rationality that governs market transactions alongside but separate from community relations. Such a perspective is radical (although it is also advocated by many theorists from less radical traditions) because it is faced by a barrage of contemporary economic discourses that suggest that our ability as communities or nations or indeed members of international organisations to organise our economies in such a fashion is severely curtailed by the growth of the ubiquitous discourse of globalisation.

DEFINING FLEXIBILITY:
THE IMPACT OF GLOBALISATION

In contemporary times countries such as the USA and the UK abound with discourses of flexibility that suggest that comparative economic advantage is derived from flexible forms of working and production. Thus the strong globalisation thesis associated with commentators such as Kenichi Ohmae (1995) suggests that nation-states in the modern world are in competition with one another for limited resources and those nations that are able to produce and work in a flexible fashion are more likely to attract investment and success in the world market. However, whilst globalisation is one of the most common concepts employed in the social sciences, there is little agreement as to its meaning. Is it a purely economic phenomenon or does it have a fundamental impact upon political and social structures? What impact do the latter in any given country have on economic success? Is the idea of an all-encompassing globalisation process overstated by those who want to vindicate liberal economic strategies? For our purposes, these questions are important because they impact on our understanding of the power of communities and the impact that the advocacy of community virtues may have on the economic arrangements of a nation-state. In this sense we need to ask whether there has been a political convergence in the world on specific liberal democratic structures and whether this negates or facilitates the ideas behind communitarian politics. Moreover if global society is more interdependent than ever before and we are embroiled in transnational forms of governance that undermine the powers of nation-states, we can question whether or not the pursuit of community is a worthwhile objective at all. Despite the dominance of the strong globalisation thesis, alternative perspectives might suggest that the nation-state will play a central part in the reorganisation of the governance of global society or that globalisation will sustain greater regionalism in which local communities may undertake some of the powers that were previously wielded at the level of the state.

One of the most notable proponents of a strong globalisation thesis has been Anthony Giddens (1998, 1999), who, despite recognising some of the problems that emanate from the process of globalisation, argues that it is an economic reality of the modern world. Thus globalisation is a phenomenon that we must grapple with though, for Giddens, we should welcome it in any case because it provides new opportunities for rethinking our systems of governance. As such, and in his role as the guru of new social democratic thinking, or the 'Third Way', Giddens rejects criticisms of globalisation as manifestations of an outdated form of social democracy (Giddens 1998: 28). In this vein Giddens, like many advocates of the Third Way in its different manifestations, retains a concern for civil society and communities. Thus he believes that globalisation is a process that will lead to a redefinition of government systems and will open up spaces for democratic renewal. He advocates a move towards new forms of governance in terms of relations between states and regions on the one hand and nation-states and transnational organisations on the other. For Giddens, such fundamental political and economic changes require a new radical agenda.

However, not all analysts of globalisation see the process in the same light as Giddens. Most notable here are Hirst and Thompson (1996), who have taken a much more sceptical stance towards these economic and political developments (Little 1998). The dominant orthodoxy on globalisation is rejected by Hirst and Thompson on a number of grounds, most notably, that it is not a new phenomenon in the history of capitalism and that there is no automatic impact of globalisation that necessitates structural changes in the economies of advanced Western countries. Thus they argue that the globalisation thesis generates alarmism regarding the ways in which industrialisation in the developing world will collapse manufacturing in the West. This is dismissed by Hirst and Thompson on the basis that there is an interdependence between Western and newly industrialised countries and the world economy necessitates a rough balance of trade whereby countries are able to offer something to one another. Thus the idea that the West will be paralysed by the expansion of economies in the less developed world does not appear to hold water. A similarly misguided idea of the alarmists ten years ago was that the West had to follow the models of the Asian tiger economies to achieve their levels of success – not surprisingly this idea has not been so prominent since the economic decline in the Pacific Rim since the mid-1990s.

Another feature highlighted in the globalisation thesis is the idea that multi- or transnational corporations are coming to dominate the global economy and that these firms will only invest in countries which can promise flexibility, that is, low wages and minimal social overheads. However, the figures Hirst and Thompson produce for Germany, Japan, the USA and the UK, for example, suggest that roughly two-thirds of manufacturing takes place within home countries and there is a heavy reliance upon consumption in the home country also. This is not to say that they don't strive for foreign markets, but it also suggests that they are not rootless. In this context, whilst transnational corporations may try to influence overheads and pay in the areas where they locate, they are also not beyond the scope of national regulation. The same point can be extended to international financial markets that are dominated by a short-term, globalising rhetoric which undermines economic stability. For Hirst and Thompson, this is not because of an inability to have effective economic governance but rather a lack of a will to govern world financial markets.

In summary, then, the globalisation thesis has been challenged on the basis that even if globalising tendencies are on the increase, this does not correlate with the drastic alarmist predictions of some commentators both on the left and right of the political spectrum. The example of the introduction of the minimum wage in the UK serves as a useful reminder of how different countries have differing socio-economic structures and how Western countries are not necessarily in direct competition with newly industrialised countries.[2] Western countries have always had different patterns of employment and public expenditure without a rather base lowest common denominator driving wages and welfare downwards. Scaremongers, particularly proponents of economic liberalism, told us that the minimum wage would cost jobs in the UK when, in fact, the opposite has been the case. All of this undermines the economic ungovernability thesis that has been popularised especially in the UK and the USA. It suggests that national government remains central to economic organisation albeit in the context of globalising tendencies and international institutions and also sub-national and regional organisations. This suggests not that the economy is ungovernable but rather that more effective governance is required that co-ordinates the national with the local and the international.

In some respects, then, the argument constructed by Giddens contains a false dichotomy between sceptics on globalisation whom he sees as traditionalists, and his own position which he depicts as radicalism. Hirst and Thompson do not argue against the need for new forms of governance of the global economy, they merely question some of the economic facts that are put forward in favour of the globalisation thesis. Giddens, however, argues that 'radical' views on globalisation are ultimately more persuasive. Importantly, though, he argues that we are wrong to focus only on the economic aspects of globalisation and that we must not neglect the social, political and cultural impact of new technology. It impacts just as acutely on the everyday lives of individuals and communities as it does on global economic systems:

> Globalisation thus is a complex set of processes, not a single one. And these operate in a contradictory or oppositional fashion. Most people think of globalisation as simply 'pulling away' power or influence from local communities and nations into the global arena. And indeed this is one of its consequences. Nations do lose some of the economic power they once had. Yet it also has an opposite effect. Globalisation not only pulls upwards, but also pushes downwards, creating new pressures for local autonomy. (Giddens 1999: 13)

This perspective feeds into communitarian concern for the renewal of local and regional politics and the demise of the centralised state as the primary location of power. However, even though Giddens is explicitly aware of the damaging impact that free trade has had on the developing world and poorer communities in the West, he still argues that the state of flux that we are living through provides opportunities for the creation of new forms of governance at the sub-state level. Whilst notionally these opportunities for democratic renewal may exist, their realisation seems much more distant. Giddens appears overly optimistic with regard to individuals and communities gaining sufficient power to take on the process of political renewal by themselves. Arguably such a process cannot be engendered without recourse to state institutions and limitations being placed on the operation of market mechanisms. This is perhaps the chief limitation of the thesis promulgated by Giddens. Economic globalisation is quite rightly presented as a reality of the modern world but there is little analysis of power relations within this new reality. Thus the process of reshaping that reality is depicted as straightforward when, in fact, there are numerous obstacles to it. Giddens wants us to reshape social and political arrangements around the accepted economic 'truths' and immutable laws of the runaway world rather than recognising the problems that these 'truths' generate for such a process. New forms of governance are expected to accommodate economic realities rather than challenge them. Here we see the hegemony of the economic over other spheres of modern life without any recognition that the demands of the economic might undermine the virtues that may be appropriate in society as a whole. If the global economy demands flexibility, we need to ask what the social impact of flexibility is. It is of little use merely asserting that economic, social and political forms must sit comfortably alongside one another – we need to recognise where they challenge and conflict with one another. In terms of community we need to identify where it complements the economic sphere and where new discourses of flexibility in the context of globalisation challenge the principles of community and civic virtues.

– COMMUNITARIANISM AND THE ECONOMY –

Francis Fukuyama's communitarianism, expressed in *Trust* (1996), moves beyond the famous economic and political arguments put forward in *The End of History and the Last Man* (1992) and centres instead on issues of culture. Thus he argues that successful economies are reliant upon the degree of trust and social capital within any given culture or society. Fukuyama suggests that America has experienced a decline of social capital insofar as older ways of spontaneously engaging with one another are decreasing. In economic terms this is problematic because trust engendered a kind of social capital which assisted the operation and organisation of the economy and functionally integrated workers within the economy. Thus Fukuyama looks towards some of the economies in East Asia and Europe to identify societies that have either high trust or low trust as their basis and the ways that this degree of social cohesion contributes to the success or failure of these economies. From this basis, he argues that the regeneration of the American economy necessitates new forms of trust and spontaneity.

These ideas owe much to the work of Robert Putnam (1995, 2001) and his influential 'Bowling Alone' thesis, whereby he argued that the breakdown of social integration and the supportive mutual associations of civil society had a negative knock-on effect on economic organisation due to the erosion of social capital. In this sense Fukuyama argues that our relationships in society with those around us have a direct effect upon the foundations of economic activity. Thus activities in civil society are not necessarily valued in themselves but are celebrated for the impact that they have on economic success. There is a suggestion that Fukuyama's perspective reflects the widespread hegemony of market discourses in modern political economy and ignores the deleterious effects of markets on some areas of social life. The thrust of his argument appears to regard community and civil society as servicers of economic imperatives, even if he does argue that they have inherent value as well in *The Great Disruption*.

According to Fukuyama trust and social capital can be defined as follows. Trust 'is the expectation that arises within a community of regular, honest, and cooperative behaviour, based on commonly shared norms, on the part of other members of that community'. From this basic cement of society, then, comes social capital:

> Social capital is a capability that arises from the prevalence of trust in a society or in certain parts of it. It can be embodied in the smallest and most basic social group, the family, as well as the largest of all groups, the nation, and in all the other groups in between. Social capital differs from other forms of human capital insofar as it is usually created and transmitted through cultural mechanisms like religion, tradition, or historical habit. (Fukuyama 1996: 26)

Here we can see a shift in emphasis from the early Fukuyama. Implicit in his earlier work was a triumphal celebration of the USA in the Reagan/Bush era, and there was little evidence of a critical stance towards the economic model that the latter embodied. In *Trust* Fukuyama appears to distance himself from the idea of *homo economicus* as a rational egoist who enters into economic transactions on a voluntary basis to further individualistic objectives. Rather he seems to believe that it is the existence of social ties between individuals which provide the foundations of the successful economy. The path of the rational egoist is, it appears, a road to economic ruin. Clearly, then, Fukuyama has taken a more critical stance towards economic liberalism than was the case in his early work, although he continues to express considerable opposition to the impact of state welfare as well. In his later work Fukuyama suggests that modern prosperous economies rely upon a blend of individualism and association. Associations and bonds of trust are not economically rational themselves (indeed they may seem rather irrational), but they give rise to the optimal economic outcomes and can therefore be seen as rational in their economic impact.

In terms of the global economy Fukuyama rather uncritically swallows the line that the contemporary world is one that is characterised by political and economic convergence in which the differences between nations are primarily attributed to cultural factors. Thus globalisation does not extend to culture in Fukuyama's eyes, and this is why we see different levels of economic performance in different countries. In this sense he argues that countries with cultures which have a particularly high level of trust and social capital will provide the model for economic success. Under the appropriate conditions of trust, 'markets and democratic politics will thrive . . . the market can in fact play a role as a school of sociability' (Fukuyama 1996: 356). The market economy then helps to provide the values and structures that hold society together – rather than merely distributing goods according to supply and demand, the market becomes a socialising agent, a force for good. This appears to neglect the rationality that characterises the operation of market mechanisms – namely the logic of growth, profit and accumulation – and the fact that they may be at odds with social objectives such as cohesion or solidarity. For Fukuyama, our social standing is based upon our pursuit of recognition that derives from our being successful in economic enterprises – a purely economic definition of social status that ignores the multiplicity of ways we derive identity and standing in modern societies.

In the global market place some countries have an advantage over others, according to Fukuyama, because they have cultures that assist the development of social capital. Thus success or failure is less a matter of politics or economics and more to do with culture. An example of this comes in Fukuyama's dismissal of former communist regimes that, because they decimated civil society and forms of civic association, will struggle. Thus their problems derive from their statism. In this sense the economic problems of Russia do not emanate from the embrace of free-market capitalism (that is encouraged by the West) but the type of state organisation that has historically existed. Cultural defects create 'delinquent communities' and these can be found on a social level in countries such as

Russia, and also in certain sectors within countries, for example the underclass in the USA, the family-based relations of southern Italy (as opposed to the more associational northern areas) and the violent ghettos of South Africa. Again, it is not the social and economic policies that are implemented in these countries that generate a lack of trust but rather the cultural background against which these policies are formulated. The contradictions of Fukuyama's position are exemplified when he discusses the USA, however. He argues that it is now suffering from a lack of trust that has seen the rise of the strong state. Social capital, he argues, can only develop beyond the state. This would suggest some kind of cultural defect in the USA that Fukuyama identifies as liberal individualism and atomisation. Instead of being hamstrung by this cultural legacy he suggests that the USA should learn from the social relations of high trust societies such as Japan. This being the case it appears that our economies are not culturally determined and therefore that, despite cultural influence, we can adopt policies to create social structures that would generate trust and social capital.

Not surprisingly then, Fukuyama can be accused of trying to have his cake and eat it. He attempts to depoliticise economic change by focusing on culture, whereas he ultimately recognises that policy can alter the economic context. What, we may well ask, is the underlying reason for this? The idea that public policy may contribute to the formula for success suggests a positive role for the state, and it is this that Fukuyama cannot abide. This fundamentally undermines his position, for he fails to explain the area in which social capital can develop and the relationship between social structures, state institutions and government policies in the process of generating social capital. This is not to criticise the notion of trust *per se* but merely to point to the political as well as cultural origins that are neglected by Fukuyama. A more policy-orientated perspective is provided by Will Hutton:

> Trust is the key ingredient to stop contract capitalism dissolving into a hire-and-fire, slash-and burn market jungle. For the more solid a trust relationship, then the more solid the implicit contract that, whatever shocks the relationship may receive, neither party is going to desert the other. Both sides are committed. (Hutton 1997: 31)

Following the work of commentators such as Putnam (1993) in his study of Italy, Hutton argues that political structures impact upon the creation of trust, and he therefore calls, for example, for the strengthening of regional and local government. The point is clear: trust is not apolitical or merely spontaneous. It can be promoted through public policy and is influenced by the social and economic structures that we institutionalise. Like Fukuyama however, Hutton does not deal with the criticism that, whilst trust may be a useful contributor to the economy through social capital, the alternative relationship, that is, of the economic sphere on community values, is not evaluated. For such an analysis we must turn to radical commentators such as O'Neill and Gorz.

The theme of evaluating the nature of work has been a constant feature in the work of André Gorz since the 1960s. As we shall see, he suggests that work is an important human activity which can provide individuals with a mode of social insertion and a vital source of membership and identity in society as a whole. At the same time, however, he has been a fervent critic of the way we work in the contemporary world. Gorz laments the divided labour markets which exist both within Western capitalist economies and in the global economic system. Thus he identifies the creation of expert elites that encompass the minority of workers and the growth of insecure, casualised or contracted work for the many that does not provide a sound foundation for identity and status. The elites are protective of their status, whilst the majority move between unfulfilling and insecure activities. The latter do not experience the same degree of rights and protection that comes from strong trade unions and regulated labour markets. At the same time as labour markets in Europe become more regulated, there is a strong temptation for transnational corporations to shift their production to less developed parts of the world that do not have the same overheads that exist in Western labour markets. Clearly then, globalising tendencies in the economy throw up new challenges for the organisation of the way we work.

There are two main consequences of this developing scenario. First, there is a drive within some Western countries, such as the UK and the USA, to minimise social overheads and labour-market regulation in order to produce attractive environments for inward investment – in the United Kingdom this has been termed 'Nissan-chasing', where working standards are driven down in order to compete with the standards in less developed parts of the world. This leaves workers open to exploitation as globalisation becomes entwined with governmental obsession with employment-based strategies of renewal. Moreover governments spend money attracting foreign companies to invest whilst most of the economic benefits that accrue from attracting these companies do not stay within the country. Second the shifting of traditional forms of work in manufacturing to less regulated parts of the world opens up Western economies to the process of tertiarisation (Gorz 1989). This refers to the expansion of the service sector of the economy that is heralded by many as the future for Western economic success.

However, Gorz has maintained for many years that the growth of the service sector does not entail a new logic in the organisation of advanced capitalist economies. Instead, what we are witnessing is the extension of Weberian notions of rationality and bureaucracy as in George Ritzer's theory of McDonaldisation (Ritzer 1996), or the expansion of old Fordist and Taylorist notions of structuring work in the service sector. The latter is most evident in the explosion of the modern phenomenon of the call centre as a source of employment in countries such as the UK:

> In the call centre, employees are subject to performance measurement and forms of work monitoring that obtain a level of management control and authority over the conduct of work that even Henry Ford would have envied. Indeed, close analysis of the interaction between the human/computer/customer interface typically reveals a level of manipulation of human relationships that places the exchanges, including the emotional signals, between worker and customer at the centre of the process of the creation of surplus value. (Poynter 2000: 152)

This passage exemplifies the ways in which the tertiarisation of advanced capitalist economies does not entail new wholesome forms of employment spreading at the expense of old and manipulative blue-collar work. Whilst manufacturing may be in decline, the logic that inspired capitalist economies has merely been displaced. Indeed Poynter argues that the ideas that inspire the call centre are now widely employed across service industry, both in the public and private spheres. This reflects the growth of a 'new managerialism' that limits the powers and autonomy of workers and finds its political manifestation in discourses of modernisation. This has accelerated some of the processes that first emerged in Britain under the Thatcherite flirtation with neo-liberal economics. The key change for Poynter is that 'the old neo-classical world of buyers and sellers is now represented as a new world of providers and purchasers, with the state being primarily concerned with setting the rules and regulations for the effective conduct of market relations' (Poynter 2000: 160).

This then is the brave new world to which Fukuyama and his acolytes believe social capital makes a fundamental contribution. We appear to need communitarian virtues of co-operation and trust to enable such an economic system to function. The irony here is manifest. Modernisation and the new managerialism in both manufacturing and services are fundamentally based on mistrust. It is because managers do not trust workers to act autonomously or take responsibility for their actions that they are monitored, subject to often spurious definitions of quality, and, in many cases in the service sector, told to follow pre-ordained scripts rather than using their own initiative or engaging in spontaneous discourse with those they come into contact with. Spontaneity which is supposed to be a valuable social or communitarian virtue is squashed at work. The rationale for this is of course economic – such managerialist practices are not in place by mistake but because they are thought to be successful and economically efficient (whether they are or not is another matter altogether). This relates to the most important aspect of Gorz's theory in recent years, namely, the existence of ideas of economic rationality that often conflict with and contradict other social virtues such as those that can be linked to community (Little 1996). This is reinforced by O'Neill (1998: Chapter 6), who points out how a virtue such as individual autonomy that is often thought to be enhanced by market mechanisms is actually often undermined. He examines the relationship between autonomy and character and suggests that they are based in reality upon social relations and structures. Thus O'Neill substantiates Sennett's less radical perspective that contemporary economic structures lead to 'the corrosion of character' (Sennett 1999). For the former, 'autonomy is not just the absence of heteronomy and the conditions that foster that character. Autonomy requires also settled dispositions and commitments that define what it is to have a character and hence the conditions in which these can develop. The market tends to undermine those conditions' (O'Neill 1998: 83). If this radical perspective is to sustain the politics of community, we need to examine the relationship between work and social inclusion.

– WORK AND SOCIAL INCLUSION –

Scepticism regarding contemporary notions of work and the hegemony of liberal market discourses permeates radical approaches to community. Thinkers such as Gorz have consistently criticised what they see as the 'ideology of work', whereby paid work is accorded greater significance in contemporary politics than any other form of activity and the possession of any kind of paid work is regarded as preferable to having no work and being reliant on benefits (Hughes and Little 1999; for a historical survey of the development of the work ethic, see Bauman 1998). Nonetheless all communitarians, whether radical or orthodox, do recognise that work is a key form of activity in modern life. The fault line between the radical and the orthodox appears to centre upon whether paid work should take priority over other unpaid activities such as child-rearing or voluntary activities in the local community. Orthodox approaches tend to attach greater significance to the former, whereas radical commentators attempt to raise the significance and priority of the latter. Nevertheless, despite their interest in unpaid activities, most communitarians tend to see paid work as central to their project. Orthodox communitarians such as Fukuyama and Etzioni and their political followers view work as an important force in maintaining the moral fabric of society. Thus not only do they regard it as a key form of social activity because it provides social goods and benefits, but they also promote paid work because it moralises individuals into virtues such as independence and responsibility. Occasionally lip service may be paid to the virtues of unpaid work, but the latter is usually treated as something which takes place in the time left over after paid work has been completed.

A recent exposition of the orthodox communitarian position on work can be found in the work of Henry Tam. He argues that there are three main reasons why citizens need paid work. These are, first, the need to produce goods and services that individuals require, second, the autonomy that comes from economic independence, and, third, the provision of individual self-esteem and fulfilment. He refers to these respectively as the economic, social and moral dimensions of community life (Tam 1998: 85). In terms of work, he argues that there needs to be a recognition of the contribution to the economy of unpaid work, insofar as it enables others to participate in paid work. However, Tam focuses more on paid work as the key economic activity and suggests that economic decision-making should not be the domain of state bureaucracies as in communist regimes or the business elites which prevail in market liberal perspectives. His ideas here correspond with those of Will Hutton (1996), insofar as he advocates a stakeholding model of economic relations:

> What is needed is a participatory economy wherein citizens and the many communities to which they belong can feed their input into a collective decision-making process. Without the effective participation of all the stake-holders, those who have the exclusive right to shape all the key decisions will unavoidably neglect others in society. (Tam 1998: 93)

Ostensibly then, Tam's advocacy of stakeholding and his concern for the value of unpaid work appears to provide a progressive dynamic to communitarian thinking. However, his solution to this problem lies in a renewal of claims for full employment, which he sets up as an alternative to the market liberal prescriptions of business elites. Thus he criticises a 'Nozickian world' in which there is little mutual trust or responsibility and where there is no understanding of the obligations that society owes to the unemployed and economically disenfranchised. For Tam, this is a reflection of much contemporary corporate capitalism in which 'workers are treated as dispensable tools, and are discarded with no support for them, their families, or the communities which have relied on their productive capacity for their vibrancy' (Tam 1998: 95). The outcome of this culture is social division between decreasing groups of elite workers and the insecure masses and inefficiencies in the overall operations of market economies.

What, then, is Tam's preferred route out of this impasse of market individualist culture? Using the work of Jonathan Boswell (1994), he suggests that there is a pressing need for a communitarian democratisation of economic decision-making. This would involve the participation of sectional interests (especially those that have been marginalised in the current climate) and public-sector groups. The obstacles to this participation would be challenged through 'the statutory enforcement of openness' whereby public spaces would be opened up and subject to public scrutiny to ensure that pertinent interest groups were properly involved in economic decision-making. The underlying virtue in this process would be the development of greater relations of trust rather than the mistrust which permeates many modern economic relationships in the hegemonic market liberal culture. For Tam, these bonds of trust and co-operation must be built up through processes of civic education whereby appropriate models of the common good and partnership would be developed. What is left unclear in this interpretation of communitarian economic strategies is a specification of the economic policies that would lead to the common good. Tam and Boswell provide what we might call a procedural model, whereby the most important factor is the method of decision-making rather than the actual decision that is reached. This exemplifies the tendency, which is especially apparent in orthodox communitarian approaches, to promote deliberative models of the public sphere which pay insufficient attention to vested interests and other sources of conflict. There appears to be a belief that participation will bring agreement on the directions of economic policy when, in fact, widened involvement may lead to increased conflict. Radical approaches to community would welcome this conflict – it is because of the exclusion of conflicting ideas on the economy that market liberal approaches have become so hegemonic in countries such as the UK and the

USA. What Tam provides us with is a hypothetical model in which this hegemony will be superseded by a democratic system of agreement. Yet there is precious little evidence of where this democratic agreement will emanate from – perspectives on economics are notoriously contestatory, so the involvement of the many rather than the few is not a recipe for concurrence.

On top of this, Tam suggests that he is mostly concerned with decision-making procedures, but his work does imply a predilection for full-employment strategies. This is not to criticise his vision of more participatory forms of economic governance *per se*, but his proposals for the future seem rather bound within rather traditional and orthodox economic theories. Indeed Tam's vision of a participatory economy in which there was greater local activism and involvement alongside local, national and international regulation provides real opportunities to open spaces for alternative forms of economic thinking to the dominant orthodoxy. Nonetheless there are signs that Tam is willing to engage with some radical ideas: he openly advocates a minimum income for all in recognition of their contribution, either through paid or unpaid work. Unfortunately this support for basic income is not developed in much detail, and the radical opportunities such a policy might open up are not explored. This is largely because Tam remains constrained by economic orthodoxy. The radical question would be to ask whether full-employment strategies are the only option for economic policy or whether opposition to the market individualist hegemony can take on alternative faces. Should we be seeking to move away from the focus on paid work and seek strategies which actively pursue the importance of unpaid activities?

In answering this question we need to identify what benefits accrue to individuals who are in paid work. Here the work of Richard Sennett is instructive in identifying changes in the nature of work in 'the new capitalism' and the impact that it has upon the character of individuals. He argues that the new capitalism is driven by flexibility and a short-termist concern for profit which undermines bonds of loyalty and trust which were previously forged by long-term association. In firms where workers are not treated with trust and commitment they are unlikely to reciprocate with strong loyalty to the firm. However, we are told that values such as responsibility and trust are key social virtues, and yet we find these principles being undermined in the sphere of work. Thus 'the conditions of time in the new capitalism have created a conflict between character and experience, the experience of disjointed time threatening the ability of people to form their characters into sustained narratives' (Sennett 1999: 31). In other words, the moral values which we, are told provide the cement of society contradict our experience of the economic sphere. For Sennett, this is a recipe for confusion and social disintegration. Paid work, then, rather than bonding society together, contributes to the demise of social capital. Where commentators such as Fukuyama and Tam argue that successful economies rely upon high levels of trust and social capital and indeed help to create these social virtues, Sennett's insights suggest that the economies that Fukuyama celebrates are actually harmful to the very virtues he wishes to promote for economic reasons. Here we see the development of a relationship of conflict and contradiction rather than mutual support. In this scenario the harmonious economic relations promoted by Fukuyama or the consensual decision-making procedures of Tam appear wide of the mark.

Does this mean that communitarians should surrender a concern for paid work? The answer appears to be no. Even those radical commentators on community such as Gorz (1994) argue that work is a key form of social activity. It is a major source of social identity and a mode of social insertion. This is evident not only in the continued importance that people attach to work but also the pride in doing one's work well that can emanate from even the most mundane and menial tasks. For these reasons, Gorz's perspective suggests that we need to provide people with access to meaningful work, that is, work which is economically rational (Gorz 1989; Little 1996). Controversially he argues that some types of work are not economically rational, such as domestic labour performed for wages for others. This is work which he believes people could just as easily perform themselves – their rationale for employing others to do their domestic chores is that it frees up their time to earn more at work than they could if they performed the work themselves and more than they pay their domestic employees. Gorz sees this as a new form of domestic slavery whereby elites employ 'servants' to perform work that is not valued in the public sphere. The question arises as to who benefits from such a scenario. In terms of flexibility it seems that the key beneficiaries are social elites of secure workers and the business sector which prizes flexibility in employees above their roles in families or communities. Gorz does not wish to trap people in family life but rather to provide them with real flexibility. This would involve providing people with real opportunities to find appropriate blends of paid and unpaid work, to balance their work activities with domestic responsibilities. It is not about trapping people in drudgery but in giving the choice of flexibility to individuals and their families rather than people being at the behest of the form of flexibility which has emanated from deregulated capitalist labour markets. Thus, Gorz wants to improve access to meaningful work, rather than seeing it hoarded by diminishing elites that have a vested interest in preventing work being more equitably shared throughout society. The question to be asked, then, when we face the discourse of flexibility which permeates many contemporary economic pronouncements is 'Flexibility for whom?'. In this vein, Sennett notes that in the dominant discourse of flexibility in the new capitalism:

> the appearance of a new freedom is deceptive. Time in institutions and for individuals has been unchained from the iron cage of the past, but subjected to new, top–down controls and surveillance. The time of flexibility is the time of a new power. Flexibility begets disorder, but not freedom from restraint. (Sennett 1999: 59)

Gorz's strategy for challenging the dominant model of flexibility is to put forward a policy of reduced working hours. Whilst this has been a long-term objective in Gorz's theory, it has also reached growing currency among greens and elements of the left throughout Europe (Little 2002). The clearest manifestation of this policy has recently come under Jospin's socialist government in France, which has pursued working time reductions (although with some concessions for businesses to offset the extra costs of implementing the policy). Gorz's theory of reduced working hours shows how such a policy could be implemented in numerous ways in contrast to economic Jeremiahs who see any such interference in markets as a recipe for inefficiency (see Gorz 1994 and Little 1998 for further discussion of the economic options Gorz outlines). Rather, reduced working hours have been shown in France to be a weapon to tackle involuntary unemployment as working hours are redistributed to those who have previously been margin-alised from labour markets. At the same time rising levels of productivity can lead to greater efficiency per hour worked, and this growth in pro-ductivity can help to sustain wage levels despite fewer working hours. Gorz also offers the possibility of the state providing a 'second cheque' to workers to supplement their income and offset any loss of wages that did result from reduced working hours.

Thus there is a multiplicity of economic options available that could facilitate communitarian objectives. In radical perspectives such as that of Gorz, we see opportunities for rethinking our conceptions of work. By reducing working hours there is the possibility of opening up time and space for individuals to engage in more activities in their communities which may be voluntary or unpaid. We also glimpse the chance of people having more choice over the blend of activities they pursue between paid work, community activities or family responsibilities. In this radical guise there are opportunities for us to try and scrutinise and change the balance of activities that are carried out by women and men. Communitarians who do not attempt to grapple with the constraints on community of deregulated labour markets, uncritical visions of flexibility and the ideology of work fail to deal with the major obstacles that present themselves to the realisation of strong visions of community. At the same time, however, approaches that focus solely on the economic sphere and the shape of markets at the expense of unpaid or voluntary work also do the pursuit of community a disservice. Clearly then, the analysis of the economic must go hand in hand with explorations of the social and this feeds into debates over proposals for welfare reform. As we shall see in the following chapter, this provides rich territory for communitarian debate, and it is reflected in not only radical approaches but also the less dynamic terrain of 'Third Way' thinking. This is evident in the words of Giddens:

> Involvement in the labour force, and not just in dead-end jobs, is plainly vital to attacking involuntary exclusion. Work has multiple benefits: it generates income for the individual, gives a sense of stability and direction in life, and creates wealth for the overall society. Yet inclusion must stretch beyond work, not only because there are many people at any one time not able to be in the labour force, but because a society too dominated by the work ethic would be a thoroughly unattractive place in which to live. (Giddens 1998: 110)

Before moving on to look at social policy concerns that might challenge the dominant work ethic however, it is important to consider briefly the relationship between work and communities.

– Work in Communities –

Thus far we have seen how there have been damaging social consequences from the pursuit of flexibility in contemporary economic arrangements. Not least we have noted how the operation of economies can undermine rather than strengthen or profit from social virtues such as trust, commitment and participation. Whilst there are methods of challenging the hegemony of flexibility as noted above, the dominance of economic rationality in modern life has also impacted strongly on the sphere of communities. In many respects, as Sennett notes, it has turned the spotlight more directly on community as the source of belonging and meaningful social relations:

> One of the unintended consequences of modern capitalism is that it has strengthened the value of place, aroused a longing for community. All the emotional conditions we have explored in the workplace animate that desire: the uncertainties of flexibility; the absence of deeply rooted trust and commitment; the superficiality of teamwork; most of all, the specter of failing to make something of oneself in the world, to 'get a life' through one's work. All these conditions impel people to look for some other scene of attachment and depth. (Sennett 1999: 138)

In this scenario the absence of social virtues from the economic domain provides a renewed focus on community as the potential venue in which social cohesion can be reinvigorated. It is the disintegration of trust and commitment in political economy that has led to the focus on these values as part of the concern of communitarianism. However, Sennett is somewhat sceptical of communitarian claims to foster social virtues. In analysing orthodox political communitarianism, Sennett argues that communitarianism 'falsely emphasizes unity as the source of strength in a community and mistakenly fears that when conflicts arise in a community, social bonds are threatened' (Sennett 1999: 143). Thus he fears that the social virtues will be threatened by a concern for community that is often defensive and exclusionary due to 'the superficial sharing of common values'. Clearly this has much in common with the agonistic model developed in the work of Chantal Mouffe. However this does not negate the concern for community *per se* – it merely serves to underline the 'reductive moralism' of orthodox communitarian approaches. Indeed further reading of Sennett's thesis suggests that he does still recognise value in the notion of community. Thus he states that 'there is no community until differences are acknowledged within it' and recognises that 'strong bonding between people means engaging over time their differences' (Sennett 1999: 143). This suggests that, despite his avowed aversion to communitarianism, Sennett does value bonds of association that combine community with the principle of difference. Moreover he implies that such bonds can inculcate the social virtues that are subject to attack from the mechanisms and ideologies of the new capitalism.

This raises two main questions. First, does this mean that the development of social virtues can *only* take place within the domain of community and, if so, must community therefore be protected from the logic of economic rationality? Second, what are the activities within community that generate social virtues and why do they do so? Following Gorz, we can say that there are virtues of membership, insertion and participation that derive from work and economic activity, but that such virtues are at best only partially realised. He suggests that we should also engage in less instrumental activities, such as those that emanate from our responsibilities to our families and also to the variety of associations and communities that we are members of.

Taking this on board, it is quite clear that many associations do engage in economic activity, but that to be successful in this sphere may require a subversion of the principles of community. In other words economic success, even for small-scale community enterprises, may require that the concerns for profit and growth mean that community values such as friendship may be relegated in priority. This is not to say that there are not community enterprises that contain bonds of friendship and association – patently, this would be absurd. Rather, following Gorz, it is possible to argue that the success of these enterprises relies upon a different logic or rationality from that of community. Markets are not in themselves virtuous, and success therein may mean placing competition and aggression at the forefront of our thinking rather than mutualism and the common good. In the appropriate environment this is not problematic – in some spheres markets are the most effective means of distributing goods and services, but this is not because they comprise social virtues but often the opposite. It may be that economic success means the subversion of social values and principles. This suggests that social life comprises a multiplicity of spheres, each of them governed and characterised by differing values. Where Gorz's theory stands out is his recognition that there is no inherent reason why economic rationality should predominate over all others. It is merely one sphere and one set of values among a multiplicity. A mature polity for Gorz would be one whereby a range of forms of association would be valued and maintained, including economic and non-economic sets of relations. Put simply, the latter would be much more likely to exemplify the principles of community than the former.

Turning to the second issue raised above, we must ask what the virtues of community are and what activities encourage them. Essentially the radical perspective on community cherishes a range of activities and principles which are based upon non-instrumental interests. The definition of non-instrumentalism employed here refers to the idea that actions are not undertaken for purely selfish ends or economic gain. Thus non-instrumental activities will be undertaken perhaps on a voluntary basis and will be for the mutual interest of the community associations of which we are a part. The rationality that underpins these activities, then, will be representative of principles such as friendship, the ethic of care, selflessness and the common interest of members of the community. People undertake community activities because they feel a pull of responsibility to the communities they belong to. Sometimes this idea of responsibility will emanate from the principle of reciprocity whereby we feel obliged to help our communities because of the benefits that we derive as members of that community. However, critics may argue that this involves self-interest or an instrumentalist attitude towards our relationships with others. It is for this reason that it is important to stress that, frequently, individuals will feel responsibility on a non-reciprocal basis. Thus we will frequently care for and act in the interests of others because of our attachment to them generally rather than because we expect anything in return from them. That this altruistic ethos exists is even recognised by critics of communitarianism such as Iris Marion Young. There is no hard and fast definition of what community activities are, but they tend to be those which exemplify altruistic and non-instrumental virtues. Radical theorists of community do not attempt to prescribe which activities should take place under the auspices of community. Rather they recognise that different communities will take on divergent forms and that the activities appropriate therein will also differ from one community to another. In terms of the relationship between economy and community, radical thinkers argue that our economic arrangements should be based around maximal opportunities for participation, although in a less time-consuming fashion than is currently the case. This would liberate time and space for individuals to engage in a wider variety of activities than the hegemony of flexibility (defined by economic rationality) allows in contemporary Anglo-American capitalisms. The freeing-up of time and resources could open new spaces for the expansion of community and a new priority for altruistic, non-instrumental principles. In short then, the pursuit of community necessitates a redefinition of flexibility to encourage individual autonomy and to challenge the hegemony of economic rationality.

– CONCLUSION –

This chapter has evaluated the various ways in which communitarian theories engage and interact with discourses on work and perspectives on political economy. This is an area that has been neglected in communitarian thinking when compared with the more developed and overt concern with various areas of social policy. As such, a coherent communitarian perspective on economic policies is much harder to discern. However, as we have seen above, communitarians do frequently advance their ideas regarding the importance of work, although sometimes this is equated too much with paid work at the expense of other types of activity. What becomes clear, as has been evident throughout this study, is the diversity of communitarian thinking, with notable differences between the advocates of orthodox communitarian perspectives and those (often not associated with communitarianism *per se*) who offer more radical approaches. The latter, I contend, have raised the more complex questions regarding how a concern for community sits alongside economic imperatives – as such they also fail to provide us with the kinds of easy answers that sometimes seem to emanate from those constrained by the boundaries of the market liberal hegemony in political economy.

Within orthodox approaches we can identify differences between those, such as Tam, who recognise the need for fundamental change in the organisation of political economy if communitarian concerns are to be met and others, such as Fukuyama, who see a seamless relationship in which economic success is reliant upon the existence of communitarian virtues that are in turn reinforced by economic success. The latter celebrates specific types of communitarian culture as the basis of modern political economy, whereas the former approach argues that a new participatory culture is required to democratise economic decision-making. Through analysis of the work of commentators such as Sennett and Gorz, Fukuyama's argument has been criticised here for failing to deal with the extent of disruption to social virtues that is caused by the hegemony of current economic thinking. Indeed, the contradictions and conflict that emerge from an economic culture of mistrust and antagonism sit uneasily with the altruistic principles that Fukuyama advocates. According to Sennett, this is a recipe for social disintegration rather than cohesion. At the same time approaches such as that of Tam have also been criticised here. He eschews the temptation to prescribe communitarian economic policy and instead presents us with a procedural argument for decision-making as communitarian political economy. Tam's ideas are criticised because they gloss over the extent of conflict on economic strategy that is likely to emanate from greater participation in decision-making (although of course the process itself is a key communitarian strategy). He underestimates the difficulty of undermining the hegemony of dominant economic thinking and reducing the powers of vested economic interests. Moreover his failure to address concrete policies for economic change leaves him with little more than communitarian aspirations, although these aspirations may themselves be valuable, such as giving more priority to unpaid activities. The suspicion remains that Tam like many orthodox communitarians remains bound by fairly traditional ideas regarding employment policy, for example. It is not surprising, then, that communitarianism appears as little more than aspirational to its critics, even when advocates promise more radical change.

To find more concrete proposals for the economy that reflect a concern for community we must turn to radicals such as Gorz. Unpalatable as they may be to those who reject prescriptive approaches to political economy, Gorz recognises that the democratisation of economic decision-making cannot be generated through mere pious wishes but requires policies designed to open participation. His proposals for reducing working hours and redistributing work to the economically disenfranchised are undoubtedly difficult to countenance in the modern economic climate but they represent a concrete attempt to challenge orthodoxy. Moreover, as events in France in recent years have shown us, even governments that are not particularly radical can intervene in economic processes in such a way. What becomes clear is that community cannot be simply asserted but rather the appropriate conditions for it to flourish must be fostered or even manufactured. The unwillingness of some communitarians to engage in this process renders them toothless and impedes the practical realisation of their concern for principles and virtues of community. The reluctance to engage in debate over the economic sphere is perhaps the most serious weakness in contemporary communitarian thinking. Moreover the failure to recognise areas of conflict between economic interests and principles of community is likely to limit the likelihood of a practical application of communitarian ideas. The extent of market liberal hegemony is perhaps underestimated and will not be understood until the challenges it throws up for the concern for community are challenged directly. Until then, the communitarian focus on issues of social policy will provide only a partial solution to the problems it identifies as central to the disintegration of modern society. At the same time, economic change alone would not deliver the promise of community. The latter can only be understood through a lens that recognises the interdependence of the social and the economic and then initialises political procedures to implement appropriate policies and decisions. This chapter suggests that this realisation is still remote in much contemporary communitarian thinking.

– NOTES –

1. This position is not one that Walzer himself develops. However, his idea of complex equality does provide spaces to debate whether such a limitation on the operation of market mechanisms would be appropriate.

2. Another example of the way in which countries may implement economic change and regulation without impairing global competitiveness is the reduced working hours initiative introduced by Lionel Jospin's government in France. For more detail on the environmental impact of this move, see Little (2002).

CHAPTER 6

Community and Society: The Implications for Social Policy

In recent times the notion of community has become commonplace within social policy and orthodox political communitarians are increasingly active participants in welfare debates. The analysis of these developments is complicated because of the way in which the appeal of community leads to its invocation by a range of different commentators with sometimes quite divergent agendas. This chapter will evaluate the ways in which orthodox political communitarians have intervened in social policy debates and contrast those contributions with radical approaches to community. Whilst examining the impact of communitarian strategies for the future politics of welfare, it will become clear that a central question over the role of the state remains unanswered in much communitarian thought. Ultimately, despite the opportunities that the analysis of community generates for the rethinking of social policy, it is unwise to overlook the importance of state mechanisms in the implementation and delivery of vital welfare services.

Part of the reason for the focus on community in contemporary welfare debates is a reflection of the unfashionable nature of statist policies in the aftermath of the Thatcher/Reagan attack on Keynesianism and the welfare state. In this sense, one of the defining features of the discipline of social policy, namely the role of government and state mechanisms in social organisation and the collective management of risk, came under widespread and often vitriolic criticism. Nonetheless, although social policy remains resilient against this attack, many thinkers on welfare have attempted to move beyond statist approaches. In the hands of the right this has reinforced their focus on individualism and the placement of responsibility for welfare provision on the shoulders of private individuals (Green 1996). In this scenario the impact of communitarianism has been ambiguous. Where it has traditionally been viewed as an intellectual opponent of individualism,

frequently communitarian solutions and policy proposals reflect individualist ideas and strategies. This has been manifest in the orthodox political
communitarianism of Amitai Etzioni and some of the policy initiatives that
have emanated from Tony Blair's Labour government in the UK (Hughes
and Little 1999). Communitarians have been at the forefront of political
debates on social inclusion that have been pervasive since the election of
Blair's government in 1997. Nonetheless, as we have seen repeatedly during
the course of this book, there have also been valuable contributions to social
policy debates by theorists with a more radical approach to community.

Community often appears somewhat illusory in social policy debates. It is
invoked often as something of an imagined body – an objective to which we
should aspire. Alternatively it can also be construed as a lost entity, that is,
as *Gemeinschaft* community. Here the debate focuses on policy proposals to
deal with the impact of industrial or post-industrial society on traditional
small-scale associations. A third way in which community has impacted
upon social policy debates has been as a site for new political initiatives to
replace state provision. This latter approach was manifest in the policies of
the Conservative governments in the UK in the 1980s and 1990s, where
community became something of a touchstone as the attack on welfare-state
bureaucracy and dependency developed. Most famously this appeared in the
policy of 'care in the community' to replace segregative institutionalisation.
For critics this amounted to little more than the expedient unburdening of
the state and raised questions as to whether there actually was a thing called
'community' to care for people. This gave the notion of community a
tarnished reputation that it has struggled to shed. This has not been assisted
by the way communitarianism has been invoked to support a range of
policies, some of which are premised upon individualist assumptions, such as
in welfare strategies, and some of which smack of authoritarianism, such as
curfews and measures against noisy neighbours. All of this has contributed
to the continued ambiguity surrounding community and the absence of
intellectual clarity on what it means. Whilst this continues to cloud the
issue, not surprisingly, the idea of community retains considerable rhetorical
and political power. As such, it will continue to inform social policy debates,
both in its orthodox form and in more radical guises. However the
continued contribution of orthodox political communitarianism is likely
to undermine the pursuit of intellectual clarity, whereas radical perspectives,
whilst more challenging, offer a more coherent approach.

– ORTHODOX COMMUNITARIANISM AND SOCIAL POLICY –

Social policy concerns have been at the forefront of orthodox political communitarianism as it seeks to find strategic initiatives to replace the welfare state. Traditionally commentators such as Etzioni have been critical of both the individualism of the new right on one hand and the culture of rights that has emanated from the welfare state on the other. Rather than recourse to a doctrinaire abstract individualism, orthodox communitarians argue for solutions to new welfare debates that prioritise the moral community. Politically this serves a dual purpose of justifying restrictions on state welfare provision and simultaneously identifying individual responsibility as the key ingredient in social welfare. This point demonstrates the ambiguity at the heart of orthodox political communitarianism – whilst it professes to be anti-individualist, it employs individualist discourses and recommends welfare strategies that owe much to that individualist tradition. Where communitarians such as Etzioni profess that their ideas are based upon the notion of a community that shares a moral culture, ultimately responsibility for complying with that moral culture lies with individuals. The picture that emerges, then, is a particular blend of conservatism and individualism that resonates closely with some of the policy initiatives that have been put forward across the political spectrum in the last twenty years or so. The ambiguity at the heart of orthodox political communitarianism has made it an attractive doctrine to politicians representing a variety of ideological positions, and this explains why it has been one of the most influential movements in recent years.

The irony of the prominent role of individual responsibility in political communitarianism is noted by Elizabeth Frazer. She argues that communitarians such as Sandel hint at an argument for the welfare state as the embodiment of a community. This is predicated upon the fact that:

> [M]embers' relations with each other are multiple rather than simple or one-dimensional. Citizens relate to each other not only politically, in a welfare state, but also economically and culturally and, crucially, so the theory goes, their relationship is to each, to all, and to the whole thus constituted. Their relationships are dense rather than loose because each is related to each. (Frazer 1999: 208)

Thus Frazer argues that even if welfare states are not predicated upon localness or face-to-face relations between individuals, they still generate a sense of community. This is guaranteed by the commitment to social welfare, that is, to the well-being of all, and the redistribution of resources to provide security for those in need. In this sense 'this degree of density and multiplexity based on sharing and commitment generates the transcendent quality of community, the spirit of community, which is also of course expressed and promoted symbolically and culturally' (Frazer 1999: 208–9). Whilst community can be manufactured in such a fashion, a genuine sense of community does require a degree of commitment. In this sense community cannot be created by simply imposing it upon people. Rather individuals must want to belong to their communities or at least understand their relationship with others. Here the welfare state can be seen to be lacking in the spirit of community in recent years, insofar as its legitimacy in some areas has been increasingly questioned. Arguably a lack of commitment to the welfare state means that it only provided an imposed sense of community. It faced resentment and criticism for the last quarter of the twentieth century and, even then, was failing to provide communitarian virtues of solidarity and co-operation. Many critics, from across the political spectrum, have viewed the welfare state as divisive rather than integrative, as keeping people in poverty rather than lifting them from it, and as ineffective in delivering its objectives. From this perspective, the view of the welfare state as the embodiment of the spirit of community appears misguided. Thus, whilst Frazer is correct to point to the view that community can be manufactured, it is less clear that the models of Western welfare states were successful in doing so.

If the Keynesian welfare state was unable to concretise political community, what is to be made of recent attempts to reconstruct Western welfare systems? Where fundamental change in welfare regimes is taking place as in parts of the United States and especially in the UK, those systems are moving away from universalism towards more targeted, selective welfare systems. Jordan (1998) argues that this signifies a move towards a new orthodoxy in the politics of welfare. Nowhere has this been more evident than in the growth of workfare strategies that are predicated upon work requirements as fundamental criteria on which the receipt of welfare benefits is based. For Jordan, this indicates a change not only in the organisation of welfare provision but, more importantly, a broader political project:

> It takes the moral high ground, and mobilizes citizens in a thrust for national regeneration. It deals in ethical principles, and appeals to civic responsibility and the common good. Above all, it bids to recreate a cohesive community, through

the values of self-discipline, family solidarity and respect for lawful authority (Jordan 1998: 1)

Of course the great irony of this search to resurrect the political community is that the dominant economic perspective in both the USA and the UK is characterised by the acceptance of the all-encompassing constraints of globalisation (Little 1998). The latter implies that there are strict limitations on governments in engaging in redistributive welfare strategies and that the demands of flexibility and comparative competitive advantage necessitate limitations on public expenditure. However, rather than being hamstrung by these developments, the new orthodoxy suggests that enlightened governments can remoralise their peoples by reinventing individual and civic responsibility. Not only would this convey comparative advantage due to the exigencies of flexible global markets, but it would also be good for the community as a whole as traditional virtues would be resurrected. Thus Third Way commentators such as Giddens point not only to the diminishing powers of the nation-state in the face of globalising tendencies, but also to the way in which it opens up new forms of governance. In this vein, he argues that 'globalisation also "pushes down" – it creates new demands and also new possibilities for regenerating local identities' (Giddens 1998: 31). This feeds into the rediscovery of political communitarianism by the new orthodoxy because, as Giddens recognises, it contributes to a renewal of individualism. Like Etzioni, this individualism does not reflect the possessive individualism of Thatcherism but focuses instead on the lifestyle diversity of contemporary society coupled with a discourse of responsibility and obligation.

Traditionally, and until recently, the Labour Party in the UK has defended principles of universalism in welfare and resisted the introduction of conditionality in social policy. However much has changed in the New Labour agenda, and many critics have noted how their strategies, notably 'welfare to work', amount to the introduction of 'workfare' into the British welfare regime, despite the government's protestations to the contrary (King and Wickham-Jones 1999: 257–9). Here we can identify that the introduction of conditionality into the post-Thatcherite welfare equation has become accepted in the New Labour agenda. According to King and Wickham-Jones, a central influence in this welfare strategy was the lessons learned from the experience of the Democrats in the USA during Bill Clinton's presidency. 'Welfare to work' carries with it the key moral sentiments of political communitarianism. The underpinning principle is tackling social exclusion and ridding society of the social costs that emanate from it. This objective would be achieved through a strategy based upon individual responsibility and obligation. A combination of incentives and penalties would be used to ensure that people did not have the opportunity to live off the welfare state whilst shunning jobs and training. Those who failed to avail themselves of the available options would face sanctions, including the withdrawal of their benefits. Whilst strictly speaking this was not a workfare scheme insofar as benefits were not paid in direct return for work performed, it introduced an element of conditionality and coercion that went against the model of universal social rights of citizenship.

'Welfare to work' also highlights New Labour's obsession with paid work as the gauge of social inclusion. However, several critics have noted that this orthodox communitarian agenda on work and welfare contains a bundle of contradictions. Thus, for example, 'New Labour's position assumes an individual can contribute to society through working as a paid childcarer but not as an unpaid mother, though both individuals carry out the same tasks and make identical contributions' (King and Wickham-Jones 1999: 277). It is clear then that behind the benign message of facilitating social inclusion, New Labour's welfare strategy is also a disciplinary measure to ensure that citizens behave in a socially and morally responsible fashion. As Dwyer (2000: 80) argues 'the New Labour government is concerned to use social policy to reward worthy citizens and discipline irresponsible ones'. The lesson is clear. New Labour expects individuals to meet the responsibilities that emanate from their membership of the community. If they do not do so, then government strategies will be used to police people into morally acceptable behaviour. The latter is strictly defined by New Labour and political communitarianism as paid work or meeting the needs of the family. However, the choice to work in the family is only an acceptable one if individuals make few claims upon the state. In other words one can be a good member of the community and not work for wages as long as you have an independent source of income, for example a partner with sufficient income to permit you to forego paid work or inherited income, and so on. As is so frequently the case then, the responsibilities that New Labour wants to enforce seem to be directed at those with the fewest resources. The implications are that individuals who want to make the choice of, for example, bringing up their children themselves find that that choice can only take place within certain stringent circumstances. The Janus-faced nature of New Labour's political communitarianism then is evident in the 'welfare to work' agenda. Where we are told to place greater emphasis on the family and to take responsibility for familial needs, the choice of doing so has severe financial ramifications due to strict criteria for benefits based on paid work.

Despite the acceptance of some of the Thatcherite economic and social model, New Labour's communitarianism moves beyond the new right. Older leftist principles of solidarity, community and fairness permeate their strategy. However, the meaning of those principles in the contemporary world of flexibility and global markets has been altered to meet new constraints. These alterations have been made, though, in the apparent belief that they can be easily adapted whilst retaining their essential meaning. This has led inevitably to a number of contradictions in New Labour's programme due to the particular model of political communitarianism that it subscribes to (Hughes and Little 1999). This is not to say that the Blair government has not realised some of the potential problems. Through measures such as the minimum wage and the Working Families Tax Credit, New Labour has attempted to 'make work pay' (Driver and Martell 1998: 109–10). In line with a new Keynesian approach, the Blair government has concentrated on the supply side of the economy with, at least in its early years, a fair degree of success. The problem with political communitarianism, then, is not so much one of strategy for economic management. In the short term New Labour has met its economic objectives and run the economy as it saw fit (although, of course, there is no guarantee that that success will carry on in the future). Thus the major criticism to be made of New Labour in terms of community is not that it has employed an unsuccessful economic strategy, but that it has taken the conscious choice to focus on paid work. As governments in other similar economies such as France have shown, there are a range of economic strategies that include the reduction of working hours (Little 2002). New Labour's advocacy of compulsion in welfare based around paid work fails to recognise how this strategy can come into conflict with the principles of community.

For this reason Driver and Martell (1998: 118–20) have asked whether, in New Labour's communitarianism, there has been something of a shift away from social democracy towards social authoritarianism. The arguments in favour of this proposition are predicated upon a number of assumptions, including the way in which reciprocity is understood for the poor and unemployed as something that must be enforced and welfare rights are seen as conditional. Moreover this is part of a social remoralising, whereby the irresponsible are educated into appropriate forms of behaviour. In practice, according to Driver and Martell, this has resulted in regressive policy-making that is at odds with much contemporary thought on the centre left but shares much with modern conservatism. Most notably they point out how New Labour's communitarianism is marked by the increased activity of government in organising social life. There seem to be few lengths to which the Blair government is reluctant to go in ensuring that its communitarianism is put into practice but a marked reluctance to legislate in other areas that might upset important supporters: 'New Labour appears to see few problems when it comes to legislating for individual behaviour, yet has fought shy of doing the same for corporate responsibility: this will be left to voluntary solutions' (Driver and Martell 1998: 119). However, Driver and Martell also recognise that it is not really the fact of government action but the nature of that action that is at the root of the problem:

> The real issue here may not be that Labour has got too moralistic at the expense of liberal permissiveness (within limits moralism is what governments are for) but that it has become more conservative and less progressive in the *content* of its moralism. (Driver and Martell 1998: 120)

Ultimately Driver and Martell argue that whilst Labour has become less attached to the traditional tenets of social democracy and increasingly moralistic in tone, it has not become practically authoritarian. In terms of social policy, this position depends upon the extent to which one believes that the focus on paid work serves to limit individual freedom and contradicts the principles of community. Most radical communitarians like Jordan and Gorz would believe that this strategy is authoritarian, whilst recognising that Labour's philosophical objectives might be more liberal. Essentially this demonstrates the contradictions within not only the New Labour programme but also the manifestation of political communitarianism that has permeated the contemporary world.

– COMMUNITARIANISM AND CRIME –

Another area of social policy where communitarian policy proposals abound is in the area of crime, criminal justice and crime prevention. For orthodox communitarianism, the state has not succeeded in controlling crime, and rises in crime demonstrate that the decline of community has been accompanied by the growth of lawlessness. To rectify this, we must look beyond abstract individualism and re-establish the frameworks which previously made communities cohesive and provided social integration. This view of the crime and law and order agenda has been widely criticised

(Crawford 1999; Hughes 1996, 1998; Young 1999). In various places communitarianism is accused of simplifying the law and order issue, pandering to right-wing and/or individualist rhetoric, advocating authoritarian criminal justice strategies, and imagining a community that bears little resemblance to the reality of complex contemporary societies. The underlying problem with communitarians such as Etzioni rests upon the fact that his bottom line in the 'diagnosis of the problem of crime and disorder and the means of their prevention always appears to be the existence of a tight and homogeneous community' (Hughes 1998: 109). However, we must also recognise that there are more radical communitarians, such as Braithwaite (1989), who demonstrate in their work that communitarianism does not necessarily entail 'moral authoritarianism' (Hughes 1996).

Crime has been a central issue in Third Way politics in the UK, and Tony Blair has sought to establish the severity of New Labour in an area that is frequently regarded as crucial in the electoral battle ground. Community appears as a central ingredient in the recipe for preventing crime on the one hand and as an option in punishing crime on the other.[1] Here again the work of Giddens is instructive. He points out that '[p]reventing crime, and reducing fear of crime, are both closely related to community regeneration' (Giddens 1998: 86). A key to this strategy is not only the usual measure of tackling serious crime such as assault and murder but also lower level crimes that contribute to declining civility and the culture of fear. For Giddens, these problems include prostitution, graffiti and gangs of young people loitering in the streets. There is some dislocation however between the problems Giddens identifies and the ways in which New Labour has attempted to tackle these issues. For example, where Giddens points out that he does not advocate increasing policing powers to take people off the streets, Jack Straw introduced powers of curfew (specifically directed towards young people) as a means of addressing this issue when he was Home Secretary. The point is that New Labour clearly is attuned to the agenda Giddens identifies, that is, the need for greater partnerships between the police and local communities to tackle crime as well as the fear and causes of crime. However, in practice, New Labour appears willing to entertain more draconian measures such as curfews that are not driven by local communities (and which might be worrying and exclusionary if they were). There is a clear difference, then, between the ideas that drive New Labour's communitarianism and its manifestation when it comes to policy-making.

Undoubtedly though, in recognising the scale of the problems, New

Labour has placed a greater emphasis on crime than previous Labour governments, and this reflects the influence of communitarianism. Thus, some commentators have argued that, regardless of the political rhetoric sometimes employed by Blair and Straw, 'the new agenda was a serious far-reaching programme to tackle crime, employing strategies far more radical than many liberal critics had . . . realised' (Charman and Savage 1999: 198–9). In terms of communitarianism this agenda included local partnerships to tackle crime and ensure community safety and strategies to challenge the prevalence of anti-social behaviour. Thus New Labour has legislated not only to recognise social crime but also to broaden notions of crime prevention to involve a wide range of groups as well as the police. In this vein, crime prevention is a task for a range of agencies within the local community. According to Charman and Savage, this clearly differentiates New Labour thinking from that of the previous Conservative administration insofar as Labour aims 'to reintegrate the offender into the community, rather than banish them from the community' (Charman and Savage 1999: 202). Whilst this idea may be apparent in New Labour's strategy, we should also remember that there are contradictions in its agenda, especially with regard to the continued advocacy of incarceration as a key deterrent in crime prevention.

Following Charman and Savage though, it would appear that New Labour's communitarianism may have given rise to a new, progressive agenda on crime. However, this appearance is less credible when we begin to scratch the surface. In terms of restorative justice the strategy to reintegrate offenders in their communities seems laudable in terms of long-term crime prevention. There has been much interest in these issues in contemporary criminology, for example, in the idea of mediation and community conferences or Family Group Conferences (FGCs) as sources of community reintegration (Crawford 1999: Chapter 5; Hughes 2001). The philosophy here is to make criminals face up to their crimes by meeting with their victims as part of the process of punishment and reintegration. Theoretically this can make criminals aware of the human cost of their actions and help victims to come to terms with their misfortune. Perhaps the most notable communitarian contribution to these debates has been that of John Braithwaite (1989, 1993). Based upon his research in Australia and New Zealand, Braithwaite has examined a form of communitarian crime prevention entitled 'reintegrative shaming' (Hughes 1998: 122). Here the community is viewed as a means of expressing disapproval to offenders of their acts and to make them accountable for their actions to the people among whom they must live. However, as Hughes notes, 'such preventative processes will only work in situations where loss of respect counts heavy' (Hughes 1998: 123). In this sense, reintegrative shaming should not necessarily be seen as a means of creating community but is more appropriately viewed as an effective system of crime prevention where strong communal bonds already exist.

One of the great dangers of reintegrative shaming is of course the way in which we define community. Crawford notes how there may well be problems with the representativeness of those who are deemed to 'lead' communities, and Hughes identifies the dangers that can emanate from majoritarianism in such a scenario. We should also be aware of the ways in which such processes could become the preserve of professional mediators who, although having a key role to play in the process, must not come to dominate the stakeholders involved in these conferences. However, the strength of conferencing strategies has perhaps been the way in which they strengthen and broaden our understanding of community. Touching upon the interests of a wide range of affected groups and seeking their representation moves us beyond the notion of community as merely local or spatial. Rather they expand our definition of community 'in that the ascription to community membership or social identity is personal and not necessarily one which carries any fixed or eternal attributes of membership. In other words, "communities of care" do not carry connotations of coerced or constrained membership' (Crawford 1999: 193). There is a sense then in which such strategies can manufacture 'community' by bringing together elements of society that may have been marginalised if we focus only on the local or spatial community. That said, it is best not to make too many grand claims for these strategies beyond their applicability to communities that are already fairly coherent. In this sense the implementation of these kinds of strategies on a broader level in different contexts could be problematic. Certainly they should not be regarded as a means of *creating* the moral community. One of the most problematic elements of Etzioni's political communitarianism is the 'virtuous circularity' (Crawford 1999: 195) of his argument whereby we are supposed to derive morality from our communities. This implies that we should invest in them as they contain elements of virtue, and in turn this will further strengthen morality in society as a whole.

Nonetheless communitarian strategies such as those of Braithwaite clearly have progressive implications as opposed to some other traditional forms of punishment such as imprisonment. However, in a political climate where politicians feel they must be seen to be severe on crime this also provides scope for more draconian policy:

> The established political parties have recently been vying to compete with each other over new policies that seek to 'name and shame' offenders particularly young people, increase parental responsibility for the crimes of their children, and criminalize the anti-social activities of neighbours. These and other initiatives have moved the 'punishment in the community' debate further forward, as they seek to activate, facilitate, and utilize existing informal control for the purposes of the formal penal system. (Crawford 1999: 54)

This demonstrates well the potential problems with communitarian strategies on crime. Where potential exists for the use of community as a reintegrative functionary, in practice it may lead to the growth of 'naming and shaming' without any preparation within the community itself for dealing with the criminals in their midst. The focus with New Labour has not been sufficiently on the community, rather it is merely assumed that it exists and offenders must be reintegrated within it. The problems are clear. If communities do not know how to or do not want to admit offenders to their community, then the potential for exclusion or violence and vigilantism is evident.

Suspicion also remains that community may be used as a proxy for other forms of punishment when the criminal justice system is creaking under the weight of overcrowded prisons. Governments that are keen to show their toughness on crime must ensure that the view is implanted in the public mind that community punishments are severe. In the current climate this is not an easy task to carry off (Garland 2001). New Labour has sought to implement its policies by stressing prison as well as a key part of its criminal justice strategy. Thus beneath the veneer of progressivism, 'unfortunately . . . Labour's insistence on remaining faithful to imprisonment as a tool for crime control somewhat undermines this "liberal" approach' (Charman and Savage 1999: 202). However, what Charman and Savage also imply is that Labour should have the courage of its progressive convictions. Thus, they suggest that the public may well be receptive to alternative strategies to imprisonment if the limitations of the prison system are demonstrated and the benefits of community-based strategies are emphasised. As a result, until 'Labour feels politically comfortable enough to "think the unthinkable" about the custodial end of law and order policy the picture will remain an uneven one' (Charman and Savage 1999: 212). The continued usage of rhetorical devices such as 'zero tolerance' to demonstrate their severity and focus on discipline reinforces the suspicion that Labour's strategy on crime is, at best, somewhat inconsistent and, at worst, potentially authoritarian when it comes to implementation.

Ultimately where New Labour has diverged from orthodox communitarianism is in a 'realist' recognition of the problems of preventing crime. Etzioni knows that a degree of crime is unavoidable but believes that in a genuinely communitarian society crime would be naturally low. Only a small group of individuals with 'no inner moral voice or only a rather weak one' would commit crimes because everyone else would be susceptible to the overarching moral voice of community that holds society together (Etzioni 1996: 146). In this scenario Etzioni reckons that neither a liberal focus on incarcerating persistent wrongdoers accompanied by some community strategies nor the conservative advocacy of the state as the agent of social order are acceptable solutions. Rather, what is required is 'moral regeneration and some law enforcement' (Etzioni 1996: 147) in which the dominant morality of community constrains the behaviour of its members, apart from those it cannot reach such as 'psychopaths' and 'sex offenders'. Adopting a 'realist' approach, one might suggest that there are many more people than Etzioni suggests that exist beyond the moral voice of community. If one accepts that society contains a multiplicity of communities, some of which have conflicting moral voices, then Etzioni's blind faith in the power of community appears misguided.

Ultimately the complex society of diverse communities must rely more heavily on the rule of law than is the case in the political communitarian vision. This is not to say that the rule of law must represent an overarching morality; there is nothing to prevent it from establishing principles of difference, recognition and respect. Nonetheless in areas of incommensurable difference then political decisions need to be made. Such a scenario may be untidy and complicated, but it bears greater resemblance to the dominant social arrangements in contemporary Western states than Etzioni's appeal to the homogeneous moral voice. In the light of this, we need to recognise that the construction of community employed by Etzioni 'is cleansed of any negative or crimogenic connotations and endowed with a simplistic and naive purity and virtue'. In short, '[r]ebuilding communities as a set of shared beliefs is not, therefore, synonymous with the creation of social order' (Crawford 1999: 153).

– RADICAL COMMUNITARIANISM AND SOCIAL POLICY –

Radical approaches to community reject the homogeneity imagined within orthodox communitarianism. By arguing for the rightful existence of a multiplicity of communities, all with valid claims for recognition and respect, radical communitarianism challenges the social policy agenda. Where the orthodox approach to community simplifies policy choices by underestimating the impact of respect for social diversity, the equation becomes more complicated in the eyes of radicals as they try to envisage policy for a complex world. A radical understanding of difference implies a politics in which conflict and antagonism are likely to remain a feature of debate. Rather than policy which unites and harmonises 'the community', radicals search for means of enabling people to express difference and challenge accepted orthodoxies. As such, it does not provide any easy answers, and indeed may well be susceptible to the traditional criticism aimed at left-wing criminologists that they tell us more about what is wrong with current strategies instead of providing concrete alternatives. Whilst there is a modicum of truth in that criticism, there is also strength to be found in the recognition of complexity and diversity and, at least, properly understanding the challenges that this generates.

Radical ideas are resonant with the critique of Third Way thinking provided by Chantal Mouffe (1998). Much Third Way theory shares common territory with orthodox communitarianism, not least the way in which both renounce their own ideological basis. Both sees themselves as above traditional political boundaries between left and right and borrow from conservatism the need to identify themselves as somehow apolitical. The Third Way and orthodox communitarianism view their own ideas as correct, as common sense rather than political ideology. Similarly right-wing communitarians such as David Green explicitly describe their defence of markets and welfare reform as 'community without politics' (Green 1996). Of the Third Way or 'radical centre', Mouffe comments that:

> they imply that we live in a society which is no longer structured by social division. Relations of power and their constitutive role in society are disregarded; the conflicts that they entail are reduced to a simple competition between interests which can be harmonised through dialogue. (Mouffe 1998: 13)

This critique is equally applicable to orthodox communitarian approaches to social policy. By assuming an overarching community, namely 'the community', they employ a one-dimensional view of policy. Even where social diversity is recognised by people like Etzioni and Tam, that difference is to be overcome within the overall community. Mouffe's point is not about the hijacking of conservative ideas or the need to challenge old leftist orthodoxies – she has no inherent problem with either. What she does object to is the rather neutered notion of politics that emerges from these strategies. Politics is reduced to a harmonisation process in which we overcome our differences in what communitarians would see as a common moral culture. Rather than difference being the basis of our social identities, it is something that we must overcome. For orthodox communitarians, our universal status as members of 'the community' must override any particular associations we may have in 'micro-communities'. For radicals such as Mouffe this neglects the vitality of difference and misappropriates the word radical for what is essentially an apolitical view of politics. Interestingly, Mouffe argues that the radical centre, or Third Way, is an example of 'the typical liberal perspective', and this reinforces the argument that the dividing line between communitarianism and liberalism is not as clear cut as some approaches to contemporary debates would have us believe.

What Mouffe identifies in these current trends is a failure of the political imagination. Democracy becomes subsumed by an overwhelming need to construct politics as the sphere of consensus. Not only is this an unattainable objective as conflict and antagonism are the very stuff of democratic politics, but it also masks more worrying political developments. Orthodox political communitarianism ends up celebrating elite politics, and this tends to generate apathy towards the formal political sphere or privatistic withdrawal from issues of public concern. The latter emerges as a combination of apathetic views of politics blended with forms of individualism which are, in themselves, intensely political. The result is political viewpoints that can find no space for expression. As the political sphere becomes closed off to ordinary participation, the antagonisms and conflicts that should characterise political engagement are channelled into private passions. The upshot of this privatism can be witnessed in vigilantism, whereby people, dissatisfied with the response of politicians to their feelings or the inability of the political arena to countenance their concerns, take the law into their own hands. The danger of orthodox political communitarianism is in providing justification for such measures. It tries to depoliticise the political and, as a result, discourages proper political debate.

An example of these privatistic trends was the moral panic over paedophiles that swept the UK in the summer of 2000. Here we saw widespread vigilantism as a response to the failure of politics. In the political vacuum and the absence of public debate, violence was committed against wrongly suspected individuals with the most instructive case being the almost laughable attack on a paediatrician who the assailants could not differentiate from a paedophile. Interestingly, Amitai Etzioni (2000a) has made a critical intervention in the debate on paedophiles. In lamenting the limitations of Megan's laws[2] that enshrine the registration of sex offenders and rights to notification, Etzioni, in characteristically nostalgic fashion, hints that such measures are not necessary in a communitarian society. Thus he states that 'in a viable community people know one another, actively gossip about each other, and watch passersby from their front porches and steps; sadly, these activities are altogether absent in many areas, and only partially present in many others' (Etzioni 2000a). Whilst there are indeed limitations in current legislation, Etzioni feels the need to express his criticisms through his model of an idyllic community. The reason behind this is Etzioni's underpinning anti-statist rationality. Against governmental strategies such as changing penal policy or introducing alternative forms of rehabilitation and reintegration, Etzioni posits his preferred solution of transferring offenders to 'a guarded village or town' once they have completed their sentences. This would operate with all the facilities of a normal town or village except that there would be no children and residents would not be allowed to leave until they were deemed no longer a danger to children.

This 'protective custody' is put forward by Etzioni to protect the public and specifically children, but, whilst it may have some impact, it would do little to prevent sex offences actually taking place. Clearly many paedophiles are repeat offenders, but we must also recognise that many are not. Etzioni's communitarian approach cannot tackle parents who have not assaulted anyone in the past but decide to attack their own children in the privacy of their own home. Why, we might ask, is Etzioni so opposed to strategies such as changing sentencing policy? Why build special towns or villages to house sex offenders rather than incarcerating them? All Etzioni offers us is the view that it would be cheaper in the long run than imprisonment. This reflects an attempt to disguise his real rationale, which is his animosity towards the state. But who, apart from the state, should have the power to implement strategies to prevent sex offences taking place? What agency, apart from the state, could be empowered to interfere in the private sphere of families where children may be at risk? Etzioni's answer appears to be the 'viable community' of gossips leaning over the garden fence to exchange information about people. There are two clearly identifiable problems with this strategy. First, we have seen in the UK how communities may react in such a situation with violence directed towards innocent victims as a result of such 'gossip'. Second there is no evidence to suggest that the idealised communities of the past that Etzioni supports had less abuse of children than is the case within the divided and fragmented communities of today. This is not to say that communities should not have a role in dealing with problems such as paedophilia but they can only do so effectively in constructive dialogue with agencies of the state. To wish away the need for the state in issues such as these leads to a dangerous misunderstanding of the violent and exclusionary capacities of communities. In the long run it may increase the dangers to children rather than reduce them.

As long as communities are viewed in the privatistic fashion encouraged by Etzioni's theories, then they would be incapable of performing the public role that he envisages. This is because Etzioni wants communities to operate along commonsense principles rather than recognising that the public sphere of politics is one of competing rationalities. The reality of complex and untidy politics does not fit in with the simple choices that communities would have regarding their own locality in Etzioni's vision. Moreover the privatistic ethos that emerges from a bastardised political sphere gives rise to exclusionary communities. Without forums for people to express their concerns perhaps it is natural for them to seek solace in their own communities and to protect them where they feel it is necessary. This is not to justify vigilante-style actions such as those alluded to above but merely to recognise them as a response to the disabilities of modern politics as it has been constructed and the disempowerment of the very community or communities to which politicians address so much of their rhetoric.

At this point it is perhaps worth unpacking again the vision of community that is employed in radical perspectives. In terms of crime prevention it encompasses a combination of certain attitudes and values that bind groups of individuals together with a recognition that those values must be fostered by local and social institutions. Thus there must be an institutional framework that provides a social and economic structure in which communities can develop. This depiction of community is dynamic insofar as it recognises that communities will be more or less strong or weak at different stages, that changing policies affect institutional structures and that these will impact upon the capacity of communities to fulfil the roles we expect of them. According to this, perspective community 'does not constitute a discursive closure. Rather, it is open-textured, allowing alternative perspectives to coalesce around it.' The latter will 'collide and produce important sites of conflict amongst and between publics and professionals, where the politics of community can be, and sometimes are, contested' (Crawford 1999: 156). This moves us beyond the limited notion of the spatial community that dominates communitarian criminology. The development and inculcation of communitarian values emerge (or not as the case may be) from a range of associations and groupings within society and not just the local, geographical community. In terms of communitarian crime prevention, for example, strategies will involve local communities alongside other relevant associational groupings and various institutions and agencies on both the local and social level.[3] The involvement of relevant groupings beyond the locality also acts against the perception of community as exclusionary, although this is, of course, a persistent fear when the notion of community is invoked.

Radical communitarians must, then, remain conscious of the requirement not to glorify the community in the way that more orthodox commentators do. The radical focus on the heterogeneity of communities must always bear in mind the fact that this may mean that the organisation of some of these communities will be problematic. Following the work of Beatrix Campbell on the gender inequalities evident within communities, Crawford notes how communities are not:

> always the utopias of egalitarianism which some might wish but are hierarchical social formations, structured upon lines of differential power relations, most notably as feminists have argued upon lines of gender, but also upon lines of ethnicity, age, class (if these categories are not in themselves grounds for exclusion), and other personal attributes and identities. (Crawford 1999: 163)

The existence of these inequalities and sources of exclusion is not, however, an argument against communities *per se*. Radical communitarians would see it as representative of some of the key modalities of modern life. That these modalities should be addressed and subject to critical scrutiny is a central element of radical theories of community. However this process must be accompanied by a recognition that individuals will associate as communities and that, by definition, there will be characteristics within communities that include people and, in many cases, exclude others. The political task is one of democratising these associations and enabling sources of association and expression for all. Wishing away the need for communities because of their contemporary manifestation within given social and economic structures is no solution. The advocacy of community may be regarded as an attempt to grapple with some of the problems of social exclusion, but it provides no guarantee that sources of exclusion will be eradicated.

The most recent expression of the radical communitarian approach to alternative social policies has been Bill Jordan's *The New Politics of Welfare*. His programme is founded upon the argument that:

> [J]ustice is not a shining prize to be awarded from on high to some political arrangements, and denied to others. It is the negotiated outcome of a dialogue over often conflicting principles, all of which apply to almost every kind of interaction; and it must be reciprocally constructed in processes of democratic compromise. (Jordan 1998: 158)

As we shall see below, Jordan's primary mode of achieving this objective is through the provision of a basic income that, he argues, would provide social justice through the recognition of both formal and informal economic activity. Before analysing that strategy, it is worth examining how Jordan's approach feeds into or from his perception of community. He recognises that the redistribution of income alone is no guarantee of community or the creation of the conditions in which communitarian values may flourish. Rather, as in Crawford's assessment, Jordan identifies the importance of broader institutional structures and facilities. Thus, rather than focusing on how to reintegrate 'deviant' communities into the wider social whole, as orthodox political communitarians argue, he suggests that resources need to be provided to enhance the development of those communities. Instead of attempting to coerce individuals into behaving in certain ways decided by the dominant morality in society as a whole, Jordan argues for the empowerment of disenfranchised communities. Thus the radical communitarian project is concerned with the politics of empowerment rather than the politics of enforcement.

Part of this strategy involves the recognition of many informal economic activities that currently take place, some of which may well be strictly regarded as criminal in contemporary society. For example, Jordan recognises the range of co-operative strategies that emerge in deprived communities to evade the economistic, paid-work-based rationality that underpins the welfare state and political communitarianism. Here the argument moves us beyond the much more limited conception of local partnerships that has so far informed the policies of the New Labour government in the UK. For Jordan, measures must be sought to legitimise some of the sources of community and co-operation that are already in existence, whilst guarding against some of the unfortunate criminal side effects that often emanate themselves from criminalisation. In the British context such moves are impeded if 'the central thrust of government policy is to replace informal activity by formal employment, or training for it, and if the rules of the benefit system are tightened to penalize paid informal work' (Jordan 1998: 185–6). Further obstacles to radical approaches to community have been thrown up by the focus on administration, managerialism, contractualisation and commercialism in contemporary policy implementation. When it comes to community relations then, 'the skills and goodwill of many professionals could be better deployed in motivating, enabling and supporting . . . than they are at present' (Jordan 1998: 187). This is not to say that such relations will always be harmonious, but moves in such a direction could further the radical communitarian agenda. The key point is the recognition that the institutional framework contributes to the development of community values and that attempts to develop community will involve complicated political processes.

The dominant political sentiment behind these radical approaches to community is expressed by Mouffe: 'the aim of democratic institutions from this perspective [agonistic pluralism] is not to establish a rational consensus in the public sphere; it is to provide democratic channels of expression for the forms of conflict considered as legitimate' (Mouffe 1998: 17). This exposes the simplicity of the orthodox political communitarian and Third Way tendency to invoke the notion of 'the people' to express their belief in homogeneity (Hughes and Little 1999). The intention of orthodox approaches then, is to do away with political contestation or at least, where it happens, for political elites to engage in the necessary dialogue. Politics becomes a dirty word and a process only to be engaged in by professional actors. But social policies should not reflect such a narrow and homogeneous agenda. Instead of imagining one dominant moral voice in attempting to deal with social concerns, policy-makers need to recognise difference and the likelihood of conflict and dissent. From this perspective, Mouffe again turns to Walzer's idea of complex equality as the source for the renewal of radical democratic politics and debates on social policy. Moreover she echoes Gorz's concerns regarding the 'crisis of work and the exhaustion of the wage society'. Like many radicals today, Mouffe sees the impact of these developments as fundamental and a reason to support the provision of a basic income:

[A] plural economy should be developed where the associative sector would play an important role alongside the market and the state sector. Many activities, of crucial social utility but discarded by the logic of the market, could, through public financing, be carried out in this solidaristic economy . . . [T]he condition for the success of such initiatives is the implementation of some form of citizen's income that would guarantee a decent minimum for everybody. This is an idea that has recently been gaining an increasing number of supporters who argue that the reform of the welfare state would be better approached by envisaging the different modalities of such an income than by replacing it by workfare. (Mouffe 1998: 22)

THE PROMISE OF BASIC INCOME THEORY _ _ AS A RADICAL COMMUNITARIAN POLICY

Basic income theory takes on many forms but is based essentially on a philosophy that advocates the provision of a guaranteed minimum income for all. This would be paid to individuals (rather than family units) and it would not be predicated upon any work requirement (past, present or future). From this fundamental premise, basic income has been promoted by a range of commentators representing numerous ideological positions to combat the crisis of the welfare state, the end of work and the desire to revitalise community (Little 1998: Chapter 5).[4] It is the latter idea, that community can be reinvigorated through the provision of a guaranteed minimum income for all citizens, that is of primary concern here. Of course, many analyses of basic income are not predicated upon communitarian objectives. Following on from the economic arguments of the previous chapter, we can see that many commentators, particularly those on the right of the ideological spectrum, tend to see basic income as a means of shoring up changing economic circumstances. This is most evident in the work of defenders of economic liberalism who regard basic income as the *quid pro quo* for the continued freeing-up of global markets (Duncan and Hobson 1995; Brittan 1996). However, even if basic income has utility in terms of dealing with the realities of new political economy (and philosophically this is one of the weaker arguments in favour of basic income), we must ask whether and in what ways it contributes to the creation or sustenance of the principles of community.

In his earlier work Jordan (1992) had advocated basic income as a policy that would strengthen community. Whilst recognising the communitarian potential of such a measure, it has also been noted that there are problems with the view that a pecuniary measure such as basic income will, by definition, bring about more communal relations (Gorz 1992; Little 1998). More recently, Jordan has reasserted his support for basic income, but he has also begun to stress the wider institutional changes that will be required to accompany basic income in the development of community. In this vein he states that 'even if basic income is a necessary condition for social justice . . . , it is not a sufficient condition for social justice (Jordan 1998: 159). Thus, in line with the strategy outlined in this book, it is important to realise the ways in which social justice emanates from a complex interaction of economic, social and political institutions. Paramount in Jordan's strategy is to address the range of activities that individuals currently undertake and to try and legitimise those that are in the 'moral economy' but are not part of the formal economy of paid work. Jordan then sees the provision of a basic income without work requirement as a means of providing legitimacy for non-market work and other activities that do not have instrumental, material gain as their primary rationality. Moreover it may contribute to a process whereby paid informal work that is performed beyond the parameters of the formal economy (and strictly criminal for that reason) could also be legitimised, given that much of this work is undertaken to top up other income in order to meet basic needs (Jordan 1998: 166). Indeed frequently this work is characterised by poor conditions, low pay and lack of protection, and individuals are 'coerced' into performing it due to the constraints imposed by work-based welfare regimes. The provision of an unconditional income could relieve the need to engage in some of this work and thereby improve the working conditions of many.

. Jordan has always regarded the freeing-up of individual time from stringent work requirements as potentially communitarian insofar as individuals would have more time to devote to activities beyond the economic sphere. As such, he believes that such a strategy could be a means of increasing choice for individuals with regard to the particular blend of activities they decide to participate in. Thus 'in order to be able to make such choices, they require some fundamental autonomy, so that they can recognize alternatives and select between them' (Jordan 1998: 172). This allows for the possibility that individuals will choose to engage in more community activities (although, of course, they might not), and Jordan sees participation therein as worthy of recognition. In this sense, for reasons of political expedience as much as anything else, there is nothing to prevent the guaranteed income being presented as a 'participation income' as long as 'participation' was conceived in broad terms to incorporate unpaid as well as paid activities (Atkinson 1996). Again, whilst this is no guarantee of community participation, it does provide the kind of official recognition of such non-market activity that could encourage more individuals to engage in it. Moreover by reducing the need for 'constrained participation' in paid formal or informal work, it could potentially furnish individuals with greater choice and opportunity.

One of the most significant critics of basic income theory for many years was André Gorz (1992), who, despite being sympathetic to the political objectives of freeing people from paid work and increasing autonomy, was sceptical of the capacity of basic income proposals to achieve those aims. His primary criticism was that basic income would not ensure membership of society as a whole because it did not attempt to redistribute paid work and open up opportunities for people to achieve a self-determined blend of paid and unpaid work. His fear was that it would further marginalise the excluded by effectively paying them off for their labour market exclusion. Moreover he feared that it would act as a subsidy for low-paying employers who would feed off the likelihood that individuals would have to top up their basic income to meet their basic needs. Last, he argued that the objective of social inclusion required a range of facilities and provisions on both a community and social level that would enable people to take advantage of the time and resources with which they would be provided. In this sense it was all very well to provide people with an income to participate in their community, but if facilities in terms of buildings, communication technologies, transportation and so on were not improved then these rights to community participation may be relatively meaningless. Indeed, without addressing the structural problems of disadvantaged communities, a basic income would provide greater benefit to people in those communities that had the infrastructure in place than the deprived communities that were most in need of social inclusion.

In his most recent work Gorz has changed his attitude towards basic income theory. Where, in his earlier work, he had shown some sympathy with the objectives of basic income theory but remained deeply sceptical of whether it could achieve those goals, in *Reclaiming Work* (1999) he readily recognises that he has shifted his stance on the issue. Now he states that:

> The granting of a sufficient basic income to all citizens must . . . be inseparable from developing and making accessible the resources which enable and encourage self-activity to take place, the resources with which individuals and groups can satisfy by their own unshackled efforts part of the needs and desires they have themselves defined. (Gorz 1999: 83)

So, whilst he now favours a basic income, it comes with the strict corollary that facilities and institutional frameworks for participation must accompany it. Gorz's change of mind is largely predicated upon economic grounds (although he has been acutely aware of the changing circumstances of work for many years). In the conditions of the new economy he now sees a guaranteed income as the most beneficial strategy for providing security by protecting people from poverty. Clearly then, he still reserves considerable criticism for minimal basic income schemes, such as those that emanate from elements of the right that offer little more than subsistence payments. The point, for Gorz, is not to devise a system that provides support for the expansion of the flexibility demanded by global capital, but rather to find a means of undermining the economistic demands that are placed upon people in contemporary Western societies. Rather than reinforcing the flexible labour market, the guaranteed income that Gorz envisages would emancipate individuals from its constraints. This would be facilitated through the strictly unconditional nature of the basic income strategy he supports. He supports unconditionality on the grounds that it is the only means of ensuring that voluntary activities are protected from the economic rationality of the formal economy.

– CONCLUSION –

Ultimately though, the success or otherwise of basic income strategies in rejuvenating community will depend upon an integrated set of measures such as urban, cultural and technological policies. Thus neither the social nor the economic domain can provide values of community in isolation from the institutional infrastructure in which policies are applied. The process of strengthening community is then intrinsically political and, as such, a matter of contention and debate. The realisation of the radical vision of community requires a political dialogue about the ends to which we direct our policies. Although seemingly more distant on the agenda than the model of orthodox political communitarianism that dominates contemporary Third Way thinking, this radical perspective on community is not less realistic in practice nor is it less philosophically coherent. What it does imply is a radical pluralistic politics, and thus a new politics of community necessitates a recognition of likely political conflict. In Jordan's words:

> The interests of groups will always conflict in various ways, and the multiplicity of conceptions of the good life will increase as societies become more diverse in their

memberships, and plural in their practices. These differences have to be negotiated in political life, and claims and conflicts mediated through democratic
processes. (Jordan 1998: 162)

It is to the analysis of the political structures to accommodate the ideals of
community that we must now turn. What should be clear is that considerable problems emerge when community is merely asserted as a replacement
for the state. Such a strategy is unfeasible in complex societies and, whilst
community may be a desirable phenomenon that we want to encourage in
policy-making, it can only be empowered as a complementary institution to
the state. This, of course, does not preclude debate about the parameters of
the state or the types of services that it provides. Indeed, according to radical
approaches to community, the debate about the state will generate considerable public dialogue and a confrontation of political standpoints.

– Notes –

1. Whilst community is invoked by New Labour in terms of crime prevention and
   punishment, simultaneously it also tends to promote a populist punitiveness that feeds
   upon the electoral popularity of discourses such as 'prison works'. The latter is discussed
   in detail in Garland (2001).
2. Megan's laws refers to legislation introduced in the United States to combat the problem
   of sex offenders in the aftermath of the murder of Megan Kanka by a paedophile.
3. An example of this kind of strategy could be the involvement of the gay community in
   the fight against hate crimes in local crime and disorder strategies. I am grateful to
   Gordon Hughes for drawing my attention to the existence of these kinds of measures in
   some local authorities.
4. There is a large and growing literature on basic income that I cannot cover in depth
   here. Nonetheless many of the key debates of the 1990s are covered in Little (1998)
   where a fuller picture of my own position is evident. What follows here will focus on the
   community aspect of these debates and more recent contributions on basic income such
   as that of Jordan (1998).

CHAPTER 7

Repoliticising Community: Towards Democratic Renewal

The difference between orthodox political communitarianism and more radical perspectives is clearly demonstrated when we examine the understanding of politics in each of these approaches. In simple terms there is an almost palpable hostility to the formal political sphere in orthodox communitarianism. For commentators such as Etzioni, the community should replace the state wherever possible as the main agent of political control in order to decentralise power and replace the inefficiency and ineffectiveness of state mechanisms. In so doing the domain of professional politicians would diminish as decision-making was relocated downwards to the sphere of community. For orthodox communitarians this would not only deprofessionalise politics but it would also depoliticise much policy-making. Because they assume the existence of a homogeneous moral community (although containing different groups within it), then decisions would be taken according to that universal morality rather than for political reasons. For this reason, orthodox political communitarians envisage a position whereby decision-making is driven by an apolitical morality that they deem to be more desirable than the self-interest of supposedly representative politicians.

Radical communitarian perspectives would share some of these sympathies but would disagree fundamentally with the understanding of politics that emerges from it. Like orthodox commentators, radicals share a degree of scepticism about the capacity of the state to understand the needs of communities or to act effectively to guarantee them. Moreover they would also concur that decision-making needs to be decentralised because they believe that there are fundamental limitations in the system of representative democracy. Therefore both radicals and orthodox communitarians would agree on the importance of devolution, decentralisation and greater ordinary participation in decision-making. However radicals do not assume a homogeneity in the nature of community or any kind of dominant moral voice. Instead they recognise that the existence of a multiplicity of communities and associations prevents such a dominant morality from developing. As such, the sphere of community is one of contestation and conflict as much as it is one of agreement. Thus, essentially, it is deeply political. Where orthodox communitarians see politics as something to be overcome to the greatest possible extent, radicals argue that the downwards devolution of power will entail more politics rather than less. The vital upshot of this is the recognition of a continued role for the state. Conflicts need to be mediated and settled because there is no overarching moral voice. In this sense, then, the state remains as the ultimate arbiter. At the same time radical communitarians agree with their orthodox counterparts that the strategy of subsidiarity should prevail. Thus decisions should be taken at the lowest, most decentralised level possible. It is only where incommensurable viewpoints clash that the state should be called upon to intervene in community affairs.

This vision of community owes much to the radical democratic theory of Mouffe (2000b). She criticises contemporary liberals such as Rawls for their advocacy of a 'well-ordered society', and this criticism can be extended to political communitarians who promote the universal moral voice as an alternative to the universal theory of justice of the early Rawls. Mouffe argues that a genuinely pluralist politics will contain considerable diversity and therefore conflict. However this does not mean that those whom we perceive as different from ourselves are automatically enemies or adversaries; we can construct the political arena around a recognition of the validity of alternative arguments to our own. This implies a more discursive understanding of politics than that of modern liberal democracy but, unlike many theories of deliberative democracy, it does not assume that participants in debates are equal or will have an equal access to decision-making. Thus the existence of a space for political dialogue does not entail that the actors therein participate on the same footing. For Mouffe, theories of the well-ordered society such as those that emerge from Third Way thinking fail to grasp power differentials that permeate contemporary societies. Thus, in terms of emancipatory politics, if we want to 'envisage the making of a new hegemony the traditional understanding of left and right needs to be redefined; but whatever the content we give to those categories, one thing is sure: there comes a time when one needs to decide on which side to stand in their agonistic confrontation' (Mouffe 2000b: 15).

This commitment to agonistic pluralism that characterises more radical approaches to community stands in contrast to the search for political consensus in orthodox political communitarianism. The latter wants to avoid criticisms that it reflects moral majoritarianism and stresses the common foundation of the moral voice of community. According to Frazer (1999: 41–2), there are three main elements of the communitarian pursuit of political consensus. First, it implies a substructure of common values and beliefs in which social differences are overridden. Second, it suggests that consensus can derive from universal participation. Third, it focuses on the way consensus can emanate from a 'human-level' politics that is taken out of the hands of self-interested professional politicians. In the light of these features of the pursuit of consensus, political communitarians are able to argue that, to borrow the title of the book by Anthony Giddens, their position is 'beyond left and right'. Radicals find this depiction of politics problematic because it presupposes that consensus is achievable. Whilst there may be more or less agreement on given issues, radicals view a situation where all in society concur on moral principles as reflective only of a homogeneous community that bears no resemblance to the reality of modern Western societies. The latter are fundamentally complex and political. In this sense it 'cannot be a feature of a theory of politics that agreement be attained or premised on the values and reasons underlying individuals' choices and conclusions regarding particular issues. This means that "politics" is a never-ending process' (Frazer 1999: 226).

In short, then, radical approaches to community disagree with the notion of consensus that is envisaged by orthodox communitarians. Radicals regard the latter as apolitical and, as such, divorced from the lived experience of Western societies today and, increasingly, societies across the world. The problem with the orthodox perspective is based upon the idea of 'the' community. By presenting community as exhaustive of 'the social', they cannot deal with the fact that there is considerable diversity in the modern world without resorting to the fabrication of an overall morality. Radicals do not equate community with society: instead society comprises many different communities (as well as a wide range of other forms of association) that confer differing identities on the individuals therein. Because each of us is a member of different communities and associations, society is made up of individuals all of whom have separate identities. In such a scenario the idea of a common moral voice appears anachronistic.

COMMUNITY AND SOCIETY:
IDENTITY AND DIFFERENCE

There is little agreement among communitarians and their critics about the meaning of community. The undertheorisation of the concept has led to a distinct absence of clarity when it comes to the politics of community. A major concern with regard to the meaning of community relates to the size and geographical space that communities are supposed to occupy. On top of this there is also a concern over the nature of the relationships that are supposed to be communitarian and how they differ from other forms of political association. Both of these issues have profound implications for the theorisation of community and the role it may be given in the political organisation of modern societies.

As we have seen, orthodox political communitarianism, such as that of Amitai Etzioni, does allow for the existence of different groups within society. Thus, it is feasible using his model to argue that there are a number of different communities within society. However, in terms of providing the overall moral voice that governs the community as a political agent, orthodox communitarians focus on community as society. In this sense they advocate a scenario whereby an overarching unified morality guides 'the' community and governs the behaviour of the range of associational groups that exist within that political community. Thus, despite the recognition that society contains divergent social groups, orthodox political communitarians are primarily interested in society as 'the' community. To make this point clear, it is worthwhile quoting Etzioni's own definition of community. He states that:

> A community is a group of people who share criss-crossing affective bonds and a moral culture. By asserting this definition, I mean to indicate clearly that communities need not be local and are distinct from mere interest groups, in that they address a broad band of human needs. People who band together to gain privileged treatment for office equipment make an interest group; those who share a history, identity and fate, a community. (Etzioni 2000b: 9)

This, I would contend, is a fairly innocuous definition of community (although it doesn't provide the full picture of Etzioni's view). In this framework there is indeed scope for a variety of different communities within a society. All that is required of a community is a shared identity that is not solely based upon self-interest and an overarching moral code that is recognised by all members. Etzioni allows for the fact that within this limited definition there is scope for conflict within the community. To this end, there is little that radicals might find constraining. However, in the same article, Etzioni adds meat to the bare bones of this definition, and here problems begin to emerge as the divergent communities appear subservient to a greater moral voice – that of society as a whole: 'communities underpin a moral culture. They define what a society considers virtuous, provide approbation for those who live up to these definitions, and censor those who do not, thus reducing the need for policing' (Etzioni 2000b: 9). Here Etzioni's agenda becomes clearer. Communities do not have their own moral culture *per se*, rather they underpin a broader morality. Thus it is the role of communities to substantiate the dominant moral culture. In this view, community is not where we experience and enjoy our differing moralities, it is the strut for the dominant moral voice of society. Community becomes the forum in which we adjudge individual behaviour and punish those who do wrong, according to the dominant morality. In this sense, communities are indeed political agents but are driven by an agenda that represents the overall social morality.

Indeed, Etzioni is very clear about what he sees as the agenda for communitarians. It is not, he says, to define this entity that we call community. Rather, it is to fill the moral vacuum created by the demise of tradition and the failure of liberals to provide a replacement to guide society. Thus there is a slippage in Etzioni's thought between 'the' community and society in the search for the moral virtues by which we should all live within any given society. To be quite clear then, orthodox political communitarianism is not really concerned with the concept of community but with the establishment of social morality. In Etzioni's words, 'there can be no community, nor a stable society, without a shared moral culture' (Etzioni 2000b: 9). This slippage between community and society is problematic for radicals, who, though they see the importance of debates over morality, are not prepared to wish away flippantly the need to clarify what we mean by community. Indeed it could be argued that the failure of orthodox political communitarians to enter these debates has contributed to not only the reception of their ideas by their critics as vague and woolly but also their political success. For example, commentators such as Frazer (1999) have noted how the whole project of communitarianism is undermined by those who focus on moral virtues rather than political agency.

To this end it is worth examining again the work of André Gorz (1999), who has attempted to fill this void by establishing a clearer differentiation between community and society. Initially Gorz (1999: 117) differentiates

nmunities, where our common endeavours are at
and constitutive communities which reflect our
ers that we were born into (otherwise known as
e and communities of fate respectively). However,
ms of community share is the communal, informal
nships therein. For Gorz, these associations lose their
ties whenever the bonds move towards the formal
uction of contracts or the institutionalisation of juridical
rules. Once bonds between individuals have to be formalised and
regulated by institutional structures, then the communal bond that holds
these groups together is undermined. It is the nature of these bonds, then,
that differentiates community from society:

> Society . . . is too large, differentiated and complex for the relations between its
> 'members' to be regulated communicatively and spontaneously. One does not
> belong to a society, then, in the same way as one belongs to a community. One
> belongs to it not as a concrete person, having, by one's origin or through co-
> operation, a shared life with the others, but as a citizen; that is to say, as an
> abstract person defined in one's universality by established, juridically formalized
> rights (and duties), guaranteed by a state. (Gorz 1999: 118)

According to this formulation of community, then, community is not
defined by locality or spatial boundaries. Rather, it is established according
to the types of relationships that individuals have in particular associations.
It may well be that these relations are best suited to geographic proximity,
but they are not defined by them. We may have common, non-instrumental
links with individuals with whom we as individuals have little direct
contact. This ably demonstrates that Etzioni's depiction of society as
'the' community is inherently problematic because it fails to recognise
the different ways in which relationships are established in different spheres.
Thus the problem with Etzioni's analysis is not his focus on virtue – Gorz too
highlights particular virtues of community – but that orthodox communitarianism is unaware of the ways in which formal relationships in society
as a whole are predicated upon a different set of principles than those of
community. Indeed, Gorz goes so far as to say that, when we look at the
virtues of the different spheres, modern society is 'the antithesis of community' (Gorz 1999: 118).

From this differentiation, Gorz goes on to make a further distinction
between what he terms 'co-operative' communities (of choice) and 'constitutive' communities (of fate). He argues that the bonds in the latter are

stronger than in the former because we are members of these communities without choice and on an equal footing. Gorz contends that we are members of religious or ethnic communities due to the bare fact of being born or inducted into these associations and that this provides all in those constitutive communities with an equal status as members. This will not be the case with 'co-operative' communities of choice in which individuals engage to a greater or lesser extent. Thus we may choose to be more or less active in the 'co-operative' associations that we elect to join, and some of the communities of which we are a part may play a more fundamental role in our social identity than others. In this sense, just as there is an element of choice over whether we join these communities, there is also a degree of choice over the extent to which we participate in them. For Gorz, this is important because it 'is quite clear . . . that in a highly differentiated modern society the communal allegiances of each individual do not exhaust his/her reality, do not define *all that he/she is*' (Gorz 1999: 120).

Gorz recognises, then, that in modern societies identity and meaning is frequently derived as much from co-operative communities as from constitutive communities. Whilst this may make communal identities less rooted than was the case when constitutive communities were the major source of identity, Gorz believes that we should encourage the expansion of co-operative communities. The alternative, he argues, would be a retreat towards an unthinking tribalism or fundamentalism in which individuals define themselves solely in relation to the associations they are born or indoctrinated into. This scenario diminishes the potential of individuals asking who they are and questioning their relationships with others. Rather, individuals may uncritically assert that they are who they are and see no need to engage with 'the other'. Radicals are sceptical of such purely constitutive identities because, even where diversity is likely to generate conflict and dissent in some areas, this does not negate the desirability of individuals engaging with those different from themselves. Only through such a political process can diverse societies manage to cohere:

> The idea of 'communitarian society' expresses nostalgia for a simple, transparent, pre-modern world in which society would operate like an originary community: each member's identity and rights would be grounded in his/her belonging to that community by birth. In such a society, that identity and those rights would depend not on what one does, but what one is – by birth . . . By elevating birth . . . into the basic criterion of each person's dignity and rights, the national-communitarian ideology makes it possible to conjure away differences of class, wealth and social position, and to repress conflicts between dominant and

dominated as attacks on the unity and cohesion of the nation and the people. (Gorz 1999: 121)

Again, this reflects the radical rejection of orthodox political communitarianism's equation of society with the depoliticised moral community. Indeed Gorz accuses what he calls national-communitarianism with a 'radically *anti-political* import' (Gorz 1999: 121). In seeking to do away with the real implications of cultural diversity, orthodox communitarians override difference with a forced unity, be that of a dominant moral voice as in Etzioni's vision, or blood and nation in nationalistic communitarian perspectives.

Gorz is not explicit enough in criticising the extent to which constitutive communities command the shape of their membership. He appears to regard constitutive communities as rather prescriptive when it comes to conferring individual identity and he underestimates the ways in which individuals can critically engage with their backgrounds. For example, individuals are perfectly capable of challenging the construction of the nationality into which they were born or the unchosen religious denomination which may be foisted upon them in childhood. Whilst undoubtedly such critical engagement bears the imprint of the constitutive community if we are to differentiate ourselves from it, we do have choices over the extent to which we are defined by the constitutive community. If one chooses to distance oneself from the communities into which we are born, then this necessitates critical engagement with a range of beliefs and practices into which we have been born or inducted. Quite simply, we can move away from the so-called communities of fate of which we are a part, but this also requires us to address the very issues which we now reject. Gorz underestimates the extent to which co-operative communities, insofar as they may demand high levels of effort and participation, often expect high degrees of cohesion and attempt to regulate the behaviour of their members. Presumably, Gorz would argue that the difference is that we have a right of exit from communities of choice, those in which we choose to co-operate. However, as noted above, we can also move away from the expected norms of those communities that are supposed to constitute us and yet, simultaneously, hold on to key elements of the identity that those communities confer upon us and continue to regard ourselves as part of them. This implies that perhaps the kind of equality of status that Gorz attributes to constitutive communities may not be reflected in practice – some people may be regarded by others or regard themselves as more 'true' to the values and foundations of a particular community than others who also belong. For example, within religious communities there may be some individuals who are seen to adhere to the requisite rules or moral guidelines to a greater degree than others. This is evident in the idea of a 'good' Catholic, for instance.

Gorz is on a firmer footing in his critical assessment of the implications of some of the relativist implications that emerge from some communitarian thinkers (he criticises the privatistic ethos in Sandel's work but spares Walzer from his critique). He rightly contends that relativism, whether cultural or otherwise, can lead to a privatistic drive in which individuals are encouraged to enjoy their individuality and experience the opportunities that pluralism provides as long as that difference is expressed in the private sphere. Here, Gorz refers to the danger of the compartmentalisation of public space in which spheres are created that allow different groups to pursue their own ends in isolation from others. Thus mere recognition of the existence of 'other' communities could actually entail enabling them to do whatever they want in their own space without giving them full access to the public sphere. In this vein, he contends that communities should have a 'common political culture and a common public space'. Moreover 'such a space will need to be established, for it does not arise spontaneously out of each community's recognition of the other's specificity. By itself, such a recognition will lead more probably to a plurality of compartmentalized public spaces than to a single common one' (Gorz 1999: 124). This reflects a radical concern with the need to manufacture a public space in which individuals recognise that their voice is merely one among the many, and, indeed, that in matters of contention their voice will not always prevail. At the same time the dialogic process must reflect a common understanding of the kind of forum in which decisions take place. This is the basis of a politics of difference that recognises that diversity must not leave us with a privatistic relativism. Rather, the 'political is the specific space in which to work out the conflictual tension between the opposing poles of community and society' (Gorz 1999: 125). For Gorz, the alternative to such a model of political relations and the public sphere is a recipe for 'authoritarian statism' or the 'strait-jacketed conformism' he links with 'national-communitarian societies'.

If, as we have seen, communities do not equate with the national community and there is also a requirement for state institutions to mediate between the conflicting moral concerns of different communities, questions arise as to the most appropriate form of political arrangements to allow such a process of mediation to take place. Perhaps the most appropriate model for the radical perspective on community is that of associational, or associative, democracy which attempts to formulate a pluralistic vision of participatory groups and associations that accommodates the realities of diversity. It is to the usefulness and applicability of such a model that we now turn.

– COMMUNITIES AND ASSOCIATIVE DEMOCRACY –

The most notable expression of theories of associative democracy has been provided by Paul Hirst (1994), who makes major claims for the potential of such a model:

> Associationalism makes accountable representative democracy possible again by limiting the scope of state administration, without diminishing social provision. It enables market-based societies to deliver the substantive goals desired by citizens, by embedding the market system in a social network of coordinative and regulatory institutions. It is a political idea that is big enough to offer the hope of radical reform, and to mobilize political energies in doing so, but it is specific enough to be developed within and added to our existing institutions. (Hirst 1994: 12–13)

According to this depiction of associative democracy, then, it is a system that can be introduced through gradualist reform of our existing political institutions in Western liberal democracies. Hirst sees this as a major strength, insofar as there is no requirement for radical upheaval or social unrest. Moreover he sees associative democracy as transcending traditional ideological divisions, and it is therefore capable of harnessing widespread support from across the political spectrum. He explicitly links it with the advocacy of civil society as the sphere of society in which a range of diverse groups and associations with different moralities and ways of life can be empowered to follow their own particular pathway to the good life. Thus associative democracy is constructed as a set of ideas and institutions that transcend the limitations of statist models of social organisation and traditional systems of representative democracy. According to Hirst, this task of moving beyond traditional political fissures should not be presented as radical in the way that some new social movements have tended to trumpet their opposition to existing forms of liberal democracy. Instead, he advocates 'the common cause that very different movements may find in gaining the freedom to build their own self-governing communities in civil society' (Hirst 1994: 14).

Clearly the associative model of democratic politics does hold potential for the radical theory of community, although, as Hirst implies, it could also provide a system for more orthodox or national-communitarian arrangements. The fact that it is envisaged as an improvement to existing institutional frameworks suggests that it would be suitable for the orthodox political communitarian project of permitting cultural difference within an overarching moral community. Nonetheless by now we are well aware of the limitations of such a theory, not least in the way it could stifle difference rather than allowing it to flourish. Hirst's emphasis on enabling different groups and associations to follow their own vision of the good is potentially radical because it does not require a common moral commitment. Rather, it focuses on a common understanding of politics as the forum through which different moralities co-exist and which enable diverse groups of people to live together in relative harmony. It promises decentralisation and participation in ways that appear to offer quite fundamental changes to the representative systems that currently dominate liberal democracies. Nonetheless it is not so clear that the pluralist conception that Hirst employs is as aware of the need to recognise conflict as is the case with more radical visions such as Mouffe's agonistic pluralism (Mouffe 2000b). As such, the utility of associative democracy for radical conceptions of community is identifiable, but, at the same time, the two positions do not equate with each other.

In Hirst's model of associative democracy the guiding principle is not to do away with functions of liberal democracy such as voting or the necessity of a regulatory state. Rather, he prefers a system in which 'as many of the affairs of society as possible are managed by voluntary and democratically self-governing associations' (Hirst 1994: 19). The key to the radical potential of such a strategy is the impact that an arrangement of this kind would have on the nature of politics. As argued in Chapter 8 however, this kind of civil society politics contains a number of different approaches. In political terms some civil society politics envisage the harmonious co-existence of numerous groups and associations. Frequently this kind of analysis goes hand in hand with theories of deliberative or discursive democracy in which differences between groups are resolved through the agreements that would be forged if groups were able to enter into perfectionist forms of dialogue. Radical democrats have often argued that such a model, notable in the work of Jürgen Habermas, is problematic because it invokes a model of discourse in which power differentials between the participants are overcome. For radical democrats, the practical applicability of such a model is highly questionable given the ubiquity and acute impact of power differentials. Thus, although most versions of civil society politics 'see such participation giving life to the body politic' (Carter and Stokes 1998: 14), there are clear differences in the way in which politics is to be invigorated. A radical view of civil society must not only note the need for different groups to actually engage with one another but also recognise that such engagement will not always yield optimally harmonious outcomes. The need for the state as the mediator of such engagements is evident, even if the state may be incapable of containing all of the conflicts that may emerge.

A role for the state in associative democracy is explicit in Hirst's proposals. He recognises that associations need to be protected if they are to carry out their democratic functions and that the state must help in the process of socially embedding market mechanisms and extending welfare provision. Nonetheless Hirst is keen to articulate the ways in which such a role for the state would not lead to authoritarianism and bureaucracy. Instead he argues that 'voluntary self-governing associations' must become the main source of political decision-making and that the defining asso-ciative principle must be that governance is devolved to the lowest possible level as appropriate in any given area. Moreover it is essential that associative democracy does not become bound up with the finality of election results or rely on simple majorities in decision-making. Rather, it is vital that governance is open and accessible and that appropriate channels of communication are used to transmit information and decisions to those who will be affected. Hirst believes that in such a model:

> Associationalism attempts to construct a political framework within which individuals and the groups they create through voluntary association . . . can pursue different public goods whilst remaining in the same society. Plural groups share a limited, but common, set of public rules and regulatory institutions, which ensure that their differing goals and beliefs can be accommodated without undue conflict or the infringements of the rights of individuals and associations. (Hirst 1994: 20)

Associative democracy will not come about accidentally nor are govern-ments likely to volunteer to devolve their powers. What is required, according to Hirst, is pressure from below, whereby associations and groups in civil society demonstrate their capacity to govern their own concerns and come together to pressurise government for the devolution of power. This, of course, recognises the necessity of governments and state institutions that are not actively opposed to subsidiarity. Moreover it also implies a commit-ment from associative groups to come together and organise politically. This is a realistic suggestion from Hirst, but it does run the risk of groups with power and influence having a greater impact on the shape of the associative structures that emerge than less powerful associations or communities. Moreover we cannot assume that governments or the state will readily give up their powers or that associative groups and communities are sufficiently organised to carry out an extended political role.

Associational theories are based upon pluralistic concerns for the promotion of diversity and difference and suggest that, as with radical theories of community, we have a multiplicity of identities that derive from the various parts of social life in which we participate. Thus, there should be greater political recognition of our membership of a range of groups and associations. These may involve our work and our locality but will also include our families, and other social networks of which we are a part, such as sports clubs, religious organisations, voluntary groups, political parties, sexual communities, charities, reading circles, social movements, pressure groups and so on. In this sense, Hirst's arguments 'make it possible to imagine a society with widespread participation in decision-making over a wide range of issues. It makes it possible to move towards radical notions of pluralist democracy' (Cochrane 1998: 260). Cochrane notes how this kind of individuated approach to social identity promotes notions of difference as being healthy in a way that rarely finds expression in the world of formal, electoral politics. Against Hirst's thesis, however, Cochrane suggests that it fails to devote sufficient attention to power differentials between different groups. Thus the latter suggests that, as is the case now, certain groups have more power in the voluntary sector and that there is an underrepresentation of ethnic minorities, women, the unemployed and the working class. Whilst this is the case, Hirst would presumably suggest that an empowered associational sector would provide greater status for the forms of association that these underrepresented groups in the contemporary voluntary sector engage in. Hirst's thesis focuses on the legitimation of a range of forms of association which are currently marginalised. At the same time it requires something of a leap of faith to believe that current inequalities would not be evident in future associative democratic arrangements.

In his later work Hirst (1998) presents his model of associative democracy as an alternative strategy to tackle the conditions fostered by the increasing automation of production and exchange, the globalisation of our economies and the problem of an ageing population. From this basis, he believes that the future problems of the welfare state are clearly identifiable today and that associational models, including a guaranteed universal citizen's income, offer potential solutions to the risks and dangers that we must tackle in the future. The first of these risks that Hirst identifies is that of structural unemployment, the growth of low-paid work that does not meet subsistence needs, and the underemployment of great swathes of the population. He sees this as the basis of social fragmentation between elite minorities and the majority of the population. The answer, he suggests, is to provide a guaranteed minimum income through a transfer payment or a tax credit that would enable everyone to participate in meeting their welfare needs. A second risk that Hirst addresses is the problem of globalisation. Of course, he is also a strident critic of the globalisation thesis (Hirst and Thompson 1996), and he suggests that there is considerable evidence that associational social provisions would not impact negatively upon our economic performance. He argues that the different strategies of welfare in 'successful' countries would imply that there is not one model that equates with success in globalised markets. In this scenario Western economies have no need to drive down the costs of welfare or the services that are provided and, therefore, it would seem that a guaranteed income would be viable.

The third risk that is dealt with in Hirst's analysis is that of the ageing population and its socio-economic implications. He believes that associational strategies can assist the transitions ahead by breaking down the barriers between employment and unemployment. Thus, he suggests that it is unrealistic to expect large sections of the population to be economically inactive and still survive on very low incomes. By allowing and recompensing different types of participation alongside a citizen's income, associationalism provides ways of preventing the social exclusion of this growing sector of society. By providing greater recognition of the voluntary sector, associationalism could make greater use of the skills and abilities of older people rather than discarding them once they reach retirement age. The great strength of Hirst's analysis is that, whether one agrees with his prescriptions or not, he has explicitly recognised the ways in which political renewal cannot be disassociated from key issues of social and economic reform. As with the radical theory of community, associative democracy is founded on the interdependence of political, social and economic issues.

Hirst's advocacy of associative democracy is focused on transcending the old private–public divide, and the impact that that dualism has on debates about future political and social organisation. Thus 'associationalism is as concerned to democratise civil society as it is to devolve the powers of state to voluntary organisations' (Hirst 1998: 86). Therefore, he believes that democratisation necessitates a rejection of the marketisation of public institutions and the unaccountable influence of private corporations in public functions. Democratisation, then, involves the empowerment of individuals to take control over their own lives in a collective fashion and to establish more localised and communitarian forms of governance. In the light of this, Hirst recognises the failings of the Keynesian welfare state but rejects the accusation that associationalism amounts to privatisation and the legitimation of possessive individualism. Like John Keane in his under-standing of civil society, Hirst recognises the importance of the state in this new structure: 'it would remain as a standard setter, inspector and determi-ner of overall funding levels' (Hirst 1998: 90). In this sense, associationalism and the advocacy of civil society are concerned with new methods of governance and the extension of welfare rather than a surrender to private provision and marketisation. Hirst claims that 'it may be the only route to social solidarity in a pluralistic and individualistic society' (Hirst 1998: 91), and in this he may be right. However, as Cochrane (1998) notes, there need to be concentrated attempts to empower those who have often been underpopulated in the realms of associational participation and this requires a recognition of some of the traditional problems of pluralism (Mouffe 2000b).

NEGOTIATION, CONTINGENCY AND COMPROMISE: TOWARDS COMMUNITARIAN GOVERNANCE?

Various attempts have been made to circumvent the traditional pitfalls of pluralist theory, such as Rawls' political liberalism or the Habermasian model of deliberative democracy. However, as Mouffe notes, these models have failed, insofar as they rely on an unworkable separation of the private and the public in the case of Rawls and a narrow proceduralism that attempts to 'preclude the possibility of contestation' in the work of Habermas (Mouffe 2000b: 90–2). Neither approach satisfies Mouffe, who argues that they insulate politics and ignore the realities of diverse societies:

> Democratic theory should renounce those forms of escapism and face the challenge that the recognition of the pluralism of values entails. This does not mean accepting a total pluralism, and some limits need to be put to the kind of confrontation which is going to be seen as legitimate in the public sphere. But the political nature of the limits should be acknowledged instead of being presented as requirements of morality or rationality. (Mouffe 2000b: 93)

If the main models from democratic theory and contemporary liberalism are problematic, then what kind of political relations are envisaged by radical democratic theory and what do they offer the theorisation of community? First of all, we should note that the radical democratic recognition of plurality and difference is untidy. It doesn't offer us clear ways of making decisions nor does it guarantee ways in which we can overcome differences in power between various associations and communities. This potential weakness is the great strength of radical democratic approaches. By rejecting perfectionism and proceduralism it provides us with a dynamic approach to politics; it genuinely invigorates political debate and attempts to engage with the dilemmas of plurality and multiple versions of the common good within society. As such, it has been influential on radical theorists of community such as Bill Jordan (1998). In his recent analyses Jordan has moved beyond his prior focus on basic income as a means of moving towards a more just society and has drawn attention to the attendant measures that would also be required to supplement a basic income approach. One of these measures is to rethink the nature of politics and participation.

Jordan refutes forcefully the kind of politics that emanates from orthodox political communitarianism and the morally authoritarian undertones that support the kinds of programmes on welfare that have emerged in the UK and USA. Here he notes how the communitarian rhetoric employed by politicians such as Tony Blair and Bill Clinton disguised the use of state institutions to coerce people into forms of behaviour that were deemed to be morally responsible. Thus, beneath appeals to individual freedom coupled with social responsibility lurks the threat of the authoritarian and intolerant state. Jordan is not convinced of the inevitability of these procedures and argues on the contrary that a basic income could be part of an empowering process that would enable individuals, many of whom are effectively disenfranchised from decision-making in the contemporary system, to participate in the most important decisions that affect their lives. Indeed, he indicates out how sociological theory points to the possibility of reciprocal forms of communication without resorting to the abstraction or proceduralism that has characterised recent contributions from political theory. For Jordan, these arguments provide evidence of forms of interaction that sustain informal communities even though the participants in these interactions may well be unequal or have differential degrees of power. In this scenario the powerful still have a 'need to legitimate their authority to the subordinate, who in turn have opportunities to subvert power by turning these justifications against those who use them' (Jordan 1998: 191–2). In this vein, he contends that 'unequal partners can construct common interests through dialogue and negotiation' (Jordan 1998: 192).

Whilst accepting Jordan's contention that a basic income may empower people and enable them to contribute in the decision-making processes that are open to them, his analysis does not necessarily explain how relations between groups and communities are going to be negotiated, especially when there may be vast power differentials between the actors. In this light Jordan might be wise to countenance his own advice that 'cooperation under circumstances of unequal power and wealth is fragile, and trust can be easily destroyed' (Jordan 1998: 192). His basic contention that social justice emerges through a process of dialogue and that inequality does not preclude the achievement of agreement is sound, but he does not provide us with the mechanism through which those from different communities are to establish the foundations of agreement when they may disagree over the nature of political engagement and the public sphere. His preferred strategy is the liberal notion of compromise, whereby difference is encouraged within 'the mutual acceptance of an agreement'. He summarises this approach as follows:

> [L]iberal compromise requires negotiation for a mutually satisfying solution, when there is a collective problem . . . to be solved. The art of compromise involves recognizing situations where the only possible solution is the second-best option for all parties . . . But above all, compromise relies on the practice of reciprocity and mutual respect in negotiation, and encourages members of a political community to accommodate each other's values and principles. It appeals to common ground that can only be constructed in dialogue, and not settled in advance; and to some underlying principles of justice, tradition and common interest. This form of compromise is a good in itself, because it supplies the sense of empowerment and inclusion, even though none of the parties can achieve all their goals. (Jordan 1998: 192–3)

This model of empowered groups engaging in debate within a framework of compromise is also reflected in Ulrich Beck's radical programme for a new politics. Building on his earlier theories of risk society and reflexive modernisation, Beck contends that a new radical democratic politics will facilitate critical reflection and participation from a range of associational groups and movements in civil society. Here he focuses on what he calls 'subpolitics', that is, the growing importance of politics beyond the formal understanding of government and the state. Thus he is concerned with the 'self-organised politics' that takes place outside of the formal political arena.

In the context of risk society subpolitics features groups with a reflexive relationship with the environment around them. In this sense there is a scepticism or a critical relationship between individuals and groups on the one hand and the traditional sources of political and social authority on the other. Beck's thesis corresponds with the radical democratic agenda precisely because it recognises and indeed encourages sources of conflict as evidence of a critical politics. This equates to a fundamentally different understanding of the political than that in the formal political arena: 'politics breaks open and erupts *beyond* the formal responsibilities and hierarchies . . . the political constellation of industrial society is becoming *un*political, while what was unpolitical in industrialism is becoming *political*' (Beck 1997: 99). For Beck, this is evidence of the reinvention of politics.

Beck's thesis on the reinvention of politics imagines the political sphere as much more fluid and less systematic than the old political organisation. Thus there is little fixity and less certainty than in orthodox understandings of politics as the formal arena of parties and parliaments. What Beck rejects, in a vein similar to André Gorz, is the nature of systems and the rules and regulations that tend to characterise systems generally. Subpolitics, on the other hand, refers to political activity that does not merely follow externally directed rules but is instead reflexive, that is, subpolitics involves attempts to change the rules of the political game. Thus subpolitics 'is measured by the *degree* and *quality* of politics' (Beck 1997: 134). Beck's depiction of the reinvention of politics as a more creative, critical set of attitudes accompanied by scepticism of established institutions is an alluring prospect for radical visions of community. However the real existence of a qualitatively superior political sphere is somewhat questionable. Beck rightly notes the growth of scepticism and cynicism with regard to the formal political arena and the individuals and parties that occupy it. Similarly his idea of a public that is critical of scientific rationality and traditional sources of authority and hierarchy is also sound. However, this does not equate with a qualitatively better politics. In many respects what we tend to see is the extension of civic privatism where individuals withdraw from political debate due to their disregard for the traditional way of doing politics. Individuals, rather than immersing themselves in the political, may retreat into a world of family, job and narrow individualistic concerns.

Of course, Beck would be right to argue that these are indeed intensely political spaces and the potential sources of new political debates. However, this does not mean that the ways in which we interact within these new political spheres is automatically a *qualitative* improvement in the nature of politics. Similarly the idea that our privatistic engagement with our narrow world could result in a rule-changing politics seems aspirational rather than a representation of contemporary reality. Nonetheless the overall rejection of the formal political arena is commonplace – the question is what replaces it? Arguably in the contemporary era there is something of a political vacuum and an absence of legitimacy in the formal processes of government. However that does not entail a replacement of a tired old politics with a new vibrant, dynamic form of participatory engagement. Where Beck is persuasive is in identifying the need to replace dying political institutions with more radical arrangements, but he must also recognise the resilience of the state and the difficulties of bringing about a programme of reform. In other words the crisis of the current system – that is, the absence of legitimacy in the public eye – does not translate into its replacement with superior institutions or better forms of decision-making.

Beck's analysis of the conditions of the new modernity is based upon doubt, scepticism and criticism. As such, it relates clearly to radical democratic politics and radical rather than orthodox theories of community. For Beck, doubt and scepticism are positive phenomena because they question old truths and the validity and legitimacy of any claims of truth. In this sense, doubt legitimises criticism and scepticism of all of our views – if we can challenge the validity of the views of others then perhaps we can accept that our own views may not be true. Importantly Beck sees this as a scenario with the potential to do away with others as 'enemies' – others become 'fellow or opposing doubters' because 'doubt implies multiple voices, opposing voices on all sides and in each of us' (Beck 1997: 169). The universality of doubt is of course dubious. The idea that we are all equally beset by doubt clearly does not characterise the contemporary world, but Beck is persuasive in arguing that the acceptance of doubt and criticism offers a basis upon which to develop the kind of compromise that Jordan advocates. Nonetheless decision-making, even if doubt prevails, must have some kind of basis in rationality. Beck recognises that new forms of rationality will emerge but also that such rationalities are not in themselves truths. Radical communitarian politics are more likely to emerge when we recognise that our rationalities are competing and may not be appropriate. We are more likely to compromise or accept our failure to have our way on a given issue when we are able to question the validity of all our rationalities. Nonetheless there is little evidence that such a culture of self-doubt exists in contemporary society. If anything, the scepticism about politics and science that Beck proclaims has led to a retreat into private certainties and a lack of willingness to countenance the fallibility of our own rationalities. If this is the case, then the creation of a politics without enemies is still remote – yet again, it is a radical aspiration rather than a representation of contemporary reality.

– TOWARDS A POLITICS WITHOUT ADVERSARY? –

It is essential for radical democratic politics and with that the radical vision of community that the renewal of politics creates new forms of solidarity. This kind of solidarity is what is referred to as 'politics without enemies' (Beck 1998) or, in more developed form, agonistic pluralism in which there is opposition and conflict but not adversaries (Mouffe 2000b). Where orthodox political communitarianism attempts to override difference and conflict by constructing and imposing moral unity, radical theories embrace conflict and argue that solidarity can emerge from the expression of our diversity and the varying rationalities that our outlooks on life generate. Mouffe expresses this perspective in forthright terms:

> A well-functioning democracy calls for a confrontation between democratic political positions, and this requires a real debate about possible alternatives. Consensus is indeed necessary but it must be accompanied by dissent . . . Consensus is needed on the institutions which are constitutive of democracy. But there will always be disagreement concerning the way social justice should be implemented in these institutions. In a pluralist democracy such a disagreement should be considered as legitimate and indeed welcome. (Mouffe 2000b: 113)

Mouffe's thesis contends that difference and conflict are necessary and welcome to a functioning pluralist democracy, but that these disagreements must be agonistic rather than antagonistic. Thus her position suggests that it is not disagreement *per se* that inhibits contemporary democracies, but, rather, it is the antagonistic fashion in which such differences manifest themselves that generates political and social problems. Therefore she contends that 'the aim of democratic politics should be to provide the framework through which conflicts can take the form of an agonistic confrontation among adversaries instead of manifesting themselves as an antagonistic struggle between enemies' (Mouffe 2000b: 117). The problem of orthodox political communitarianism is that it pretends that confrontation can be overridden by the dominant morality. By trying to circumvent disagreement and present a politics in which conflict does not and need not occur, orthodox communitarians reject pluralism and diversity (regardless of the rhetoric they employ). A genuinely democratic pluralism must recognise the unavoidability of confrontation and dispute. The challenge, then, is to construct ways of overcoming such conflict in the process of reaching decisions and avoiding social fragmentation. Communitarianisms (or liberalisms for that matter) that want to constrain such expressions of plurality to the private sphere lead to exclusionary outcomes. A system that decides *ex ante* what ideas and rationalities are to govern the public sphere cannot accommodate diversity in an inclusive fashion. The system of public expression is itself subject to conflict and debate. There is no universal set of institutions or principles to which all societies can adhere and thereby guarantee pluralistic democracy and diversity.

What then are to be the forms of deliberation that allow society to function? If conflict is unavoidable, how will society be held together? Clearly the answers to these questions will not be clear cut if they can be answered at all. What must be rejected is the idea that we can reach a harmonious consensus on these issues. By their very nature these questions lead to disagreement rather than consensus. There is no one rationality that can provide the answers to these questions but merely competing perspectives on the preferred system to meliorate these disagreements. For theorists such as Mouffe this leads to a rejection of models of deliberative democracy such as those developed (in different ways) by Habermas and Rawls. Thus, she argues that there are no universally applicable procedural criteria that can circumvent power inequalities that exist within pluralistic societies. Moreover attempts to find a rationality that encapsulates these universal procedures merely reflect the beliefs of certain individuals and groups and are therefore interpretations of rationality rather than empirical facts. Just as diverse societies will generate disagreement, so such competing views on the world will lead to competing rationalities. The attempt to assert the legitimacy of one over any other reflects certain vested interests rather than universality or impartiality. To this end, Mouffe asserts that 'it is not by providing arguments about the rationality embodied in liberal democratic institutions that one can contribute to the creation of democratic citizens. Democratic individuals can only be made possible by multiplying the institutions, the discourses, the forms of life that foster identification with democratic values' (Mouffe 2000b: 96). From this perspective, the critique of liberal democratic theory constructed by deliberative democrats is accepted. What is not is the way that they replace orthodox theories of liberal democracy with their own alternative procedures and rationalities. In short Mouffe argues that we need to put 'the emphasis on the types of *practices* [of democracy] and not the forms of *argumentation*' (Mouffe 2000b: 96).

Importantly, Mouffe sees power as inescapable insofar as it is 'constitutive of social relations'. The fallacy in models of deliberative democracy, then, is their attempt to construct political spaces in which power relations either do not exist at all or are irrelevant in that public sphere. It is this critique that forms the foundation of 'agonistic pluralism'. If power is unavoidable, the political programme becomes one in which power is reconstructed to become more compatible with democratic values. However it also recognises that the system that would emerge from this basis would be imperfect, that is, that there is no political system that can provide an ideal method of reconciling power and democracy. Thus the former is always likely to compromise the latter. In this sense there is no precise definitive form of democracy, although we can still argue whether societies are more or less democratic. For Mouffe, antagonism and hostility are inescapable in social relations characterised by diversity, and the role of politics is not to establish a democratic consensus or rationality – she regards this as impossible – but to find ways in which we accept difference but don't regard those different from us as adversaries. Thus others with alternative views should be treated as 'legitimate opponents'; they have just as much right to hold to their own rationalisation of the world as we have. This involves a commitment to allow others to express their values in the public sphere (as long as they, too, are committed to such an expression on the part of others). Furthermore, it suggests that everyone must be aware that their own rationality will not always prevail.

Mouffe's argument relies upon the political transformation of the antagonism that will always arise from incommensurable value pluralism into 'agonism'. Here she suggests that antagonism constitutes relations between enemies, whereas agonism refers to disagreements between legitimate adversaries. The system she envisages, then, seeks to channel antagonism into a recognition of the value of disagreement to democracy:

> [T]he ideal of a pluralist democracy cannot be to reach a rational consensus in the public sphere. Such a consensus cannot exist. We have to accept that every consensus exists as a temporary result of a provisional hegemony, as a stabilization of power, and that it always entails some form of exclusion. The ideas that power could be dissolved through a rational debate and that legitimacy could be based on pure rationality are illusions which can endanger democratic institutions. (Mouffe 2000b: 104)

– Conclusion: A Political Programme? –

Critics might justifiably ask where all of this leaves us. The radical democratic model and the radical view of community do not provide us with an ideal type of the kind of political arrangements that such theoretical perspectives favour. This is a reasonable criticism, but there is no reason why this position is inherently weaker than those that present universal models of procedural justice or communicative rationality. The strength of radical democracy lies in the recognition that the practicalities of the real world are not reflected in more orthodox perspectives. The greatest weakness of political communitarianism is its failure to recognise that the 'community' that it constructs as the key agent of the cohesive society is a fallacy. Imposing homogeneity or universal theories of rationality detaches the political commentator from the realities of pluralist societies. The radical model doesn't provide clear answers to the problems of organising diverse societies or the limitations of liberal democracy, but perhaps that is because those answers do not exist.

Lest it be argued that the position outlined here results in a mélange of relativism, we should be clear about the radical approach to community and its implications for democratic politics. It is intensely political. It wants to spread the expression of different perspectives in the public sphere. It does not see diversity as a private issue but wants to open up the public sphere to an ever increasing set of political perspectives. It is a recipe for a partici-patory politics, but in the sense that we need to open up more avenues for political expression – politics is not merely about making decisions but about a real process of deliberation in which the agreement of all is unlikely. This, it is suggested, would be facilitated by a recognition that participation in the public sphere is not currently assisted by social and economic provisions in most Western liberal democracies. The argument constructed here implies that we need to encourage and enable people to participate in their communities and to bring their perspective to the negotiating table. The reality is that such negotiation will sometimes reap rewards but at times it will not. In some cases a dilution of principles through compromise will be the result of negotiation, in others values will be so incommensurable that such a compromise is impossible.

Following this model, it is clear that the appropriate political arrange-ments themselves will be a source of conflict and a process of negotiation. They will not be perfect whatever arrangements can be agreed upon, but they will be subject to change through continual, ongoing engagement of adversaries. It may well be true that the arrangements that emerge will represent the wishes and interests of powerful groups in society, as is the case today. However, the radical communitarian politics examined in this book suggest different ways of empowering different groups in society. By recognising the impossibility of constructing a political system without reference to social and economic power differentials, the radical theory of community attempts to facilitate challenges to the dominant hegemonic political order. Certainly it does not provide all of the answers to the many difficult questions we face, but it does envisage a political process towards change that is arguably more grounded in reality than either liberal universalism or orthodox political communitarianism.

CHAPTER 8

Pluralism, Community and Civil Society

The democratic renewal of liberal democracies has become a commonplace theme in contemporary political theory. This suggests that there is a widely held view that there is some kind of democratic deficit in advanced capitalist societies. Moreover it reflects an acceptance of the need to rethink political structures to meet the requirements of an increasingly complex world. In this context there has been a new awakening of interest in the idea of civil society. Communities often feature in civil society theories insofar as the latter are frequently concerned with ways in which groups and associations co-exist in the conditions of pluralism and diversity. Because civil society theory focuses on the sphere of life beyond the reach of the state and the private domain of the individual, it is not surprising that discourses on community might emerge within it. However, the existence of communities within civil society is often implicit, and they are rarely differentiated from other types of group or association. In this sense the utility of civil society for the advancement of community needs to be examined. This chapter explains how the theory of civil society has evolved in recent years and the ways in which, despite its potential as a source of furthering community, it also throws up obstacles to the realisation of community.

The impetus for the re-emergence of the idea of civil society in contemporary politics emanates from the failure of state socialism as practised in former communist regimes on one hand and the problems that have become evident in the market-driven experiments in some Western countries since the 1980s on the other. Nonetheless there has been little agreement regarding how the process of democratisation might manifest itself. However, one common theme has been the focus on civil society as the social sphere in which political renewal might take place (see, for example, Hall

1995; Cohen and Arato 1994; Gellner 1994; Seligman 1992). In these works and others civil society has emerged as a vital space in any democratic society. An example of this trend is provided by Giddens:

> The democratising of democracy also depends upon the fostering of a strong civic culture. Markets cannot produce such a culture. Nor can a pluralism of special-interest groups. We shouldn't think of there being only two sectors of society, the state and the market-place – or the public and the private. In between is the area of civil society, including the family and other non-economic institutions. Building a democracy of the emotions is one part of a progressive civic culture. Civil society is the arena in which democratic attitudes, including tolerance, have to be developed. The civic sphere can be fostered by government, but is in turn its cultural basis. (Giddens 1999: 77–8)

These comments incorporate some of the key dimensions of the new theory of civil society. Giddens recognises the limitations of orthodox pluralist theory and the problems for civic culture that are generated by the hegemony of market discourses. Moreover he also states the case for the interdependence of the state and civil society as opposed to traditional approaches that have emphasised their separation. According to the latter perspective, civil society has been regarded as the social sector that is beyond the jurisdiction of the state but also contains associations that are outside of the private sphere of the individual. Thus, historically, civil society has been depicted as a site for the operation of markets that can be freed from regulation by the state. From this we can see how the debate over civil society has been marked by ambiguity over the public or private nature of civic relations and the impact of markets upon civic culture. In this sense a thorough rethinking of civil society must contain both a political and an economic dimension.

The approach adopted here sets out from the supposition that civil society is not a given in any particular society, but that the form that it takes depends upon the relationship with the state at any one time. Thus civil society can be strengthened or weakened through political initiatives. This stands in contrast to theorists, such as Francis Fukuyama (1996), who regard civic structures as essentially culturally defined and are less prepared to countenance the political manufacture of civic culture. On the left, especially under the influence of Gramsci, civil society had been flagged up as a key factor in the reproduction of capitalism. The latter is not achieved through the control of the state alone or the economic base, but rather it is also facilitated through a range of forms throughout society in which capitalist hegemony is maintained. Thus capitalist reproduction was cultural and social as well as economic. Power is wielded and maintained through an integrated set of institutions imbued with particular values and not merely by market mechanisms alone. Thus many on the left have had to accept that markets cannot be eradicated or wished away and therefore, 'we are all going to have to live with some mix of market and state orchestration. The difficult question is what mix suits each society' (Taylor 1997: 68). It is in this context that we see why civil society has become such a deeply contested concept in the social sciences. Civil society is not a simplistic 'politics-free sphere', but rather it seems that the 'definition we accept of civil society will have important consequences for our picture of the free society and hence our political practice' (Taylor 1997: 77). Thus the nature of social pluralism and the possibilities for a multiplicity of communities existing alongside one another depend as much upon political factors as historical developments or cultural predispositions towards a diverse and pluralised form of civil association.

The focus on civil society, evident in the work of commentators such as Fukuyama (1996, 1999) and Giddens (1998, 1999) in recent times, represents a reassertion of the primacy of the third sector, that is, the ill-defined sphere that lies between the state and the individual. As we have seen, for Fukuyama, the regeneration of civil society would provide the trust and social capital that would assist the successful working of the economy. Thus, the social glue or cement of society would not be provided by the state nor could we rely upon isolated individuals to formulate spontaneously the kinds of relationships that assist companies to work most efficiently. From Fukuyama's perspective, we need bodies such as churches and charities, communities and local associations that ground people in civil society. According to this model then, civil society is not merely an end in itself, but rather it is viewed as a part of society that assists economic operations, and indeed it is the sphere in which markets are able to operate free from regulation or state intervention. In this sense there is an obvious attraction of civil society to conservative and/or liberal theory, and it has been used similarly by centre-left theorists, such as Giddens (and politicians such as Tony Blair), who try to offer a radical new politics without providing fundamental challenges to the hegemony of globalised markets (Hughes and Little 1999).

An initial problem that emerges here is the assumption that communities and other associations in civil society are ready and able to provide the democratic function that cannot be supplied by the bureaucratic state, market mechanisms or private individuals. Charles Taylor (1997) has noted the difference between the view that civil society exists if there are bodies free from state power and more radical perspectives in which society is organised by free organisations. Arguably commentators such as Fukuyama conflate these two positions in assuming that, because civic associations exist, it is a relatively simple step in empowering them to take up key roles in democratic organisation. Similarly, Giddens has constructed a 'third way between left and right' that rests upon enabling civil society to carry out the democratic functions that have been flawed in both traditional social democracy and economic liberalism. Even in these moderate centrist proposals for civil society, there is an acceptance that many advanced capitalist societies in the contemporary world demonstrate unacceptably high levels of fragmentation and social disintegration. This is the territory on which radical commentators have entered the debate and taken an increasing interest in civil society theory.

Theorists such as John Keane (1988, 1998) have analysed civil society as a forum that may be able to rectify both the limitations of the state and the failings of market-based economies. From this radical perspective we need to challenge the relationships between the state, civil society and markets on the basis that civil society should be empowered because of the importance of associations therein, whereas Fukuyama's liberal-conservative thesis sees civil society as worthy of special consideration because it would shore up market economies. Where Fukuyama argues that civil society complements markets, radicals such as Gorz argue that 'there can't be democracy without a much more substantial civil society comprising a set of self-organized public activities recognized and protected by the state. Socialism was born out of a conflict between civil society and the market' (Gorz 1994: 83). Gorz's argument expresses the need for a political engagement between the state and bodies in civil society rather than the anti-statist perfectionism of traditional pluralism. This radical view of civil society sees it as a highly differentiated and particularistic environment that enables individuals to pursue a multiplicity of forms of membership and inclusion. For Gorz, there is a role for political institutions within the state to enable diversity to flourish. In this sense the existence of particularism and diversity in civil society is predicated upon a universal guarantee from the state that we can find a multiplicity of forms of membership. Thus, universalism is viewed as a facilitator rather than an opponent of particularism and diversity. Keane hints at a similar position in arguing that 'while a more democratic order cannot be built through state power, it cannot be built without state power' (Keane 1988: 23).

In Keane's early work there was a somewhat optimistic vision of civil society as the environment in which radical democratic ideas could flourish. There was relatively little discussion of the problems that might emanate within civil society – instead it was presented as the antidote to the problems of the market and the state. Perhaps this was not surprising given the apparent problems of communism in Eastern Europe and its imminent downfall, along with the social problems that were evolving in the context of the Thatcher–Reagan flirtation with free-market economics. However, whilst still a passionate advocate of civil society as a venue for political and social regeneration, Keane's later work would be more focused on the potential problems of this process as well as the benefits which would accrue from its implementation. With this in mind we should be wary of accounts of civil society in which it is celebrated as the antidote to the failings of statism and economic liberalism. In complex societies such simplistic solutions are unlikely to work, and it seems clear that the democratic renewal of the public sphere will generate new sources of political conflict rather than harmony and consensus.

The Challenge of Democratising Civil Society and the Public Sphere

As we can see, much debate on the nature of civil society relates to its place with respect to the state on one hand and the economic sphere on the other. Many recent attempts have been made to argue for a civil society that is freed from the administrative bureaucracy of the state system (as in the work of Habermas 1996) and/or the economic rationality of markets (Gorz 1989). According to these theories, civil society should be encouraged as a sphere of dialogue and identity, an area in which solidarity can develop free from external rationalities associated with markets or the state. These perspectives have been challenged by Keane (1998), who believes that these narrow definitions of civil society as economically passive disempower the groups and associations therein because they would be deprived of the property resources that bring power. He also believes that the Habermasian approach neglects the positive freedoms that can be generated through the economic sphere. Thus, the latter is more than a sphere of necessity, and indeed Keane suggests that, like Fukuyama, the success of the economic sphere is related to the extent of its embeddedness in civic cultures of trust and social capital. However, by Keane's reckoning, there are also limitations to the integrative possibilities of markets by themselves, and therefore there is a role for civil society alongside market mechanisms:

> 'market failures' . . . demonstrate that markets cannot create social order because the vital ingredients of social order cannot be produced by market interaction. Where there are no markets, civil societies find it impossible to survive. But the converse rule also applies: where there is no civil society, there can be no markets. (Keane 1998: 19)

Thus, Keane sees civil society as an integrative mechanism that has a symbiotic relationship with markets – the two rely on one another to perform different social functions. He sees civil society as the means through which collective actors exercise the power to influence and affect social and political structures. However in his later work Keane has also turned his attention to the impediments to this kind of participation, and he notes some of the problems of violence and incivility that characterise contemporary societies. As such, he identifies the challenges for theorists of civil society and recognises the dangers that arise from existing social and political arrangements. Whilst he remains a fervent supporter of the potential of civil society in invigorating the public sphere, he is also reluctant to glorify it as the great hope for a renewed democratic polity.

Keane published *Reflections on Violence* in 1996, which marked a more critical appraisal of civil society than had been the case in his path-breaking work of the 1980s. In this book he attempted to get to grips with a broader global understanding of the different forms of civil society that exist in the world. Thus he tackles the misguided perception that civil society is a feature of the developed Western societies and not the developing world. In this sense he suggests that in the global system nations are interlinked and that liberal democracies comprise violent and non-violent elements, much the same as other parts of the world. In this sense democracy, in itself, is not a guarantor of non-violence. Indeed, given the risk society thesis described by Ulrich Beck (1992), the fear and/or experience of violence may be more acute in Western societies than in other parts of the world. Historically then, there has been a tradition of violence and cruelty within civil society, but this has not prevented the rediscovery and popularity of civil society in contemporary political debate as an antidote to despotism and Soviet-style totalitarianism. Keane is critical of liberal perspectives that depict civil society as a sphere of liberty freed from political power, as in the work of Ernest Gellner (1994). Thus, whilst an ideal-type civil society may be a sphere of equal opportunities and scope for self-improvement, the very complexity, diversity and pluralism that it encourages also contains sources of conflict and violence. In the words of Hall, 'civil society is thus a complex balance of consensus and conflict, the valuation of as much difference as is compatible with the bare minimum of consensus necessary for settled existence' (Hall 1995: 6).

Keane, then, has moved somewhat from his position in the 1980s in pointing out that there is a negative side to civil society. There is, he suggests, a history of incivility that has accompanied the process of 'civilisation'. Nonetheless Keane believes that, on the whole, the historical process of civilisation has been characterised by progress from incivil society towards greater civility and a decrease in some forms of violence. At the same time what can also be identified is the way in which the discretionary use of violence has been located within the modern state for specific ends such as obtaining justice or preserving rights. In this sense the state in modernity has tried to take violence out of the arbitrary domain of civil society and provide a legal monopoly of force. Despite this, however, Keane argues that the history of the twentieth century – 'the long century of violence' – has demonstrated the limitations of the evolutionary approach to civil society. Thus he points out that violence has always existed in civil society, and that civil society can regress into uncivil society. In other words, there is no evolutionary pathway from uncivil to civil society but that political decisions can impact upon social relations in such a way as to create new sources of violence.

Keane uses this perspective to examine the ways in which we use terms such as civilisation. Analysing the work of Norbert Elias, he describes how the belief has arisen in the West that the developed world is more civilised than less developed countries. Keane argues to the contrary in stating that that viewpoint is both myopic and arrogant. Elias argues that theories of civilisation developed alongside the growth of the modern state – thus it was the process whereby force was legally monopolised by the state that brought about the decline of violence. The modern state grew within the context of an international system in which war (or the threat of war) became central to the civilising process. States attempted to engender civilising tendencies and adopted less bellicose attitudes to others because of the threat of violence from other states. According to this viewpoint then, the modern state was civilising, both within its sphere of jurisdiction and beyond on the wider international level. Keane believes there is considerable mythology surrounding this model. The modern state, he argues, has historically been shown to employ violent and barbaric methods both on its own citizens and towards other states. This is a fundamentally modern development wherein states attempt to pursue and acquire power over their internal peoples and also the peoples of other states. The threat of this kind of incivility is wielded by states through 'the rational-calculating use of violence' to ensure the compliance from groups of people over whom the state exercises its power. It is precisely for this reason that Keane wants to strengthen civil society against the power of the modern state by demonstrating the 'limitations of barbarism'. Thus he states of civil society that:

> There, in areas of life underneath and outside of the state, it can empower its followers by stimulating their awareness that large-scale organisations, such as transnational firms and state bureaucracies, even violent ones, ultimately rest upon the molecular networks of power of civil society – and that the strengthening and transformation of these micro-power relations necessarily affect the operations of these large-scale organisations. (Keane 1996: 103–04)

Keane's message is that the long century of violence and the continuation of violence and uncivil wars, often fought on issues of religion and nationality, should teach us that democratisation must focus on institutions below the level of the state. It is only through establishing and empowering institutions of civil society that the state can be prevented from continuing to exercise power in ways that sometimes leads to violent and uncivil outcomes. At the same time, a civic culture that promotes diversity and particularism and is opposed to attempts to impose universal moral standards must also recognise that conflict may emerge. Civil society, then, may be promoted as an alternative to state power, but, at the same time, it is not a panacea for the problems that exist in contemporary societies.

– DIVERSITY, PLURALISM AND CIVIL SOCIETY –

The potential of civil society for the advancement of pluralism and equality has been highlighted in communitarian terms most notably by Michael Walzer (1983, 1992). Walzer has been a critic of the radical left because, he argues, it has traditionally either 1) glorified the state and the wider political community as the primary site of action, or 2) resorted to a utopian economistic belief in the primacy of co-operative work as the unifying feature of the relationship between the state, civil society and individuals (Walzer 1992: 91–4). Thus Walzer, in rejecting both these critiques of pluralism, advocates a potential regeneration of civil society as the venue in which individuals can participate pluralistically in social life. He believes that this provides a framework for 'a project of projects' under which citizens can regain lost powers and influence over politics and the economy through small-scale activities and decisions made in the domain of civil society. This would spawn 'a new recognition . . . that the good life is in the details' (Walzer 1992: 107). Walzer's argument suggests that civil society can become the location in which market organisations and state organisations can compete and co-operate, free from the constraints that previously bound their interactions, such as bureaucracy. In this scenario the state could develop a framework for a value-free civil society that would be an arena in which a variety of bodies and institutions (including those of the state and market-oriented firms) could operate freely (see also Walzer 1995).

There are two key criticisms to be made of Walzer's perspective with regard to the radical rethinking of community and civil society. First, his supposition of a value-free civil society neglects the particular principles and values that are imbued within state institutions and market mechanisms. To suggest that civil society would be a neutral venue in which profit-making bodies or state regulation would seamlessly interact appears to overlook the actual rationality that impels the forces of the state or markets. Walzer's position neglects power differentials between consumers and presupposes the absence of vested economic interests. According to Keane (1996, 1998), the promotion of civil society must not overlook the propensity of conflict leading to uncivil tendencies manifesting themselves in violence. Thus civil society must not be idealised as the location of unadulterated interaction between equally endowed groups who come together with benign, altruistic intentions. Whilst this is indeed a desirable scenario, it overlooks not only uncivil tendencies created by individuals and groups, but also the ways in which incivility and violence can be generated by state institutions and the unfettered operation of market mechanisms. In this sense, a radical democratic perspective must recognise that the advocacy of civil society as a strengthened sphere implies plurality and difference that may be integrative in some cases but also holds the potential for the expression of conflict (Keane 1998).

The second critical point with regard to Walzer's argument is his failure to identify the role of the state in manufacturing a civic space in which the state would not have primary jurisdiction and where the particular logic of market mechanisms would not dominate other principles such as friendship, voluntarism and co-operation, which are related to community. This criticism does not merely apply to Walzer's conception of the macro-political level. In *Spheres of Justice* (1983) he conflates the pursuit of recognition in the eyes of others with economic activity in a form that suggests that individuals' source of recognition lies in competitive relations with regard to others. Of course, this assumption is manifest in much economic activity (especially in the domain of work-for-wages) but pays insufficient attention to the recognition and status that can (and should) be derived from non-economic activities. Thus O'Neill argues that Walzer wrongly conflates recognition with economic value, and that economic status does not necessarily embody any notion of virtue: 'Appearance is something that is vied over by competitors in a market. The idea of independent worth disappears' (O'Neill 1998: 108). This implies that independent worth becomes subsumed by work-based definitions of identity and value in contemporary Western societies. A more radical theory of community, on the other hand, suggests that some of the most important virtues that individuals acquire and demonstrate are more likely to be manifest in non-economic sectors of social life.

Nonetheless Walzer's argument remains useful for theorists concerned with a radical rethinking of pluralism, insofar as it recognises the importance of the state in fostering the conditions under which the expansion of civil society can take place. Moreover he also identifies the need for associations with political agency if a more democratic civil society is to emerge. In this sense civil society remains a domain of political contestation between groups with differing objectives in mind. This is not to say, however, that civil society should be reinvigorated to provide a new sphere of interaction between the state and the market as Walzer implies. Rather, civil society should be designed to encompass a kind of pluralist micro-politics that, although likely to influence major social and economic decision-making, is not dominated by state regulation or economic values. This suggests 'a process of rebuilding associations from below, by political campaigning and voluntary action in civil society' (Hirst 1995: 111). Similarly, Walzer implies a kind of associationalism whereby economic actors operate in civil society alongside communities that do not have economic objectives as their primary aim. This underestimates the hegemony of the logic of market mechanisms. Walzer fails to grasp the ways in which economic rationality spreads its pervasive influence into other spheres of life and comes to dominate in areas where its specific logic is not necessarily the most appropriate rationality (see Little 2000).

A more radical pluralist viewpoint than Walzer's would require a sphere for community action that was actually protected from economic values. The reason for this is straightforward; where communities, as defined upon the principles identified here, such as compassion, friendship, co-operation and mutual obligations, operate on the basis of non-economic objectives, bodies or associations acting for economic ends cannot have the principles of community at heart. The efficient pursuit of economic imperatives such as profit and growth cannot *prioritise* virtues such as voluntarism and friendship. The implications of this position should be clear: the *prioritisation* of community necessitates a sphere free from the direct control of the state and the pernicious influence of market mechanisms – this is what O'Neill refers to as a non-market order (O'Neill 1998). This is not to say that we should try to eradicate market mechanisms. On the contrary, there must be a highly important area of interaction and regulation between the state and the market, but a separate civic sphere for communities must be created in which the principles of community would prevail. Although Keane (1998: 16–19) is sceptical of attempts, such as that of Habermas, to draw concrete lines between political and economic systems on the one hand, and a sphere of freedom in civil society on the other, he does recognise that 'market forces tend to spread into every nook and cranny of social life, thereby violating its plurality of voices and identities' (Keane 1998: 19; see also Hirst 1994). The question then remains over the strategy that theorists of civil society should follow in addressing the pervasive spread of market values with their potentially deleterious effect on civic virtues. One possible answer that we will address in due course is the idea of a multiplicity of public spheres in which different values could predominate. This approach is based on the recognition that 'individuals no longer inhabit a single "public sphere", nor is their citizenship conferred upon them through a singular relationship with the state' (Rose 1999: 178).

The analysis of civil society theories such as those of Walzer and Keane offers a timely corrective to the dominance of economic thinking in modern politics. Where neither of them subscribe to the view that it is essential to manufacture an identifiably non-economic sphere, they do imply that it is important to resurrect opportunities for micro-political influence. However, both fail to explain how a sphere of micro-politics might be protected from the economic rationality of markets. The danger remains in the work of both Walzer and Keane that the public expression of civic virtues might be overridden by the logic of the economic. An alternative view is expressed by O'Neill:

> The tendency to picture social and economic life in terms of either an all embracing centralised planning board or the governance of market norms

underplays the way both can disrupt other important institutions in which knowledge is embodied and distributed and through which individuals' activities are coordinated. The classical notions of politics as an association of associations deserves to be revived if for no other reason than to stand as a corrective to this picture. (O'Neill 1998: 159)

Implicit in this cry for the rejuvenation of associational politics is a recognition that the prominence in political debates of arguments over state regulation and market freedoms is an indicator of the economism of orthodox political discourses. Nowhere is this more evident than in the explicit attempts of Tony Blair's Labour government in the UK to tackle the acknowledged problem of social exclusion through a waged-work-based strategy that ignores the sources of integration and social co-operation that exist beyond the formal economic sphere. Indeed, we might argue that work-based theories of social integration pander to economic liberal perceptions of individual worth. Whilst, undoubtedly, the opportunity to work is a central feature of debates surrounding the future of citizenship, especially with regard to economic rights (Little 1998), the focus on this type of activity to the exclusion of others (primarily unpaid) serves to cloud judgement on the nature of social solidarity. Rather than relying wholly on economic and work-based interpretations of the ingredients that bring social integration, radical approaches to the conceptualisation of civil society should recognise that the bonds that hold society together – the relations of solidarity that exist to a greater or lesser extent in any given society – are as much derived from non-economic activities (if not more so) than the traditional concerns of political economy. Moreover the radical reinterpretation of these relations of solidarity should recognise that the bonds within society as a whole do not emerge fully formed as a by-product of our economic arrangements. Rather, they must be created and policy initiatives in both the economic and social domains will impact upon the nature of the social relations that exist. As such, the radical rethinking of pluralism and civil society should recognise that the promotion of a politics of difference must engage with the social and economic conditions in the world today.

– Civil Society and New Modernity –

As we saw in the previous chapter, the influential German social commentator Ulrich Beck (2000) has attached considerable significance to new forms of technology and their social and economic implications. He argues that a post-industrial society is coming into being and that we are entering an era in which many of the old certainties of the modern world will be swept away to be replaced with a culture of doubt. This involves an acceptance that the orthodoxy of right and wrong is undermined and that there will be a greater emphasis upon the multiplicity of ways of understanding the world in which we live. The unifying universalistic logic of the state becomes less applicable and this provides new scope for the more particularistic environment of civil society. Thus Beck states that 'doubt points the way to a new modernity. It is more modern than the old, industrial modernity we know. The latter, after all, is based on certainty, on repelling and suppressing doubt' (Beck 1997: 173). This is a reflection of the complexity of contemporary politics, whereby older notions of universalism will be replaced by a realisation that the concretisation of the universal lies in an understanding of the particular. Moreover, this complexity undermines traditional sources of authority and proffers opportunities for a reflexive engagement with contemporary political debates. Here the idea of civil society is a social space in which the multiplicity of political ideas and perspectives can interact.

Beck argues, in a similar manner to André Gorz (1999), that the system of work that characterised capitalist modernity is breaking down and, as a consequence, the value system of society that has traditionally relied on orthodox understandings of work is becoming increasingly irrelevant. Beck believes that the risk of unemployment is now ubiquitous and universal and that this 'post-work society' requires a new democratic order. Thus, according to Beck, we cannot ignore the growing problems of Western capitalism, not least the threat to democracy that emanates from new patterns of unemployment and underemployment. He argues that Western capitalism has always linked political freedoms to material security and that citizenship and democratic participation has been predicated upon notions of full employment. Whilst politicians continue to employ the rhetoric of the latter, a new reality is beginning to emerge that undermines democracy. Capitalism is increasingly jobless – growth no longer brings more employment – and little public finance exists to rectify this situation. Thus, For Gorz:

> It has to be recognized that neither the right to an income, nor full citizenship, nor everyone's sense of identity and self-fulfilment can any longer be centred on and depend upon occupying a job. And society has to be changed to take account

of this . . . The place of work in everyone's imagination and self-image and in his/
her vision of a possible future is the central issue in a profoundly political conflict,
a struggle for power. (Gorz 1999: 54)

In this context, Beck calls for greater recognition of 'public work', which he
sees as 'an odd blend of politics, care for others and everyday cooperation'
(Beck 1998: 60). He believes that this can feed into new forms of active
democracy in which decentralisation and citizen participation are the key
guiding processes. Put simply, Beck sees this as a recipe for the rejuvenation of
civil society in which we should invest and delegate authority. The empowerment of civil society would involve measures to try and give status to unpaid
work and activities within the private and public spheres that were carried out
without remuneration as a primary purpose. For Beck, this would provide the
material and cultural foundations for 'individualism coupled with solidarity'
(Beck 1998: 60). Like many contemporary radical commentators, Beck
expresses some support for a form of guaranteed minimum income payment
for citizens as a means of supporting this investment in social capital.

In this context it is important to return to the perspective on civil society
that is provided by John Keane in *Civil Society* (1998). In this work Keane
demonstrates how complex civil society is and he reiterates that we should
be wary of theories which suggest that civil society can be separated off from
the economy or a broader political society. Thus he suggests that it is
problematic to view civil society as a sphere of freedom whereas the
economy or the state comprise the realm of necessity. Similarly, Keane
rejects the Habermasian dichotomy between the system and the lifeworld,
and argues that in an era of individualism and pluralism conflict and
confusion between the two are likely to occur. Thus civil society is regarded
as a venue in which conflict takes place and is resolved or contained – it is in
this sense deeply political. According to Keane's theory, then, civil society is
'a signifier of plurality' (Keane 1998: 53), and this means that we need to
avoid justifying civil society on the basis of substantive grounding principles
or foundations such as justice, rights or utility. At the same time it is the
venue in which these kinds of values should be debated and evaluated;
Keane is therefore not seduced by the 'abyss' of relativism. Instead, he
proffers a need for new forms of political thinking through which institutions can be created that facilitate democracy. This democracy must
recognise plurality and difference: 'democracy has to live with those who
are unfriendly to democracy. It has to tolerate the intolerant. It has to take
pity on those who know no pity' (Keane 1998: 61).

Keane rejects the Marxian perspective that theorising civil society is a bourgeois enterprise and critically argues against Marxist ideas regarding the inherently problematic nature of the state and civil society. Where for orthodox Marxists both the state and civil society must be overcome, for Keane, both must be strengthened and democratised. Whilst he associates problems of violence and incivility with the operation of the state, he realises the necessity of state mechanisms in facilitating political structures that could empower a democratised civil society. Thus he sees the civic bond between individuals as one of the forms of association that play a part in any healthy democracy and the latter implies a plurality of perspectives followed by free citizens. Moreover, if these associations are to be facilitated, then the role of the state is paramount in ensuring that the requisite services are provided:

> [D]emocracy . . . requires various governmental and non-governmental social policies (in fields such as health, education, child care and basic income provision) which prevent the market exchanges of civil society from becoming dominant and thereby ensure that citizens can live as free equals by enjoying their basic political and civil entitlements. (Keane 1998: 88)

This necessitates a rethinking of the relationship between the state, the economy and civil society. There has been a long tradition of theory that attempts to differentiate and protect civil society from both the state and the economy, but Keane makes the case for a more integrated approach. Thus he suggests that rather than a singular entity, we need to envisage three different types of public sphere: the micro-public, meso-public and macro-public spheres. The first refers to small group or associational relations on a sub-state level, the second entails larger groups interacting on the nation-state level, and the third refers to political disputation on the global, supranational level. Issues will filter across these levels and individuals may participate in different ways in these overlapping domains. For Keane, we must legitimise each of these spheres to vindicate a diversity of forms of public/civic activity. Thus we must enable people to participate democratically within a range of associations – from small local communities to international social movements. This diversified view of civil society is another reflection of the complex nature of associations beyond the state and the variety of ways that humans interact with one another.

Implicit in Keane's argument is that non-economic activities should be encouraged and legitimised. However, he does not provide a counterbalance to the pervasive influence that market mechanisms have on civic life, nor does he provide a solution to the deleterious affect markets can have on the possibilities of legitimising the non-market order. In this sense, his theory of civil society can be criticised for failing to give significant weight to the dominance of the economic dimension and the obstacles that it provides to the expansion of civil society. His theory of different levels of public sphere is useful in demonstrating the wide range of associations that we have on different levels and he implies that non-economic activities should be valued. However, he does not suggest that we need to protect rights to non-economic activity explicitly through guaranteeing a sphere of life in which market mechanisms will not predominate. Thus, his interpretation of the interaction of the economy and the public sphere is problematic. His theory is primarily focused on the political sphere, and yet the different types of structures that he identifies therein could apply to the economic as well. Thus, if we can assert that there are differing levels of public sphere that comprise the relationship between civil society, individuals and the state, then it is also possible to suggest that a distinction could be made between economic and non-economic activities as well. In this sense we could have spheres of life in which market mechanisms predominate or where paid work is the primary form of activity, and, at the same time, others that would be protected from the particular logic and rationality that emanates from modern economic concerns.

Like many commentators analysed in this book, Keane hints at support for a basic income (although in little detail), and yet he fails to capitalise on the opportunities that basic income could open up for limiting economic rationality and vindicating life activities and communities that do not have instrumental gain as their prime objective. Such is his focus on political structures and institutions that the possibilities opened up by social and economic developments for democratic renewal do not feature as prominently in Keane's work as they should. The potential for dealing with the social and economic issues raised by 'the end of work' thesis is expressed in more detail by Barber:

> Globalizing markets and anti-governmental paranoia have obscured our civic vision, making it hard for us to see that there is a place for us between big government and commercial markets, where citizens can breathe freely and behave democratically without regarding themselves as passive complainers, grasping consumers, or isolated victims. (Barber 1998: 10)

– CIVIL SOCIETY, GOVERNMENT AND THE MARKET –

Two different perspectives on the relationship between civil society and markets and the state are beginning to emerge that transcend divisions between the orthodox and the radical. The first view which is evident in the work of Fukuyama and Giddens and, more radically, Keane and Walzer does not attempt to protect civil society from the influence of market rationality (although some of them recognise the detrimental impact that markets may have on civic virtues). The second view, evident in the work of radicals such as Gorz and O'Neill and more mainstream commentators such as Barber, is that civil society should be constructed as an arena in which market logic should not prevail. Given the earlier discussions of the first perspective, the last section of this chapter will examine the arguments put forward for separating markets and civil society.

Benjamin Barber (1998) identifies three main approaches to civil society that he characterises as the libertarian, communitarian and strong democratic perspectives. The libertarian viewpoint is criticised because it relies upon a view of civil society as a synonym for the private sector, in which the market prevails as the mediator of differing private individual freedoms. It rejects the interference of government in issues that are not deemed to be a matter of public concern. The communitarian viewpoint is criticised by Barber for the opposite reason. Rather than civil society being a surrogate for the private sector and a negative view of individual liberty, communitarians 'think of civil society as a zone where people interact and are embedded in communities, and they treat it as the condition for all social bonding' (Barber 1998: 23). Obviously this resonates with some of the ideas which have been discussed during the course of this book, especially with regard to the embeddedness of individuals in various bonds of association. However, Barber is quick to point out that there is a paradox of communitarianism insofar as it is made possible by pluralistic values whilst simultaneously containing potentially exclusionary features. Thus 'democratic community is certainly no oxymoron, but community has ideal attributes that resist democracy, while democracy makes demands that can undermine community' (Barber 1998: 25). Clearly this comment corresponds with our earlier critique of the moral authoritarianism in some orthodox political communitarian perspectives, however we should be careful not to dismiss communities *per se* when they may well, given the appropriate environment and civil society, correspond fairly closely with democratic virtues. Nonetheless Barber is correct to identify the problems that develop when civil society is represented as the public domain of a unified community. As such he rightly notes that, whilst community is not inherently exclusionary, in practice it has often been manifest in authoritarian or hierarchical forms. In this sense, the libertarian and communitarian perspectives on civil society are problematic for Barber because they are constructed around a public–private divide that reflects an outmoded agenda on government and markets. Thus 'neither the libertarian nor the communitarian model serves as effectively as it might to make the revitalizing of civil society a condition for taming markets, civilizing society, and democratizing government' (Barber 1998: 16).

What, then, of Barber's third approach? He depicts this as the strong democratic perspective that is founded upon the idea of civil society as the space between government and markets. This stance represents an attempt to grapple with the plurality of identities that individuals have and the differing purposes to which they apply their skills and talents. As such, Barber does not want to deny the benefits that may accrue from market interactions or strong inclusive communities, but rather he wishes to recognise the multiplicity of associations to which individuals belong. Thus he foresees not only a strong public sector in which regulation by government institutions is prominent and a private sector in which market exchange may be the dominant form of interaction, but also:

> a third domain mediating between them, sharing the virtues of each. This third, independent sector is defined by its civic communities – their plurality is its essence – which are membership associations that are open and egalitarian enough to permit voluntary participation. (Barber 1998: 34–5)

Barber is aware that a perfectionist account of relations in civil society is unlikely to survive the scrutiny of comparison with the real world, and thus, whilst he does want to promote openness and voluntary participation, he recognises that this may not always be the case. Most important, though, is the way in which civil society could combine some of the virtues of the public and private sectors. In Barber's eyes civil society must try to engender the openness of the public realm with the voluntarism and lack of coercion that he sees as characteristic of the private sector. It is this interaction that he regards as the key process in achieving democracy, that is, a society marked by pluralism and a degree of equality. The latter vision of civil society is certainly one that moves beyond orthodox communitarianism and provides an environment in which radical theories of community could flourish. The existence of a multiplicity of communities (some of which may not be as open or voluntaristic as a perfectionist account would suggest as the ideal) provides a basis for people to engage in a degree of choice over which associations they belong to in civil society. For this reason 'pluralism is the condition of liberty in a strong democratic civil society. More is better' (Barber 1998: 36).

Barber's model of civil society can be criticised for exaggerating the harmonious relationships that might ensue from a strong democratic civil society. He offers us little by way of a challenge to the expansionist horizons of economic rationality whereby the values of 'the market' are spread widely throughout society and come to dominate spheres of life where those values are wholly inappropriate. Perhaps he underestimates the proselytising zeal of the ideology of work and its proponents in the fields of economics and politics. This is not say that he is not aware of the problems of modern political economy. Indeed, under the influence of Rifkin's 'end of work' thesis (2000), Barber points out the paradoxes in contemporary discourses on work and welfare and notes the economic policies of Lionel Jospin's socialist government in France as an attempt to grapple with some of these contradictions. However, he appears to offer more of a diagnosis of the problems of civil society than a remedy for the social and economic problems which impair it (Barber 1998: Chapter 5). This is not to reject his model but merely to suggest that sterner governmental action than he implies may be necessary to create a space in which market values do not prevail. Thus his advocacy of civil society as a space between government and market is appropriate but perhaps does not grasp the ways in which this space must be protected against the power of the private or public sectors (Gorz 1999). His statement that 'civil society is . . . public without being coercive, voluntary without being privatized' (Barber 1996: 271) does not explain how exactly those values are to be cultivated without them becoming coercive or privatistic. Without being an ideal solution, a guaranteed income of some kind might provide a buttress against the expansionism of the state and markets into a potential civic sphere by empowering people to make lifestyle choices that are not governed by alternative rationalities (Barber discusses stakeholding and a participation income very briefly in Chapter 5 of A Place For Us (1998)).

The question that Barber needs to address, then, is what are the conditions under which strong democratic civil society can develop? As is evident in the following passage, he articulates how it might constrain governments and markets but does not explain how this situation might arise:

> Interposed between the state and the market, it [civil society] can constrain an obtrusive government without ceding public goods to the private sphere; at the same time, it can dissipate the atmospherics of solitariness and greed that surround markets without suffocating in an energetic big government's exhaust fumes. For *both* government *and* the private sector can be humbled a little by a growing civil society that absorbs some of the public aspirations of government, without casting off its voluntary character as a noncoercive association of equals. (Barber 1996: 274)

To be fair, Barber is aware that the assertion of civil society and strong democracy is not a sufficient condition of their realisation. Nonetheless his suggestion that his proposals do not 'entail a novel civic architecture' (Barber 1996: 274) raises questions over the extent to which he is genuinely offering an alternative to current arrangements. He is quite right to recognise that bodies such as communities and associations already exist and perform an important role in society. If this is the case, though, we must then ask why it is that these communities and associations do not presently perform the function of the regulatory civil society that Barber imagines. The answer may lie in the reality that the pervasiveness of markets and the expansionism of government may not reside happily alongside a strengthened civil society. Barber argues that we need a 'civic forum' in which the participating voice of civil society can be heard. Thus the articulation of the public voice would help to rein in government and markets. But, as we have argued in the course of this book, the voice of civil society, of community, is unlikely to be unitary or consensual. Indeed, it is the condition of diversity that would allow civil society to be strengthened, but this negates the possibility of a singular public voice emerging. In this sense we need to recognise the role of civil society in the process of governance, but also the need for the state to arbitrate where incommensurate voices are unable to reach agreement.

Such a process of strengthening civil society does rely upon government and politics. The political will is required to formalise the process – that it will just occur is wishful thinking and it underestimates the power of vested interests. It is important to avoid merely advocating civil society as a substitute for the requirement for a democratic political process and the need to convince people of the desirability of a civic forum of the kind that Barber envisages. In short, despite his awareness of the socio-economic issues involved, Barber focuses mainly on the political forms that would enable civil society to flourish. Democratisation and diversified governance are regarded as mainly political exercises. The theories examined through the course of the book suggest that a meaningful conception of community, and civil society as the space in which communities find their voice, must be framed within economic and social policies as well as the formalities of political processes. To do so, we must recognise the obstacles to civic participation upon which big government and markets have established their hegemony and legislate to limit their spheres of jurisdiction.

CONCLUSION: CREATING DEMOCRATIC CIVIL SOCIETY

It should be clear that there are numerous perspectives on civil society and, most importantly, on the relationship between civil society, government and markets. Despite the multiplicity of perspectives on civil society, it has been most notable as an idea that has allowed a new imagining of the public sphere (Misztal 1996: 212). In the hands of communitarian orthodoxy, civil society is a sphere in which a civic voice can be expressed because there is only one community with a shared moral concern. However, most analysts of civil society look beyond this narrow vision of community and recognise that there will be a plurality of voices and different moral concerns if a healthy civil society is to emerge. Insofar as it contributes to a democratic politics, then, civil society contributes to solidarities predicated on difference because it is 'forged out of alliances between people who are different' and 'sees community as constructed in an explicitly political realm. It is "constructed" that is the key word here, implying a process based on different constitutive elements that may continue to be in tension' (Phillips 1999: 108). In the hands of commentators such as Habermas and Barber, there is a suggestion that these differences do not prevent the articulation of a civic voice. However, it has been suggested here, in line with notions of agonistic pluralism, that civil society would be a sphere of disagreement as much as one of a cohesive public voice. Indeed the strength of civil society, according to the latter perspective, is that conflicting perspectives can be expressed through our chosen associations, but that these conflicts need not result in antagonism between enemies. In terms of community, similar ideas are articulated by Rose:

> [C]ommunities can be imagined and enacted as mobile collectivities, as spaces of indeterminacy, of becoming. To community as essence, origin, fixity, one can thus counterpose community as a constructed form for the collective unworking of identities and moralities. Once more, this is to suggest the possibility of an

explicit and agonistic ethico-politics, where the values of different forms of life
would be directly at stake. (Rose 1999: 195)

Thus we see the first major dividing line on civil society is that between
those who regard it as a sphere in which a form of unity emerges out of
difference and those who see the actual expression of difference as the
source of solidarity and do not require civil society to generate a universal
public voice. It is the latter perspective that holds potential for the
expression of a radical politics of community.

The second major dividing line in civil society theory relates to the
relationship between civil society and markets. Where it is generally
accepted that a strong civil society would be independent of state governance (although there is difference on how this might manifest itself), there is
considerable disagreement on the link between economic interactions and
civil society. There are a multiplicity of fault lines on this issue. Economic
thinkers such as Francis Fukuyama see a symbiotic relationship between
civil society and the economy whereby they reinforce one another and
generate social virtues which underpin economic success. This view is blind
to the social disintegration and disruption that is caused by markets,
especially as they expand into ever more areas of social life. Others such
as Anthony Giddens and John Keane advocate civil society without
challenging the operation of market interactions therein. They are merely
one set of relations (albeit not necessarily the most civic ones) within a
range of interactions. This view is grounded in reality but is problematic
insofar as it does not engage with the damage that pervasive market
interactions have on social life. They do not merely co-exist alongside
other relations but tend to spread their tentacles as widely as possible in
order to widen and reproduce spheres of profit and growth. This issue has
been addressed by Benjamin Barber, who argues for a civil society constructed around the openness of the public sphere and the voluntarism of
the private domain. However, Barber does not really address economic and
social policies, and focuses instead on the politics of civil society. Again this
runs the dangers of underestimating the ways in which markets can pose just
as much a threat to the health of civil society as overweening government
and heavy-handed regulation through state bureaucracy.

Between these differing views on civil society we can outline a perspective that offers genuine possibilities for the realisation of the principles of
community. In his recent work Keane (1998) has outlined a theory of
different levels of public sphere to recognise a variety of different types of

association. Whilst he does not extend this argument to the role of the economic, it is possible, following Gorz (1989, 1999), to argue for a differentiated public domain in which markets have their place but where there are also spaces constructed for non-economic, non-instrumental associations or communities to operate. The means of achieving such a goal need not entail the construction of overt barriers between different public spheres but, by using social policies to guarantee incomes for security, by using economic policies to redistribute work and assist social inclusion, and by using political reforms to construct more participatory forms of governance, we see possibilities for radical reform. Such a process is difficult, and a perfect model will not emerge, but this appears to offer the most constructive imagining of community and civil society. Unlike orthodox communitarianism, it does not attempt to impose moral unity and certainty, but instead it thrives on diversity and forms of solidarity that are not predicated upon a unitary moral culture. In short, such an understanding of civil society provides the most appropriate model for contemporary societies that are characterised by complexity.

Conclusion

The analysis of the concept of community provided in this book does not lead to a definitive statement of what community looks like or how it is to be inculcated. In many respects we reach the end of the book with more questions than answers. Nonetheless this is an inevitable consequence of a thorough evaluation of community. Discourses on community have been obscured by the way in which the concept has been subsumed within debates on communitarianism. This is problematic because, on the one hand, the philosophical analysis tends to offer little by way of strategies for practical enactment, whilst, on the other, orthodox political communitarianism tends to lose sight of the political implications of diversity and value pluralism. In the lacuna that emerges between these two elements of communitarian thinking, critics have been able to attack the pursuit of community as an incoherent project and question the utility of community as a valuable and achievable political concept. This book has attempted to rethink the way in which we understand community and asserted its importance and validity in the face of critics from across the ideological spectrum. In so doing, however, the argument has resisted the temptation to provide a tight, prescriptive definition of community. Rather, the interpretation here suggests that community takes on a multiplicity of forms and that these will vary in their make-up and constitution. The problem that then emerges is how to accommodate such a loose understanding of community in our social, economic and political arrangements.

The process of outlining the complexity of community has been the main objective of the book. If, at the outset, it was argued that it has been neglected as a concept, in conclusion we can say that when community is subjected to more thorough evaluation, a rather complicated picture emerges. However, rather than trying to override this complexity by manufacturing a mythical definitive community, the analysis has suggested that we should try to accept community for what it is. In other words, it cannot be strictly defined and any attempt to do so tends to oversimplify the various forms of community that exist. After all, if communitarians are critical of liberals for creating an abstract self that is antecedently individuated, then they should be careful not to impose an equally imagined abstract community with little real foundation in the realities of the modern world. It is for this reason that such a broad understanding of community has been employed here. Of course, the question might arise as to why we should be interested in community if it takes on so many forms that we think it futile to assert definitive principles. The answer is that within the variety of communities that exist certain principles and virtues tend to be exhibited. At the same time many of these virtues appear to be under attack in the contemporary world, such is the hegemonic power of economic rationality and pervasive spread of the logic of markets. Thus, the advancement of community as a political concept seeks to justify and validate virtues such as care, compassion, altruism and obligation in the face of the prevailing conditions of modern societies that often undermine these practices.

Clearly this model of community is not perfectionist but focuses instead on finding strategies and spaces that allow communities to experience these virtues. However, a non-perfectionist model must be careful not to eulogise community. On the contrary, we must realise that the empowerment of communities will give rise to vices as well as virtues and give rise to dissonant voices. Thus community should not be promoted as a panacea to whatever problems exist in contemporary societies. However, it can be advanced as a part of the process of grappling with the difficulties that diversity and incommensurable value pluralism can give rise to. Such a process does not provide answers or solutions to these problems but merely recognises that they will emerge in one form or another, regardless of the policies and practices in which we engage. This is a highly political model of community, insofar as it does not attempt to superimpose an overall morality that must govern all or a set of political structures that can solve definitively the problems of value pluralism. In this sense the way of dealing with these problems is part of the political debate itself; ideal political institutions are not imposed but are instead the subject of political dialogue. Similarly the social and economic measures that have been discussed in the course of this book are about facilitating the conditions upon which all groups in society are able to participate fully in these political debates.

However, the policies that are employed to achieve the latter objective will also be the subject of political discourses and conflict. Thus, unlike many perfectionist theories of community, the approach favoured here has been one that tries to open up political debate to further participation and critical engagement.

The overarching theme of the book is that such participation and critical engagement is unlikely to be advanced in the context of the expansion of market discourses. In this sense we require a 'moral vocabulary' that enables us to open up dialogue on ethical problems to replace the impoverishment of debate by 'the language of markets and choice' (Pinkard 1995: 114). There is, of course, an appropriate space for the latter but, following Walzer, there are also other spheres of justice in which such language is not so fitting. Of course, the process of defining where market discourses are appropriate and where they are not is part and parcel of the path towards democratic renewal itself. Again, there is no perfectionist model but merely an attempt to open out political debate and enable greater involvement in the decision-making process. This overall objective is neatly summarised by Kallscheuer, who argues that we need to 'accept the process of modern individualization and fragmentation of social spheres, but . . . try to reintegrate modern society by means of a process of self-government, which would develop the pluralism of life-spheres without abandoning the demo-cratic hopes of (classical) modern philosophy in a common good' (Kallscheuer 1995: 141). From this perspective, community remains a vibrant and dynamic concept. Whilst it may have been appropriated by a range of commentators and politicians to substantiate widely differing ideological objectives, it retains a critical power. The failure of these attempts to commandeer community to serve other ends do not make the concept unimportant or less alluring. Instead, they crystallise the need to restate community and reopen dialogue on its possible meanings. At the very least, even if the normative contents of this analysis of community generate equal amounts of support and opposition, I hope to have con-tributed to the vital process of the renewal of critical discourses on community.

Bibliography

Abrams, P. (ed.) (1978), *Work, Urbanism and Inequality*, London: Weidenfeld and Nicholson.

Aristotle (1996), *The Politics and the Constitution of Athens*, ed. S. Everson, Cambridge: Cambridge University Press.

Atkinson, A. B. (1996), 'The Case for a Participation Income', *The Political Quarterly*, 67, pp. 67–70.

Atkinson, D. (1994), *The Common Sense of Community*, London: Demos.

Avineri, S. and de-Shalit, A. (eds) (1992), *Communitarianism and Individualism*, Oxford: Oxford University Press.

Barber, B. R. (1996), 'An American Civic Forum: Civil Society between Market Individuals and the Political Community', *Social Philosophy and Policy*, vol. 13, no. 1, Winter, pp. 269–83.

Barber, B. R. (1998), *A Place For Us: How to Make Society Civil and Democracy Strong*, New York: Hill and Wang.

Barry, B. (1995), *Justice as Impartiality*, Oxford: Clarendon.

Bauman, Z. (1998), *Work, Consumerism and the New Poor*, Buckingham: Open University Press.

Baumeister, A. (2000), *Liberalism and the 'Politics of Difference'*, Edinburgh: Edinburgh University Press.

Beck, U. (1992), *Risk Society: Towards a New Modernity*, London: Sage.

Beck, U. (1997), *The Reinvention of Politics*, Cambridge: Polity Press.

Beck, U. (1998), *Democracy without Enemies*, Cambridge: Polity Press.

Beck, U. (2000), *The Brave New World of Work*, Cambridge: Polity Press.

Blair, T. (1996), *New Britain: My Vision of a Young Country*, London: Fourth Estate.

Boswell, J. (1994), *Community and the Economy: The Theory of Public Co-operation*, London: Routledge.

Braithwaite, J. (1989), *Crime, Shame and Re-integration*, Oxford: Oxford University Press.

Braithwaite, J. (1993), 'Shame and Modernity', *British Journal of Criminology*, vol. 33, no. 1, pp. 1–18.

Brittan, S. (1996), *Capitalism with a Human Face*, London: Fontana.

Brown, A. (1986), *Modern Political Philosophy: Theories of the Just Society*, London: Penguin.

Campbell, T. (1988), *Justice*, London: Macmillan.

Carling, A. (1996), 'Prosperity, Autonomy and Community: John Gray on the Market, Politics and Values', *Imprints*, vol. 1, no. 1, pp. 26–45.

Carling, A. (1999), 'New Labour's Polity: Tony Giddens and the "Third Way" ', *Imprints*, vol. 3, no. 3, pp. 214–42.

Carter, A. and Stokes, G. (eds) (1998), *Liberal Democracy and its Critics*, Cambridge: Polity Press.

Carter, J. (ed.) (1998), *Postmodernity and the Fragmentation of the Welfare State*, London: Routledge.

Charman, S. and Savage, S.P. (1999), 'The New Politics of Law and Order: Labour, Crime and Justice', in M. Powell (ed.) *New Labour, New Welfare State?*, Bristol: The Policy Press.

Cochrane, A. (1998), 'Globalisation, Fragmentation and Local Welfare Citizenship', in J. Carter (ed.) *Postmodernity and the Fragmentation of the Welfare State*, London: Routledge.

Cohen, J. and Arato, A. (1994), *Civil Society and Political Theory*, Cambridge, MA: MIT Press.

Compston, H. (ed.) (1997), *The New Politics of Unemployment: Radical Policy Initiatives in Western Europe*, London: Routledge.

Conway, D. (1996), 'Capitalism and Community', *Social Philosophy and Policy*, vol. 13, no. 1, Winter, pp. 137–63.

Crawford, A. (1999), *The Local Governance of Crime*, Oxford: Oxford University Press.

Crow, G. and Allan, G. (1994), *Community Life: An Introduction to Local Social Relations*, Hemel Hempstead: Harvester Wheatsheaf.

Dean, J. (1996), *Solidarity of Strangers*, Berkeley: University of California Press.

Driver, S. and Martell, L. (1998), *New Labour: Politics after Thatcherism*, Cambridge: Polity Press.

Duncan, A. and Hobson, D. (1995), *Saturn's Children: How the State Devours Liberty and Prosperity*, London: Sinclair-Stevenson.

Dwyer, P. (2000), *Welfare Rights and Responsibilities: Contesting Social Citizenship*, Bristol: The Policy Press.

Ellison, N. and Pierson, C. (eds) (1998), *Developments in British Social Policy*, London: Macmillan.

Etzioni, A. (1993), *The Spirit of Community: Rights, Responsibilities and the Communitarian Agenda*, New York: Crown.

Etzioni, A. (ed.) (1995a), *New Communitarian Thinking: Persons, Virtues, Institutions, and Communities*, London: University Press of Virginia.

Etzioni, A. (1995b), 'Old Chestnuts and New Spurs', in A. Etzioni (ed.), *New Communitarian Thinking*, London: University Press of Virginia.

Etzioni, A. (1996), *The New Golden Rule: Community and Morality in a Democratic Society*, New York: Basic Books.

Etzioni, A. (2000a), 'Isolate Them', *The Guardian*, 19 September.

Etzioni, A. (2000b), 'Banding Together', *Times Literary Supplement*, 14 July.

Everson, S. (1996), 'Introduction', in Aristotle, *The Politics and the Constitution of Athens*, Cambridge: Cambridge University Press.

Fletcher, G. P. (1996), 'The Case for Tolerance', *Social Philosophy and Policy*, vol. 13, no. 1, pp. 229–39.

Fowler, R. B. (1995), 'Community: Reflections on Definition', in A. Etzioni (ed.), *New Communitarian Thinking: Persons, Virtues, Institutions and Communities*, London: University Press of Virginia.

Frazer, E. (1996), 'The Value of Locality', in D. King and G. Stoker (eds), *Rethinking Local Democracy*, London: Macmillan.

Frazer, E. (1998), 'Communitarianism', in A. Lent (ed.), *New Political Thought*, London: Lawrence and Wishart.

Frazer, E. (1999), *The Problems of Communitarian Politics*, Oxford: Oxford University Press.

Frazer, E. and Lacey, N. (1993), *The Politics of Community: A Feminist Critique of the Liberal-Communitarian Debate*, Hemel Hempstead: Harvester Wheatsheaf.

Fukuyama, F. (1992), *The End of History and the Last Man*, London: Hamish Hamilton.

Fukuyama, F. (1996), *Trust: The Social Virtues and the Creation of Prosperity*, London: Penguin.

Fukuyama, F. (1999), *The Great Disruption: Human Nature and the Reconstitution of Social Order*, London: Profile.

Garland, D. (2001), *The Culture of Crime*, Oxford: Oxford University Press.

Gellner, E. (1994), *Conditions of Liberty: Civil Society and its Rivals*, London: Penguin.

Giddens, A. (1998), *The Third Way: The Renewal of Social Democracy*, Cambridge: Polity Press.

Giddens, A. (1999), *Runaway World: How Globalisation is Reshaping our Lives*, London: Profile.

Goodin, R. E. and Pettit, P. (1993), *A Companion to Contemporary Political Philosophy*, Oxford: Blackwell.

Goodin, R. E. and Pettit, P. (eds) (1997), *Contemporary Political Philosophy*, Oxford: Blackwell.

Gorz, A. (1989), *Critique of Economic Reason*, London: Verso.

Gorz, A. (1992), 'On the Difference between Society and Community, and Why Basic Income Cannot by Itself Confer Full Membership of Either', in P. van Parijs (ed.), *Arguing for Basic Income*, London: Verso.

Gorz, A. (1994), *Capitalism, Socialism, Ecology*, London: Verso.

Gorz, A. (1999), *Reclaiming Work: Beyond the Wage-Based Society*, Cambridge: Polity Press.

Gray, J. (1995), *Enlightenment's Wake: Politics and Culture at the Close of the Modern Age*, London: Routledge.

Gray, J. (1997), *Endgames: Questions in Late Modern Political Thought*, Cambridge: Polity Press.

Green, D. (1993), *Reinventing Civil Society*, London: Institute of Economic Affairs.

Green, D. (1996), *Community Without Politics: A Market Approach to Welfare Reform*, London: Institute of Economic Affairs.

Gutmann, A. (1992), 'Communitarian Critics of Liberalism', in S. Avineri and A. de-Shalit (eds) *Communitarianism and Individualism*, Oxford: Oxford University Press.

Habermas, J. (1996), *Between Facts and Norms*, Cambridge, MA: MIT Press.

Hall, J. A. (ed.) (1995), *Civil Society: Theory, History, Comparison*, Cambridge: Polity Press.

Harvey, D. (1993), 'Class Relations, Social Justice and the Politics of Difference', in J. Squires (ed.) *Principled Positions*, London: Lawrence and Wishart.

Hirst, P. (1994), *Associative Democracy: New Forms of Economic and Social Governance*, Cambridge: Polity Press.

Hirst, P. (1995), 'Can Secondary Associations Enhance Democratic Governance?', in E. O. Wright (ed.), *Associations and Democracy*, London: Verso.

Hirst, P. (1997), *From Statism to Pluralism*, London: UCL Press.

Hirst, P. (1998), 'Social Welfare and Associative Democracy', in N. Ellison and C. Pierson (eds) *Developments in British Social Policy*, London: Macmillan.

Hirst, P. and Thompson, G. (1996), *Globalization in Question*, Cambridge: Polity Press.

Hollenbach, D. (1995), 'Virtue, the Common Good and Democracy', in A. Etzioni (ed.) *New Communitarian Thinking: Persons, Virtues, Institutions, and Communities*, London: University Press of Virginia.

Hughes, G. (1996), 'Communitarianism and Law and Order', *Critical Social Policy*, Issue 49, vol. 16, no. 4, pp. 17–41.

Hughes, G. (1998), *Understanding Crime Prevention: Social Control, Risk and Late Modernity*, Buckingham: Open University Press.

Hughes, G. (2001), 'The Competing Logics of Community Sanctions: Welfare, Rehabilitation and Restorative Justice', in E. McLaughlin and J. Muncie (eds) *Controlling Crime*, London: Sage.

Hughes, G. and Little, A. (1999), 'The Contradictions of New Labour's Communitarianism', *Imprints*, vol. 4, no. 1, Summer, pp. 37–62.

Hutton, W. (1996), *The State We're In*, London: Vintage.

Hutton, W. (1997), *The State To Come*, London: Vintage.

Jordan, B. (1976), *Freedom and the Welfare State*, London: RKP.

Jordan, B. (1989), *The Common Good*, Oxford: Blackwell.

Jordan, B. (1990), *Social Work in an Unjust Society*, Hemel Hempstead: Harvester.

Jordan, B. (1992), 'Basic Income and the Common Good', in P. van Parijs (ed.) *Arguing for Basic Income*, London: Verso.

Jordan, B. (1996), A Theory of Poverty and Social Exclusion, Cambridge: Polity Press.

Jordan, B. (1998), The New Politics of Welfare: Social Justice in a Global Context, London: Sage.

Kallscheuer, O. (1995), 'On Labels and Reasons: The Communitarian Approach – Some European Comments', in M. Walzer (ed.) Toward a Global Civil Society, Oxford: Berghahn.

Keane, J. (1988), Democracy and Civil Society, London: Verso.

Keane, J. (1995), Tom Paine: A Political Life, London: Bloomsbury.

Keane, J. (1996), Reflections on Violence, London: Verso.

Keane, J. (1998), Civil Society: Old Images, New Visions, Cambridge: Polity Press.

Kenny, M. (1996), 'After the Deluge: Politics and Civil Society in the Wake of the New Right', Soundings, no. 4, pp. 13–27.

King, D. and Stoker, G. (eds) (1996), Rethinking Local Democracy, London: Macmillan.

King, D. and Wickham-Jones, M. (1999), 'Bridging the Atlantic: The Democratic (Party) Origins of Welfare to Work', in M. Powell (ed.), New Labour, New Welfare State?, Bristol: The Policy Press.

Kukathas, C. (1996), 'Liberalism, Communitarianism, and Political Community', Social Philosophy and Policy, vol. 13, no. 1, Winter, pp. 80–104.

Kumar, K. (1978), Prophecy and Progress: The Sociology of Industrial and Post-industrial Society, Harmondsworth: Pelican.

Kymlicka, W. (1992), 'Liberal Individualism and Liberal Neutrality', in S. Avineri and A. de-Shalit (eds), Communitarianism and Individualism, Oxford: Oxford University Press.

Kymlicka, W. (1993), 'Community', in R. E. Goodin and P. Pettit (eds), A Companion to Contemporary Political Philosophy, Oxford: Blackwell.

Lent, A. (ed.) (1998), New Political Thought, London: Lawrence and Wishart.

Lister, R. (1997), Citizenship: Feminist Perspectives, London: Macmillan.

Lister, R. (1998), 'Citizenship and Difference: Towards a Differentiated Universalism', European Journal of Social Theory, vol. 1, no. 1, July, pp. 71–90.

Little, A. (1996), The Political Thought of André Gorz, London: Routledge.

Little, A. (1997), 'Flexible Working and Socialist Theories of Welfare', Imprints: A Journal of Analytical Socialism, vol. 1, no. 3, March, pp. 37–56.

Little, A. (1998), Post-industrial Socialism: Towards a New Politics of Welfare, London: Routledge.

Little, A. (1999), 'The Politics of Compensation: Tom Paine's "Agrarian Justice" and Liberal Egalitarianism', Contemporary Politics, vol. 5, no. 1, March, pp. 63–73.

Little, A. (2000), 'Environmental and Eco-social Rationality: Challenges to Political Economy in Late Modernity', New Political Economy, vol. 5, no. 1, pp. 121–34.

Little, A. (2002), 'Working Time Reductions', in M. Cahill and T. Fitzpatrick (eds), Greening the Welfare State: Theories, Critiques and Reforms, London: Palgrave, forthcoming.

Lodziak, C. (1995), *Manipulating Needs: Capitalism and Culture*, London: Pluto Press.

MacIntyre, A. (1981), *After Virtue: A Study in Moral Theory*, London: Duckworth.

MacIntyre, A. (1992), 'Justice as a Virtue: Changing Conceptions', in S. Avineri and A. de-Shalit (eds), *Communitarianism and Individualism*, Oxford: Oxford University Press.

McLaughlin, E. and Muncie, J. (eds) (2001), *Controlling Crime*, London: Sage.

Mason, A. (ed.) (1998), *Ideals of Equality*, Oxford: Blackwell.

Mason, A. (2000), 'Communitarianism and its legacy', in N. O'Sullivan (ed.) *Political Theory in Transition*, London: Routledge.

Mendus, S. (1989), *Toleration and the Limits of Liberalism*, London: Macmillan.

Miller, D. (1992), 'Community and Citizenship', in S. Avineri and A. de-Shalit (eds) *Communitarianism and Individualism*, Oxford: Oxford University Press.

Miller, D. (1995), *On Nationality*, Oxford: Oxford University Press.

Miller, D. (1998), 'Equality and Justice', in A. Mason (ed.), *Ideals of Equality*, Oxford: Blackwell.

Miller, D. (2000), *Citizenship and National Identity*, Cambridge: Polity Press.

Miller, D. and Walzer, M. (eds) (1995), *Pluralism, Justice and Equality*, Oxford: Clarendon Press.

Mishra, R. (1999), *Globalization and the Welfare State*, Cheltenham: Edward Elgar.

Misztal, B. A. (1996), *Trust in Modern Societies*, Cambridge: Polity Press.

Mouffe, C. (ed.) (1992), *Dimensions of Radical Democracy: Pluralism, Citizenship, Community*, London: Verso.

Mouffe, C. (1993a), *The Return of the Political*, London: Verso.

Mouffe, C. (1993b), 'Liberal Socialism and Pluralism: Which Citizenship?', in J. Squires (ed.), *Principled Positions*, London: Lawrence and Wishart.

Mouffe, C. (1998), 'The Radical Centre: A Politics without Adversary', *Soundings*, Issue 9, Summer, pp. 11–23.

Mouffe, C. (2000a), 'For an Agonistic Model of Democracy', in N. O'Sullivan (ed.) *Political Theory in Transition*, London: Routledge.

Mouffe, C. (2000b), *The Democratic Paradox*, London: Verso.

Mulhall, S. and Swift, A. (1997), *Liberalism and Communitarianism*, Oxford: Blackwell, second edition.

Nicholson, L. (ed.) (1990), *Feminism/Postmodernism*, London: Routledge.

Nicholson, P. (1995), 'Aristotle: Ideals and Realities', in B. Redhead, *Plato to NATO: Studies in Political Thought*, London: Penguin/BBC Books.

Nisbet, R. A. (1969), *The Quest for Community*, Oxford: Oxford University Press.

O'Brien, M. and Penna, S. (1998), *Theorising Welfare: Enlightenment and Modern Society*, London: Sage.

Ohmae, K. (1995), *The End of the Nation State*, London: HarperCollins.

O'Neill, J. (1995), 'Polity, Economy, Neutrality', *Political Studies*, vol. 43, no. 3, September, pp. 414–31.

O'Neill, J. (1998), *The Market: Ethics, Knowledge and Politics*, London: Routledge.

O'Sullivan, N. (ed.) (2000), *Political Theory in Transition*, London: Routledge.

Paine, T. [1776] (1987), 'Common Sense', in M. Foot and I. Kramnick (eds), *The Thomas Paine Reader*, London: Penguin.

Phillips, A. (1996), 'Feminism and the Attractions of the Local', in D. King and G. Stoker (eds) *Rethinking Local Democracy*, London: Macmillan.

Phillips, A. (1999), *Which Equalities Matter?*, Cambridge: Polity Press.

Philpott, J. (ed.) (1997) *Working for Full Employment*, London: Routledge.

Pinkard, T. (1995), 'Neo-Hegelian Reflections on the Communitarian Debate', in M. Walzer (ed.), *Toward a Global Civil Society*, Oxford: Berghahn.

Plant, R. (1974), *Community and Ideology*, London: Routledge and Kegan Paul.

Plant, R. (1991), *Modern Political Thought*, Oxford: Blackwell.

Powell, M. (ed.) (1999), *New Labour, New Welfare State? The 'Third Way' in British Social Policy*, Bristol: The Policy Press.

Poynter, G. (2000), ' "Thank You For Calling": The New Ideology of Work in the Service Economy', *Soundings*, Issue 14, Spring, pp. 151–60.

Putnam, R. D. (1993), *Making Democracy Work: Civic Traditions in Modern Italy*, Princeton, NJ: Princeton University Press.

Putnam, R. D. (1995), 'Bowling Alone: America's Declining Social Capital', *Journal of Democracy*, 6, pp. 65–78.

Putnam, R. D. (2001), 'Let's play together', *The Observer*, 25 March.

Rawls, J. (1972), *A Theory of Justice*, Oxford: Clarendon Press.

Rawls, J. (1992), 'Justice as Fairness: Political not Metaphysical', in S. Avineri and A. de-Shalit (eds), *Communitarianism and Individualism*, Oxford: Oxford University Press.

Rawls, J. (1999), *A Theory of Justice*, revised edition, Oxford: Oxford University Press.

Raz, J. (1986), *The Morality of Freedom*, Oxford: Oxford University Press.

Reeve, A. (1997), 'Community, Industrial Society and Contemporary Debate', *Journal of Political Ideologies*, vol. 2, no. 3, pp. 211–25.

Rifkin, J. (2000), *The End of Work: The Decline of the Global Work-Force and the Dawn of the Post-market Era*, London: Penguin.

Ritzer, G. (1996), *The McDonaldization of Society*, London: Pine Forge Press.

Rose, N. (1999), *Powers of Freedom: Reframing Political Thought*, Cambridge: Cambridge University Press.

Sandel, M. (1982), *Liberalism and the Limits of Justice*, Cambridge: Cambridge University Press.

Sandel, M. (1992), 'The Procedural Republic and the Unencumbered Self', in S. Avineri and A. de-Shalit, *Communitarianism and Individualism*, Oxford: Oxford University Press.

Sassoon, D. (1996), *One Hundred Years of Socialism: The West European Left in the Twentieth Century*, London: I. B. Taurus.

Seligman, A. (1992), *The Idea of Civil Society*, New York: Free Press.

Selznick, P. (1994), *The Moral Commonwealth: Social Theory and the Promise of Community*, London: University of California Press.

Sennett, R. (1999), *The Corrosion of Character: The Personal Consequences of Work in the New Capitalism*, London: W. W. Norton.

Shanley, M. L. and Narayan, U. (eds) (1997), *Reconstructing Political Theory: Feminist Perspectives*, Cambridge: Polity Press.

Soros, G. (1998), *The Crisis of Global Capitalism*, London: Little, Brown.

Spicker, P. (1996), 'Understanding Particularism', in D. Taylor (ed.), *Critical Social Policy*, London: Sage.

Spragens, T. (1995), 'Communitarian Liberalism', in A. Etzioni (ed.), *New Communitarian Thinking: Persons, Virtues, Institutions, and Communities*, London: University Press of Virginia.

Squires, J. (ed.) (1993), *Principled Positions: Postmodernism and the Rediscovery of Value*, London: Lawrence and Wishart.

Tam, H. (1998), *Communitarianism: A New Agenda for Politics and Citizenship*, London: Macmillan.

Taylor, C. (1989), *Sources of the Self: The Making of Modern Identity*, Cambridge, MA: Harvard University Press.

Taylor, C. (1991), *The Ethics of Authenticity*, London: Harvard University Press.

Taylor, C. (1992), *Multiculturalism and 'The Politics of Recognition'*, Princeton, NJ: Princeton University Press.

Taylor, C. (1997), 'Invoking Civil Society', in R. E. Goodin and P. Pettit (eds), *Contemporary Political Philosophy*, Oxford: Blackwell. Originally published in C. Taylor (1995), *Philosophical Arguments*, London: Harvard University Press.

Taylor, D. (ed.) (1996), *Critical Social Policy: A Reader*, London: Sage.

van Parijs, P. (ed.) (1992), *Arguing for Basic Income: Ethical Foundations for a Radical Reform*, London: Verso.

van Parijs, P. (1997), *Real Freedom for All: What (if Anything) can Justify Capitalism?*, Oxford: Oxford University Press.

Walzer, M. (1983), *Spheres of Justice: A Defense of Pluralism and Equality*, New York: Basic Books.

Walzer, M. (1992), 'The Civil Society Argument', in C. Mouffe (ed.) *Dimensions of Radical Democracy*, London: Verso.

Walzer, M. (ed.) (1995), *Toward a Global Civil Society*, Oxford: Berghahn.

Ward, H. (1996), 'Green Arguments for Local Democracy', in D. King and G. Stoker (eds) *Rethinking Local Democracy*, London: Macmillan.

Weeks, J. (1993), 'Rediscovering Values', in J. Squires (ed.), *Principled Positions*, London: Lawrence and Wishart.

Weeks, J. (1996), 'The Idea of a Sexual Community', *Soundings*, no. 2, pp. 71–84.

White, S. (1997), 'Freedom of Association and the Right to Exclude', *The Journal of Political Philosophy*, vol. 5, no. 4, December, pp. 373–91.

Willetts, D. (1994), *Civic Conservatism*, London: The Social Market Foundation.

Williams, G. (1991), *Political Theory in Retrospect: From the Ancient Greeks to the 20th Century*, Aldershot: Edward Elgar.

Wright, C. (2000), *A Community Manifesto*, London: Earthscan.

Wright, E. O. (ed.) (1995), *Associations and Democracy*, London: Verso.

Young, I. M. (1990a), *Justice and the Politics of Difference*, Princeton, NJ: Princeton University Press.

Young, I. M. (1990b), 'The Ideal of Community and the Politics of Difference', in L. Nicholson (ed.), *Feminism/Postmodernism*, London: Routledge.

Young, I. M. (1993), 'Together in Difference: Transforming the Logic of Group Political Conflict', in J. Squires (ed.), *Principled Positions*, London: Lawrence and Wishart.

Young, I. M. (1995), 'Social Groups in Associative Democracy', in E. O. Wright (ed.), *Associations and Democracy*, London: Verso.

Young, J. (1999), *The Exclusive Society: Social Exclusion, Crime and Difference in Late Modernity*, London: Sage.

Index